WOMEN ARTISTS

and the

PRE-RAPHAELITE

MOVEMENT

ALL·HER·ROBES·WERE·BLACK·WITH·A·LONG·WHITE·VEIL·ONLY·

WOMEN ARTISTS

and the

PRE-RAPHAELITE

MOVEMENT

JAN MARSH & PAMELA GERRISH NUNN

VIRAGO

ACKNOWLEDGEMENTS

The authors would like to thank the following for their assistance: Caroline Arscott; Julia Atkins; Anthony Beasley, Bristol Central Library; Mary Bennett; Nichola Bird; Ione Brett; John Brett; Judith Bronkhurst; Noelle Brown, Ashmolean Museum; Anne Christopherson; Sarah Colegrave, Sothebys; Peter Cormack, William Morris Gallery; Mrs Imogen Dennis; Jane Eade, Phillips; Betty Elzea; Rowland Elzea and Iris Snyder, Delaware Art Museum; Cathy Gordon, de Morgan Foundation; Julian Hartnoll; Joan Hervey, Witt Library; Michael Hickox; Lady Iddesleigh; Misses Joyce and Myra Kendrick; Mrs Susan Lowndes Marques; the late Lady Mander and Montague Smith, Wightwick Manor; Jeremy Maas; Patricia McCaldin, Forbes Europe Inc.; Sir Ralph R. Millais; Joan Mitchell; Ann Moore; Peter Nahum; Evelyn Newby, Paul Mellon Centre; Mr and Mrs R. A. O'Conor; Nell Penny (for the Index); Kate Perry, Girton College; Niky Rathbone, Birmingham Reference Library; St Monica's Home of Rest, Bristol; Beryl Sells; Margaret E. Stokes; Lady Susan Stow-Hill; Virginia Surtees; Vivien Tubbs, Fitzwilliam Museum; Norma Watt, Castle Museum, Norwich; Glennys Wild and Stephen Wildman, Birmingham Museums and Art Gallery.

We should also like to thank all those individuals and institutions who have provided and given permission to reproduce photographs; acknowledgements are given with the List of Illustrations.

Published by VIRAGO PRESS Limited 1989
20–23 Mandela Street, Camden Town, London NW1 0HQ

Copyright © Jan Marsh and Pamela Gerrish Nunn 1989

A CIP catalogue record for this book
is available from the British Library

Photoset in Great Britain by
Rowland Phototypesetting Limited
Bury St Edmunds, Suffolk and printed by
Butler and Tanner Limited, Frome, Somerset

design by Elizabeth Van Amerongen

Front Cover: Kate E. Bunce, *Melody (Musica)*, c.1904. Oil on canvas, 74.5 × 50 cm. Birmingham Museum & Art Gallery.

JESSIE M. KING

1. Queen Guenevere 1904

CONTENTS

PREFACE

This book has two main aims: to recover and reveal the women artists of Pre-Raphaelitism and reinstate them in the history of the movement, and at the same time to begin a reappraisal of the assumptions on which that history has been founded.

The image of woman is the perceived motif of Pre-Raphaelite art. Despite landscapes, portraits, history and genre subjects, images of women – often simply faces of women – are the most frequent representations in the paintings – so much so that at a popular level today, in the closing years of the twentieth century, the term 'Pre-Raphaelite' can refer not to a style or period of painting, but to a specific feminine look, chiefly because, more than anything else, Pre-Raphaelite pictures depict women.

The popular inference from these images is that Pre-Raphaelite painting was created by men who discovered beautiful but unknown women – literally picking them up on the streets, as the legend goes – and transformed them into icons, immortalising them on canvas, before or after taking them to bed in the time-honoured tradition of the artist's sexual as well as professional relation to his models.

Implicitly, this account asserts that women were the subjects of art, not its producers: that they formed the content of Pre-Raphaelite painting but were not its creators. Yet, in the course of our previous respective researches in nineteenth-century art history and biography, both significant fields for the understanding of the Pre-Raphaelite phenomenon, we have become aware that, as in so many other areas of knowledge, the names and achievements of a number of women who were painters in the Pre-Raphaelite mode have been lost or suppressed, so that their contributions to the movement have virtually vanished from view. Today, a general account of Pre-Raphaelitism may include more than forty male artists and fewer than five female names, or often none at all. The ambitious exhibition 'The Pre-Raphaelites' at the Tate Gallery in 1984, for example, covering the years 1848–70, contained work by twenty-eight men and one woman.

Our first task therefore has been to recover these missing figures and restore them to the history of Pre-Raphaelitism. Even at such a simple level, however, the task assumed by the feminist historian is not easy, since so little information on their lives and works has survived, yielding tantalisingly fragmentary accounts of their careers. Although we have succeeded in discovering a great deal of new information, our restoration of these artists is pioneering and provisional. Much further work remains to be done.

In the standard account of Pre-Raphaelitism, the work of women has not been given the same status as that of men, and the difference can be gauged by the disappearance of their names during the twentieth-century when the reputation of Pre-Raphaelitism as a whole declined and fell into a pit of disregard between the Old Masters and the 'new masters' of Modernism. In this climate even work by the 'great' Pre-Raphaelites such as Millais, Rossetti and Burne-Jones was despised. The women's disappearance needs stressing: much of our time has been devoted to primary research, in establishing dates of birth and death and places of residence, or to finding titles and locating works of art. In many cases the pictures discovered are still not easily accessible, and few have been previously reproduced. The lives and works even of obscure male artists are seldom so difficult to recover.

We have researched the careers of three generations of artists whose work belongs to Pre-Raphaelitism in its various phases over half a century, to discover how they fared, in terms of successful production, exhibition, sales and critical reputation, during their own lifetimes. We have restricted our study to two-dimensional and pictorial art, concentrating on painting, photography, illustration and stained glass, a range of media that well illustrates both the continuity and the variety of Pre-Raphaelitism's extended span. This means that women whose creative work was chiefly in design arts – such as May Morris – receive only passing attention here.

In rescuing these artists from oblivion, we have also aimed to locate them within nineteenth-century British painting in general and assess their relationship to the Pre-Raphaelite movement. As has often been demonstrated, the criteria of art criticism have hitherto excluded from the pantheon almost all female artists (as well as black, peasant and proletarian artists working outside the high-art pathways), and we do not therefore aim merely to insert the women into the interstices of the dominant histories, but to understand and analyse their work and its reception in relation to the gender ideology of its time. That is, we do not intend to label their work 'good' or 'fair' or even 'better than you thought'. The value systems that have prevailed in art history, defining excellence in terms of masculinist paradigms which suppress the significance of gender, have been progressively revealed and challenged by feminist scholarship. Thus the ranking of artists in terms of quality is not our central concern here. Rather, our inquiry is into what kind of art women produced within the Pre-Raphaelite framework, and how the history and definition of Pre-Raphaelitism must be rewritten to acknowledge it.

To show, as we do, that women were among the producers and creators of Pre-Raphaelite art is, in part, to challenge the definition of Pre-Raphaelitism, and we therefore begin with a short outline of how the men of the movement were perceived and described in their own time and in subsequent histories of art – an outline that forms the anteroom to our own hall of discovery and interpretation.

A note, here, on names, since the surname convention is still obstinately masculine in many people's minds, and to refer to women artists in this way risks their being confused with brothers, fathers or husbands. Nevertheless we have elected to use surnames and, where necessary, to distinguish the male relatives by their first names. A related issue is the choice of surname for women who changed their professional names on marriage. Since it is hardly feasible to use both names, we have chosen, for consistency's sake, to use the name by which each artist first became known. Evelyn de Morgan thus appears throughout under her original name of Evelyn Pickering. A small problem still remains with Lucy and Catherine Madox Brown, who shared the same surname, and the occasional use of baptismal names has been inescapable.

ILLUSTRATIONS

BLACK/WHITE

~

COLOUR PLATES

'DIRECT

SERIOUS
AND
HEARTFELT'

EMMA SANDYS

2. Viola *c.*1870

*T*he standard history of Pre-Raphaelitism now current focuses on the seven men who formed the famous Pre-Raphaelite Brotherhood, or PRB, in 1848; on three of those men in particular: William Holman Hunt, John Everett Millais and Dante Gabriel Rossetti; on their immediate associates such as Ford Madox Brown and Arthur Hughes; on John Ruskin, the leading critical spokesman for the movement in its own time; and subsequently on the 'sons and heirs' of Pre-Raphaelitism: Edward Burne-Jones, William Morris, J. M. Strudwick and J. L. Byam Shaw, together with their indirect relations such as J. W. Waterhouse and Aubrey Beardsley. Interwoven with this cast list is a commentary on the women who were the models and muses to this creative dynasty.

In effect, the term Pre-Raphaelite has come to describe a style rather than a school or group of artists, and its uneven and sometimes contradictory qualities are explained in terms both of its variety of painters and of its longevity, as over fifty years the style was adopted and adapted by succeeding generations of artists.

As artists, these men were very diverse in their work and careers, and historians of Pre-Raphaelitism have tended to champion one or other of the original PRBs, describing the movement in terms of heroes and villains, achievement and betrayal. Nevertheless, they are considered collectively as exponents of a tendency in nineteenth-century British art that was and is recognisable through certain linked characteristics. There is a continuing dispute, however, over what is to be included under the Pre-Raphaelite umbrella, and how widely the definition can be applied both in terms of artists and dates. What, then, was Pre-Raphaelitism? How did it appear to its contemporaries, and what has it subsequently been seen to signify? Enthusiasts and detractors have their own, not always congruent views.

Purists restrict Pre-Raphaelitism to the work of the Brotherhood, whose formal structure had dissolved by 1853, or rather to work produced by the PRBs and their associates – including here less well-known artists such as F. G. Stephens, James Collinson, W. H. Deverell, C. A. Collins, Thomas Seddon, John Brett, etc. This strict definition covers a short time span, up to around 1860, by which time Millais had by common consent abandoned the Pre-Raphaelite mode, and Rossetti had begun to paint in a different style. However, the defining limits are commonly more elastic: in the 1984 Tate Gallery exhibition the time span was extended to include all of Rossetti's career as well as work by Frederick Sandys, Simeon Solomon, Spencer Stanhope as well as, most crucially, Burne-Jones. In this exhibition, the 'effective end of Pre-Raphaelite painting' was identified with the death of Rossetti in 1882. Other accounts usually also include 'later followers', that is, artists working up to the turn of the century, showing links with Symbolism, Decadence and Art Nouveau.

Our definition of Pre-Raphaelite is even more generous in terms of dates, including works produced after 1900. In extent, therefore, it is closer to that of Percy Bate, who in 1899 published a history of *The English Pre-Raphaelite Painters, their Associates and Successors* which included, under the heading 'Pre-Raphaelitism Today', a large number of contemporary artists, and concluded that the movement was still full of vigour, since 'the principles of Pre-Raphaelitism remain as essentially true as when first promulgated, and work equally good ought to be the result of an honest acceptance of them'.[1] We recognise that work in the Pre-Raphaelite mode was still being produced in the early years of the twentieth century by the last generation of the movement, artists born in the 1870s. And we identify two earlier generations, the first beginning Pre-Raphaelitism in the mid-century, the second continuing it through the 1860s and 1870s.

The first, founding phase of Pre-Raphaelitism has always been easiest to see and define. 'Essentially, here were three enterprising and variously (but hugely) gifted young men,' explained Alan Bowness in the Tate Gallery catalogue, 'feeling that English art was at a low ebb and that they had a unique opportunity of doing something about it.'[2] This is the stuff of the Pre-Raphaelite legend: rebellion against stale aesthetic norms and the revitalisation of British art. By coincidence of dates, the PRB has often been linked to the 'year of revolutions', as 1848 became known from the upsurge throughout Europe of demands for more representative government. In Britain, the Chartist movement's swan-song demonstration in that year was witnessed by Millais and Hunt, but the political transformation from an aristocratic to a bourgeois ruling class had already taken place, and the mid-century was notable not for radicalism but for commercial and imperial expansion, and for the consolidation of power by the rising middle class. This period also saw the establishment of the modern professions, in whose ranks the aspiring artists of the PRB belonged.

The new middle classes, to legitimate their access to power, cultivated social mobility through merit, and advocated a new moral code based on probity, diligence and a religious ardour that ranged from Evangelicalism to High Church Tractarianism and conversion to Catholicism. Several early Pre-Raphaelite works were criticised for 'papistical' tendencies, and it is important to note that religious faith remained one of the mainsprings of the movement, despite later shifts of focus. Similarly, philanthropic and political activities expressed concern for the weakest members of society, while the 1832 Reform Act, extending the vote to male householders, was followed by the emergence of feminist protest against the legal and social inequalities suffered by women in Britain, together with demands for their right to education, employment and professional training. Against this background, the account of Pre-Raphaelitism's genesis by William Rossetti, originally one of the Brotherhood's number and its self-appointed chronicler, aligns it firmly with this modern, middle-class, post-1848 Britain:

Being little more than lads, these young men were naturally not very deep in either the theory or the practice of art: but they had open hearts and minds, and could discern that some things were good and others bad – that some things they liked, and others they hated. They hated the lack of ideas in art, and the lack of character; the silliness and vacuity which belong to the one, the flimsiness and make-believe which result from the other. They hated those forms of execution which are merely smooth and prettyish, and those which, pretending to mastery, are nothing better than slovenly and slapdash, or what the PRBs called 'sloshy'. Still more did they hate the notion that each artist should not obey his own individual impulse, act upon his own perception and study of Nature, and scrutinize and work at his objective material with assiduity before he could attempt to display and interpret it; but that, instead of all this, he should try to be 'like somebody else', imitating some extant style and manner, and applying the cut-and-dry rules enunciated by A from the practice of B or C. They determined to do the exact contrary.

The regeneration of a moribund and compromised British art was to be attained through a return to artistic integrity, achieved through different kinds of truth: truth to materials, truth to knowledge and imagination, and that truth to individuality which is called originality. In sum, wrote William Rossetti, the Pre-Raphaelite aims were:

> 1. To have genuine ideas to express; 2. to study Nature attentively, so as to know how to express them; 3. to sympathize with what is direct and serious and heartfelt in previous art, to the exclusion of what is conventional and self-parading and learned by rote; and 4., and most indispensable of all, to produce thoroughly good pictures and statues.[3]

Looking back to Italian, German and Flemish art in the early Renaissance (Hunt recalled how they looked at engravings of fourteenth-century Italian frescoes, admiring the 'naive traits of frank expression and unaffected grace' and desiring that 'a kindred spirit should regulate our own ambition'[4]) these 'lads' selected for their Brotherhood – which was as much a social club for impecunious young friends as an aesthetic school – the idiosyncratic 'Pre-Raphaelite' name that came to label the whole movement. In the look of their art they attempted to abjure the sophistication, the visual gratification and the virtuosity of Raphael (at that time the most venerated of Renaissance artists) and his successors. In their place angular and linear drawing aspired to purity of form and a realism which could convince by resemblance to seen experience, not by the recognition of pictorial formulae.

The most striking feature of early Pre-Raphaelite works is their difference from preceding and surrounding pictures in Britain, notably those exhibited at the Royal Academy summer show and at lesser exhibitions in London and provincial centres. However, the conventions embodied in the teaching and practice of the Royal Academy were already under attack in liberal cultural circles, and Pre-Raphaelitism should be seen as only one aspect of this challenge, conspicuous because easily ridiculed. Prevalent prescriptions divided subjects into categories: history painting with heroic or religious subjects, portraiture, landscape, genre painting (scenes of everyday life), and so on. This was a hierarchy of genres, with history painting ranking at the top and still life at the bottom. There was also a hierarchy of media, oils being rated higher than watercolours, and one of size, large pictures being more important than small ones. Within the picture, there were Academic prescriptions as to composition and design which included complex ideas of visual perspective, use of chiaroscuro and modelling, receding planes and pyramidal structures, derived from the Renaissance and eighteenth-century practice. Figure painting, based on ideal undraped bodies – especially the heroic male nude – was still regarded as the highest mode, and flower painting the lowest, with copies being a species of art work deemed too humble even for inclusion on the ladder.

In contrast to this allegedly timeless consensus on fine art, the products of early Pre-Raphaelitism – their first exhibited paintings and the articles and illustrations in their

JULIA M. CAMERON
3. William Rossetti 1866

short-lived magazine *The Germ* – attest to interwoven strands of reaction, ambition and experiment. The results were pictures in vivid colour (derived from their technique of painting onto a wet white ground), studiedly naturalistic poses and gestures, a high-minded and poetic cast of subjects, together with disconcertingly mundane figures rendered with honesty and plainness (and mostly drawn not from ideal models but from the artists' own friends and relations) and a wealth of moral and typological symbolism. These were works of art which *The Times* dismissed as 'extravagances' that 'disgraced' the walls of the Academy in 1850, which Charles Dickens, in a celebrated attack on Millais's *Christ in the House of his Parents*, described as 'mean, repulsive and revolting',[5] and of whose authors the *Athenaeum* remarked: 'Abruptness, singularity, uncouthness, are the counters with which they play for fame'.[6] Other critics recognised with less asperity influences from the German Nazarene group and the examples of William Blake and William Hogarth.

At this point John Ruskin, author of *Modern Painters*, took up the critical banner of Pre-Raphaelitism, acting as friend and patron to the artists and through his writings promoting his ideas of what the new movement promised. 'Pre-Raphaelitism has but one principle,' he proclaimed, 'that of absolute, uncompromising truth in all that it does, obtained by working everything, down to the most minute detail, from nature and from nature only.'[7] This he perceived as the happy result of his earlier exhortation to young artists in the first volume of *Modern Painters* (1843):

> Go to Nature in all singleness of heart, and walk with her laboriously and trustingly, having no other thoughts but how best to penetrate her meaning, and remember her instruction; rejecting nothing, selecting nothing, and scorning nothing.[8]

Ruskin's support reflected wider enthusiasm for the Pre-Raphaelite impulse. In 1850, the *Illustrated London News* reviewer noted with some peevishness that 'a glance at some of the minor exhibitions now open will prove what really clever men have been bitten by this extraordinary art-whim'.[9] Over the next few years, up and down the country, followers were rapidly recruited to Pre-Raphaelitism as if aroused by a breath of fresh – and radical and modern – air. Regional centres of the style became established in the new industrial cities of Manchester, Birmingham, Liverpool and Leeds, where patrons and exhibiting societies and, later, the municipal art galleries built with civic pride and prosperity, welcomed the advent of Pre-Raphaelitism. Here, it was felt, was a new respect for landscape painting, an invigorated religious art, and a modern literary pantheon to replace the old inspirations: Keats, Tennyson, Shelley, Browning.

For early Pre-Raphaelite subject matter was drawn – in a time of increasing national consciousness – from the British heartland: Shakespeare, the Bible, and the modern poetry of English Romanticism. Nor was the social conscience ignored; a handful of pictures in the early 1850s dealt, albeit discreetly, with modern life issues such as illegitimacy, prostitution and emigration. Social realism, however, shared equal places with fantasy, romance and religion, all treated with fidelity to nature, whether of landscape or human form. Thus Millais's picture of *The Woodman's Daughter* (who was seduced by the squire's son) followed immediately on his fairy image of Ariel whispering to Ferdinand, while Hunt painted and exhibited in the same year both his image of Christ as *The Light of the World* and his picture of a fallen woman and her paramour, *The Awakening Conscience*.

What united them was the vivid immediacy of a technique which sought to bring both past and present to life. For modern society invoked various aspects of the past as models for the present. One wave of the tide on which Pre-Raphaelitism swam to shore celebrated the so-called early Christian era, whose culture was thought to exemplify the simple piety desired but seldom found in the modern world. Also favoured was the medieval age, in which work and community seemed to its apologists to shame the unequal and alienating relationships of industrial society, with its much discussed problems – pollution, poverty, prostitution. Later these appeals to the past, in which class and gender antagonisms might be obscured through the evocation of times when such issues were not perceived to exist, led, inevitably, to escapism.

Controversy over the new style of painting continued, fuelled by the challenge from photography which, pretending only to copy the seen thing, led many art lovers to hope that painting would put this upstart image-maker in its place precisely by asserting its own ability to do more than faithfully reproduce the reality of the material world. Thus the conservative voice, the mouthpiece of Academicism and the Renaissance tradition, insisted that real art was not about truth but beauty, not about facts but ideals, not about copying but imagining – and that Pre-Raphaelitism failed on all these counts.

Yet by 1864 Pre-Raphaelitism was no longer an issue but a fact of British art. This was the view of the critic P. G. Hamerton, reflecting on what he saw as 'the reaction from Pre-Raphaelitism' in the *Fine Arts Quarterly*:

> The father and mother of modern Pre-Raphaelitism were modern literary thought and modern scientific investigation of the facts of nature . . . the marks of the sect were intellectual and emotional intensity, marvellous power of analysis, sensitiveness to strong colours, insensitiveness to faint modulations of sober tint, curious enjoyment of quaint-ness and rigidity in arrangement, absolute indifference to grace, and size, and majesty . . . Pre-Raphaelitism was a strong and beneficial reaction from indolent synthesis to laborious analysis, and from mental inactivity to new thought and emotion – a great sharpening of the sight and rousing of the intellect, and even a fresh stimulus to the feelings.[10]

This was indeed demonstrated, although not deliberately, by the independent exhibitions that had been mounted by the first generation of Pre-Raphaelites and some younger followers, firstly with an untitled show held in Russell Place in 1857, and then with the establishment in 1858 of the Hogarth Club specifically to provide a Pre-Raphaelite head-quarters, where like-minded artists and supporters could meet and view the work together in a Pre-Raphaelite exhibiting society. Although it lasted only until 1861, the Hogarth Club effectively passed the baton from the first to the second generation of Pre-Raphaelite painters. When Hamerton's comment was written, Pre-Raphaelitism was entering into a new and different phase, like a snake shedding its skin, actively developing from the Ruskinian fervour of the 1850s to an art practice more in line with the evolving Aestheticism of the 1860s and 1870s. This is now often seen simply in terms of Rossetti's artistic evolution and coterie of followers. 'It was Rossetti who was to give Pre-Raphaelitism a completely new lease of life in the 1860s,' wrote Alan Bowness in 1984, describing how the artist put aside 'any serious attempt at modern moral subject matter, [and] was happy to pursue his cult of feminine beauty'.[11] But Rossetti was not the only Pre-Raphaelite, and the influence of

Madox Brown, with his teaching, historical interest, fluid brushwork and liking for dramatic scenes remained equally important.

In this period a younger generation of artists, prominent among them Burne-Jones, William Morris, Frederick Sandys and Simeon Solomon, took up and altered the Pre-Raphaelite aesthetic to create a dreamier vision of the past, based on legend and fantasy. In this phase Pre-Raphaelitism contained more characters and less landscape, more imagination and less fact, more decoration and less piety, and a diversity of materials, means and methods by which to express these changing concerns.

Subject matter in this second wave of Pre-Raphaelitism typically included figures from Arthurian and medieval romances, poetic compositions full of vague symbolism, and single half-length female figures in allegorical guise. Nature was revered less for the wonder of its seen form and more as the bearer of spiritual meaning, or as a decorative background to legendary scenes. The detail of imagined reality was preferred to the Ruskinian ideal of observed actuality.

Just as the early phase was marked by personal connections and social contact, so the second phase was notable for friendships and partnerships, together with the links forged through tuition. Madox Brown encouraged his students to emulate his interest in history painting, while Rossetti adopted many of the medieval enthusiasms of his own pupils Morris and Burne-Jones. There was also, from the mid-1850s onwards, an interest and commitment to joint or shared production. In 1862 a number of the artists, with other friends, founded the firm later known as Morris & Co., which aspired to close the gap between art and life by producing artistic and pictorial work for domestic and ecclesiastical interiors; hence, in due time, the emergence of the Arts and Crafts Movement, to which the history of Pre-Raphaelitism is linked.

In this second stage of Pre-Raphaelitism, there was the same disparity between the work of individual Pre-Raphaelite artists, together with some blurring at the edges. Some artists, notably G. F. Watts, shared allegorical themes with the Pre-Raphaelites, while others, like J. M. Whistler, were also concerned in the development of a new aesthetic not bound to descriptions of the actual and mundane. By the mid-1860s the style had lost its iconoclastic character. At the same time, many artists, including Hunt and several of Ruskin's most ardent followers, remained faithful to literal Pre-Raphaelitism long after the painstaking depiction of every leaf and vein had ceased to be part of the vanguard of modern art.

Individual life spans and careers did not, of course, fall neatly within the developing structure of Pre-Raphaelitism we have presented. In addition, artists working in the capital would often develop at a different pace from provincial artists, because of the difference in their immediate cultural environment and commercial opportunities. Nor did contemporary commentators always see it in such terms. Thus while William Rossetti, for instance, wrote in 1871 of a positive addition to the Pre-Raphaelite story of a younger generation of Madox Brown followers just emerging into the exhibition field, in 1873 the critic of the *Saturday Review* still apparently using the judgements of the 1850s, declared himself 'glad to add that the present [Royal Academy] Exhibition makes known the final extinction of that pretentious and mistaken school'.[12]

To the third generation of Pre-Raphaelites, who began exhibiting in the 1880s and 1890s, Rossetti was a newly revealed hero, for after his death in 1882, following several years of seclusion, his later pictures were exhibited for the first time in retrospective shows. Biographies appeared, and his brother began the lengthy process of publishing Gabriel's poetry and correspondence. The poems, especially the translations of early Italian poets in the circle around Dante, became a favoured source for later painters. During this period, Ruskin's artistic influence declined, and it was above all Burne-Jones who became the main living influence or leader of Pre-Raphaelitism. His developing style gave comfort to those reluctant to reject the entire classical tradition, while his famous words 'I mean by a picture a beautiful romantic dream of something that never was, never will be – in light better than any light ever shone – in a land no-one can define, or remember, only desire'[13] clearly encouraged Pre-Raphaelitism's final withdrawal from portrayal of the modern world into the realms of imagination and mystical symbolism. The essentially outdated persistence of Pre-Raphaelite elements, together with Symbolist influences and a late-Victorian passion for pictorial narrative, which has been fairly described as 'abundant outpourings, full of religious and mythic quests, anguished lovers and tormented souls,'[14] nevertheless continued to dominate the work of a large number of British artists in the early part of the twentieth century.

Yet in another respect, a characteristic feature of third generation Pre-Raphaelitism is its deployment of the diversity of media. It embraced the 'art as life' doctrine of Morris as well as the 'art as heaven' attitude of Burne-Jones. Pre-Raphaelite pictorial styles spread into stained glass, embroidery, enamels and other decorative arts. Its venues, too, were as diverse as its material forms: the RA's hegemony was waning, and Burne-Jones's work had helped establish the Grosvenor Gallery (opened 1877) in London as the most avant-garde of the annual exhibitions, representing the new Aesthetic style as well as that of Pre-Raphaelitism, even if the Grosvenor was as much an overgrown clique as the RA had been in its days of influence. In the 1890s the Grosvenor's role was continued by the New Gallery.

By this date Pre-Raphaelitism was one of several tendencies in British art including the Neo-Classicism represented by Alma-Tadema, the symbolic allegory of G. F. Watts, and Whistlerian Aestheticism. The so-called Decadent school, best known through Beardsley, which seemed to many to have close relations with later Pre-Raphaelitism, had closer lines of influence from French Symbolism, while the avant-garde label was now claimed by the New English Art Club painters who had looked to French Impressionism rather than to British art of the 1850s and 1860s for their brushwork and inspiration.

The deaths in the 1890s of some of the great men of the movement's earlier incarnations gave rise to reflections on the winding path Pre-Raphaelitism had followed over half a century. Madox Brown died in 1893, Morris and Millais in 1896, Burne-Jones in 1898. Retrospective exhibitions, catalogues raisonnés and double-volume biographies followed. In 1898 the Studio, the new art magazine committed to Aesthetic and Arts and Crafts ideas, considered the state of Pre-Raphaelite art in the light of the current exhibitions of Rossetti's work at the New Gallery and Millais's at the RA. It was fifty years since the founding of the Brotherhood by these and five other young men.

The Studio's views were given in the form of a dramatic dialogue. The first speaker, welcoming the opportunity to reconsider the two artists, chides the contemporary generation for being 'apt to think that the latest Rossettis, and Mr Aubrey Beardsley, represent each pole of the Pre-Raphaelite ideal' and reminds them that it was originally 'a synonym for realisation, verification, materialisation, as Ruskin put it'. Another voice notes the recent European fashion for Pre-Raphaelitism, also ignorant or forgetful of the style's beginnings: 'I fancy the Continent takes Pre-Raphaelitism to mean Burne-Jones and the cult of the sunflower, Walter Crane's and Kate Greenaway's toy-books, [Christopher] Dresser's designs and Liberty fabrics, Morris wall-papers and the Arts and Crafts movement down to the latest *Studio* artists.' The first voice embraces this perception, declaring: 'No matter what the Pre-Raphaelite Brotherhood actually meant, or what Mr Ruskin put forward as their creed, the movement we see developed today is deeper and broader than they guessed. It began before them and it has lasted beyond them.' For this speaker, Pre-Raphaelitism had proved itself by its resilience: 'a sudden innovation as a rule expires by the reaction it provokes, but a quiet advance, such as the Pre-Raphaelite idea shows today, if it seems far away from the letter of the early Millais and Rossetti, is, in the main, a logical evolution of the spirit of those two artists'. In conclusion, he saw Pre-Raphaelitism generating the new century's art.[15]

As we have seen, in 1899 Percy Bate still considered the movement full of strength and promise. Certainly Hunt's autobiography and testament to the original aims of the movement, *Pre-Raphaelitism and the Pre-Raphaelite Brotherhood*, was well received in 1905, rearousing many of the ancient controversies. But the chief focus of artistic interest and innovation had undoubtedly shifted. The year 1910 saw the first Post-Impressionist exhibition in London, provoking as much hostility and abuse as the original PRBs. Although several of the artists associated with the style in its third phase continued their personal engagement with Pre-Raphaelitism until their deaths well into the new century, it was generally considered a spent force even before the First World War, having been absorbed into Symbolism and Art Nouveau.

It will not have escaped notice that this account of the Pre-Raphaelite movement has omitted almost entirely to mention any women's names. This is not quite the standard view, since women are generally accorded a significant place in the history of Pre-Raphaelitism, as models, sources of inspiration and provokers of discord. 'Girls had now entered the Pre-Raphaelite circle,' wrote Bowness of the year 1851, 'and the close group of young men was breaking up.'[16] In both popular and scholarly accounts of the school, women play a prominent role in the biographical sections, but few if any are named as artists. The Pre-Raphaelite enterprise remains, in most versions, very much a masculine affair. In this the twentieth century is guilty of some gender bias. Individual members of the PRB, as we shall see, often noted and praised the work of female contemporaries, while in later years women Pre-Raphaelites were relatively well represented in exhibitions. Percy Bate illustrated the work of six women in his total of fifty-three artists. On the whole, however, the story, as told, is one of male innovation and achievement.

Yet there were women present at virtually every stage of the Pre-Raphaelite story, whose work adds a dimension to our understanding of the movement and whose neglect prevents a full assessment of Pre-Raphaelitism. Our task here has been to reinstate these artists, to enquire what Pre-Raphaelitism meant to them and how their work was received. In order to do so, we start by returning to the middle of the nineteenth century to consider the situation facing women artists at that date.

THE

FIRST

GENERATION

1848–65

ANNA E. BLUNDEN

4. Uncle Tom's Cabin 1853

Aspiring women artists in the early 1850s were in a very different position from the young men of the Brotherhood. Their ambitions were constrained by practical, social and ideological considerations, and by many specific obstacles and exclusions. It was, however, a period when issues of gender were under intense debate, and when custom and convention were systematically challenged. The position of women within the arts at the time of Pre-Raphaelitism's birth must therefore be seen against the broader background of the 'woman question', involving legal status, equality, education and employment.

These issues were highlighted by the first national censuses in 1841 and 1851, which revealed a surplus of single women in the British population and suggested that an increasing proportion would never be able to marry. Compounded by statistics indicating that men in the middle and upper classes were more likely to marry at a late age or not at all, thus further reducing potential partners for middle-class girls, this aroused anxiety on many counts. On the one hand, it gave rise to the idea that single middle-class women might of necessity legitimately search for decorous ways in which to earn their own living, while on the other it raised the spectre of women competing directly with men in economic spheres and occupations. Demands or even polite requests for equality led to fears that male authority and thence superiority in society, government, and the family might be eroded. In this atmosphere, the promotion of the bourgeois ideal of the wholly domestic woman (the 'angel in the house') functioned both to keep women within their traditional roles, and to oblige them to compete against each other in the contest to win a husband. At basic and sophisticated levels gender attitudes of the time thus conspired against the woman who would be an artist.

Progress in this endeavour was, in the first instance, determined by the attitudes of her family, where the father, generally speaking, held the power to decide whether or not any money would be expended on teaching a daughter to paint. Girls' education was widely regarded as a maternal responsibility and usually consisted of basic literacy and numeracy together with moral and religious instruction and a good deal of practical housewifery such as making and mending clothes. Other lessons, notably music and French, were purchased from specialist tutors, and the most widespread form of art training available to women was instruction from a local drawing master, who might visit pupils at home and whose teaching would be to an amateur level only, aimed at producing not professional skills but attractive accomplishments for young women entering marriage and society.

Social attitudes inhibited serious or devoted study, for daughters were expected to be at the beck and call of their mothers and other relatives, always available for domestic tasks and social visits, in a manner that was not demanded of sons. Young men, especially within the ranks of the middle classes, were on the contrary expected to apply themselves with industry and ambition to their chosen career. Financial outlay on male education and training was seen as a sound investment, but a waste of money for girls. The practice of art required space and materials, yet few young women except in very wealthy families enjoyed either the luxury of their own room in which to work, or the money with which to buy brushes, paints and canvas.

Beyond the home, an organised and respected art training was hard to obtain. The Royal Academy, whose Schools offered the only credible fine-art training to a professional level at that time – and one that was free of charge to those who qualified – was in practice a gentlemen's club; it ran its educational arm as a recruiting ground for the freemasonry and monopoly of male artists. The government Schools of Design – among them a Female School – were intended for artisans and designers, and were reluctant to give places to the many women who were seeking to become fine artists: in 1848, for example, the Female School in London had fifty-five pupils and eighty awaiting admission. Later in the year, the authorities argued that 'in the Female School it is not expedient to encourage painting in oil' and that all paintings on a large scale were 'decidedly objectionable . . . incurring useless and unprofitable expenditure of the pupils' time and labour'. Female students were to be restricted to drawing on a small scale, and 'to such designs for manufactures and ornamental work as can be undertaken by females' rather than to the practice of fine art.[1] The public art schools thus denied a fine-art training to women, while the private schools and academies tended, especially in London, to be crammers for the RA and therefore did not regard girls as their proper students. Even independent study in private collections, or from 1824 at the National Gallery, depended on social contacts and, fundamentally, on a woman's artistic interests being taken seriously by the men of her acquaintance.

In all ways, therefore, the woman who seriously sought art training was faced with obstruction, dismissal or at best condescending indulgence from the various men and male institutions that governed the gates to the arenas of art.

The only women not so hindered by the general lack of formal fine-art education for women before the mid-century were those born into a professionally artistic family, where the idea of a female artist was likely to be not only conceivable but unobjectionable, and no money was required for her training, since she would learn in the parental or fraternal studio, using equipment already to hand. Indeed, in these situations an aspiring daughter or sister could be a positive asset, employed as a studio assistant to prepare canvases and so on. In this respect, the family of a professional artist could represent a survival of the pre-industrial household economy well into the nineteenth century. The separation of workplace and home was characteristic of the age, however, and it was becoming common for painters to rent studios elsewhere, with a corresponding diminution of opportunities for female relatives to learn and share in the production of art.

For a significant few, study in France, Germany or Italy was seen as an alternative if expensive solution to the barrenness of the British situation. This was, obviously, an option only for women with control of their own financial resources – very rare in the middle classes of the time – or whose fathers held liberal views and had no more pressing demands on their funds. Such ventures had to be chaperoned and tended to last for a few months only: some family matter, which a daughter was obliged to heed, would be bound to call her home – a marriage, birth, illness, death or financial misfortune. So, despite the possible ways of obtaining the necessary instruction, the vast majority of young women wanting to become artists in the middle of the century were obliged to make do with what they could scrape together in the way of training. Many remained acutely conscious of their lack of instruction, especially in the important fields of anatomy and perspective as well as in technical finish, and the demand for art education continued as a major issue within the debate about women and art for several years to come.

The tone and terms of this debate were set by the actions of women themselves, not only aspiring artists but also amateurs and writers on art like Anna Jameson and Harriet Grote. An early contribution to the campaign was Anna Mary Howitt's book *An Art Student in Munich*, published in 1853, which demonstrated the lengths to which a woman had to go in order to obtain a fine-art education worthy of the name. Arriving in Munich in 1850 with the intention of studying, she reported that 'admission to the Academy, as we had hoped, we find is impossible for women'. She therefore became a pupil in the studio of Wilhelm von Kaulbach, but the sense of discrimination, with its inevitably restricting consequences, recurred later in a conversation with a male painter, to whom Howitt enthused about the city. 'But, observed he, there is one feature in Munich life from which you, as a woman, have been cut off – the jovial, poetical quaint life of the artists among themselves . . .'[2]

The lack of this camaraderie – so well attested to in the diaries and reminiscences of the young men associated with the Pre-Raphaelite Brotherhood, with their convivial gatherings, impromptu visits to each other's studios, and late-night conversations – represented a further disadvantage for women, who lost the personal and professional benefits of friendship and acquaintance among other artists, and the advice, criticism and stimulation that came from such 'jovial' contacts. Elsewhere in Howitt's writings is the dream of a women's college for education in the arts, but although some women-only classes were established by feminists – Howitt's friend Eliza Fox started one in the 1850s, for instance – the vision was never realised.

The next hurdle facing the aspiring woman was that of exhibiting her work. As with education, by the 1850s the inequities of exhibition were also being exposed and challenged. Few women artists featured in the prestigious London exhibitions. In 1848, for instance, the Royal Academy exhibition included 1474 works by 853 exhibitors; of these, 126 works were by 77 female exhibitors, a ratio of less than 10 per cent, typical of the period. It is difficult to judge from such figures how many women failed to gain acceptance at the RA show but the 278 women listed as professional artists in the 1841 census had grown to 548 by 1851, and their work evidently formed only a tiny proportion of the exhibits in the principal London shows. A fair number of these artists may, of course, have been recognised in the provincial localities where they lived and worked, and where annual exhibitions by the local society of artists or even, as in Bristol, by a regional academy, might allow a woman to build up a portrait practice or an audience for local landscapes, but overall local exhibiting societies were no more welcoming to women than the RA was.

The 1830s had seen a burgeoning of such societies and institutions in the British provinces, designed to promote the professional practice of local artists by encouraging local patronage. But, given social attitudes, few women were accepted by their male peers as equally needy of such a facility. Men feared the stigma of amateurism which they assumed female practitioners brought with them, so that while women might be welcome in principle, it tended to be on the assumption that their participation was different in kind. In practice, women wanting to exhibit with the local society probably had a professional need to gain a reputation and earn a living, but where a membership system operated, women were often restricted to a special status marking them as different (and less serious), as honorary members or – baldly as if self-explanatory – lady-members. Some local associations simply excluded women; even in those which did not, female participants were seldom more than half a dozen in a total membership of, say, fifty. In addition, social custom again tended to exclude these few women from the educational and mutually critical exchange – not to mention useful gossip regarding possible patrons and sitters – which helped the male artist to develop his work in such a circle.

London set the acid test of success, however, and most artists hoped eventually to show and become known in the capital. Thus the degree of discrimination against female artists exercised by the London exhibition societies was crucial. The RA, although a major obstacle to women's progress in terms of their exclusion from studentship and membership (the coveted initials RA and ARA were badges of professional attainment that significantly affected earning power), did not require membership since in its annual exhibition pictures and sculptures were selected anonymously by a jury of Academicians. There therefore existed, in theory at least, an open chance that a female artist's work would be accepted for exhibition, if it was entered. Of course, given women's low self-esteem, especially in an environment that defined women as incapable of great art, a good deal of uncharacteristic ambition and determination were required to submit work to the Academy in the first place, and some women did so only under pseudonyms. Moreover, there was widespread and justified criticism of partiality and favouritism among the selectors, with a strong 'old-school tie' system in operation, comprising established Academicians and their respective followers and toadies. So-called outsiders – non-members of the RA – would always be treated with less respect (the work of full RAs was accepted automatically, without submission to the jury), and this elite always obtained the best places for their exhibits. In all these areas, women simply possessed less influence. However fine their work, it was competing against men with vested interests in their own success.

The lesser exhibition venues were the Society of British Artists (SBA), the British Institution (BI), already in some decline, and the two watercolour societies, the Old Watercolour Society (OWS) and the New Watercolour Society, later the Institute of Painters in Watercolour. Both the BI and the SBA operated a membership system which allowed women to exhibit while reserving full membership for men. The two watercolour societies were more chauvinistic because more rigorously self-interested. That is to say, the BI and SBA had started out with ostensibly public-spirited aims – to offer greater opportunities for artists to exhibit their work – while the OWS and its scion the New existed to promote only the interests of their members; no outsider was allowed to exhibit in their shows. Restricting the number of female members controlled the number of female exhibitors. This was hard, when watercolour was, by common consent, a medium suited to women artists, and when a critic could write of the New's 1847 show that 'in truth, it is in no small degree indebted to the talent of its female members for the popularity it enjoys'.[3] Yet the figures tell their own tale:

at the OWS, in 1850, the ninth female artist and the hundredth male were elected to membership; while at the New, the same year saw eleven female members to ninety-three male.

The self-styled Free Exhibition was established in 1848, offering freedom from the perpetual cliques in the membership societies, and thus another available venue for unestablished artists. It was, however, not free of charge and so still presented the female artist with some practical difficulty; artists hoped to find buyers not only to make a profit but also in order to pay the costs of exhibition itself. The establishment of the Society of Female Artists in 1857 was one attempt at a solution, offering an additional exhibition venue and bringing into focus many aspects of the issue of women's relation to art. The following year, when the Hogarth Club was founded as a new exhibiting society specifically for artists of the Pre-Raphaelite persuasion, women members were not invited. This was a significant disadvantage, since successful exhibition in London depended at least partly on being in with the right people, who were of course almost exclusively male. The barriers of Victorian etiquette had to be surmounted or circumnavigated by female artists trying to approach the charmed circle. The attraction of the Academy, indeed, was for many female artists not so much its superior prestige as a venue but its possibility of anonymity and relatively impersonal entry into exhibition.

Once accepted, work needed to be seen and noticed. The RA exhibition was so vast that publicity tended to go to the names already known to the critics, with the public responding in their appraisal of the exhibition along the lines recommended by the press. Again, women artists, for many reasons finding their work inconspicuously placed in the larger exhibitions and unmentioned in the journals, had little opportunity for the smoking room fraternalism by which a male artist might ensure a reviewer's attention. There were no female critics in the 1840s and 1850s, although the feminist press which began in the late 1850s did make a point of attending to women's work at the shows it reviewed. The *Art Journal*, with its liberal approach, made an effort to give credit where the editor felt it was due, and this was occasionally of benefit to a woman, but since habitually only a small proportion of exhibits at any show would be mentioned, few women artists attracted more than cursory notice. In the later 1850s and early 1860s, they drew some pointed attention as a controversial group, but even then the proportion of critical space given to their exhibits was very small. And social custom prevented them from enjoying the kind of mutual self-promotion common among male artists.

In sketching in the background to the study of women artists in the first era of Pre-Raphaelitism, it is finally relevant to consider those who were already established in the late 1840s, before the woman artist became a contentious figure. In the catalogues of London exhibitions in this period and the pages of the monthly *Art Journal*, by far the most conspicuous of the handful of female names is that of Margaret Geddes Carpenter. Born in 1793, she began exhibiting in 1814 and enjoyed a steady popularity thereafter, showing regularly until her death in 1872. Essentially a portraitist, she varied her output of such prosaic commissions with fancy pictures (that is, imaginative, often sentimental or anecdotal 'fancies') and figure compositions of a fashionable sort and, although neither remarkable nor unconventional, she was a good artist in the post-Reynolds mode practised by most of her contemporaries. In other words, she was as good as her male colleagues of the time and

had she been a man would no doubt have been elected to the RA and even attracted royal patronage – a sure passport to fame. When with the rise of feminism the sexual politics of art began to be questioned, Carpenter's name was the most frequently cited both as evidence of women's professional ability and as proof of female achievement left unrewarded.

Other women artists of the 1840s acknowledged in press and showroom were, for the most part, practitioners in genres seen to be both modest and feminine – still life, portraiture, landscape and copying. This configuration of inferiority and gender suitability left male predominance unthreatened, despite the achievements of a number of now-forgotten women such as Emma and Mary Ann Sharpe, Fanny Corbaux, the six Rayner sisters and the five Nasmyths. Otherwise, the field was thin: significantly, in the most important event of public art of the decade, the competition for the mural decoration of the new Palace of Westminster, only one female artist's entry was noted, that of Ambrosini Jerome, and it went unrewarded. Nevertheless, these women did practise their art, for decades, and must therefore have found patrons enough to survive. The collectors of the 1840s whose taste for contemporary art laid the basis for Pre-Raphaelitism's patrons – Robert Vernon, John Sheepshanks and others – signally failed, even so, to acknowledge the female artists of their day, and Carpenter was usually the only woman represented in their collections.

By the mid-1850s, the situation was showing signs of change. Education, exhibition and fundamental questions of what constituted art as opposed to craft, pastime or imitation, and what role skill, imagination and originality played in creative practice, became important topics of discussion in the art press. One notable gain for women was initiated in 1859 when the Royal Commission investigating the RA was considering the question of women and art. Attempting to seize the moment, a group of women initiated a petition signed by thirty-eight female artists, both established and struggling, which was presented to the Academicians, requesting that they open the Schools to women. For the petitioners, the fact that the RA offered free tuition was as important as its status. Belatedly, fear of bad publicity and waning sympathy for discrimination persuaded the RA to allow female students from 1861, when an aspiring artist named Laura Herford forced its hand by passing the entrance examinations with work submitted under an initial and thought by the judges to be the work of a man. Even then, a quota system to limit the numbers of female students was shortly afterwards instituted.

The beginning of the decade had laid the ground for this demand. While previously female artists had appeared to present no threat to the status quo, being too few in number to attract much attention, either negative or positive, in the years after 1848 the position of women as a whole became an issue, and female artists part of that vast discussion. At the same time as, and in the first wave of Pre-Raphaelitism, a generation of women made their way into British art, provoking and participating in changes which exercised conservatives, liberals and radicals alike.

Women had not, of course, even been considered as possible members of the Pre-Raphaelite Brotherhood itself. Even as a contributor (under a pseudonym) to *The Germ* and fiancée of an actual PRB as well as sister to two more, Christina Rossetti was excluded from the circle by virtue of her sex. Yet she too was eager to study art, as were other female relatives like Judith Agnes, the wife of J. E. Millais's brother William, and Holman Hunt's sister Emily, who became his pupil in the mid-1850s. A sense of excitement was nevertheless felt in many quarters when the new movement became the talking point of the RA exhibition in 1850. In April of that year a letter from Bessie Parkes, a feminist and friend of Anna Mary Howitt, illustrated the impact of the PRB; she wrote:

> If you can, get a sight of the 'Germ', a small publication put forth by a set of crazy poetical young men in London, artists mostly, who call themselves the 'Pre-Raphaelian brethren' [sic] and seek in all things for the 'simplicity of nature' which is uncommonly simple and soft. But they are full of true feeling in spite of their craziness and in one of the first numbers is a lovely poem called 'The Blessed Damozel' (what a title) worthy of the very best company . . . Of course their confederation (one of them wanted to hang out a board with the PRB!) must come to an end, but I expect something from the component atoms.[4]

Four years later, Barbara Leigh Smith, an aspiring artist in the same feminist circle, responded with similar enthusiasm to the Pre-Raphaelite impulse and paintings at the RA (and incidentally expressed the single-mindedness she felt the pursuit of art demanded). 'Dearest Bess,' she wrote,

> Anna Mary says my little oils are *very good* for first productions from nature. My landscape is very PRB . . . I think you will like them very much . . . My head is full of pictures and I shall be a selfish cove all the summer for I must work out a grand picture – landscape and one figure – which is in my head distinct . . . What do you think of Hunt's 'Conscience Awakened'. What does it mean?[5]

Although Leigh Smith was not to become a fully fledged Pre-Raphaelite artist, her adviser and guide Anna Mary Howitt did so with ability and enthusiasm.

Although her career is by no means typical of those that will be detailed here, Anna Mary Howitt (1824–84) is the nearest thing to a female Pre-Raphaelite, *tout court*. Her work in painting and drawing was inspired by modern German art, the study of nature, and the desire to produce a challenging and up-to-date art; she moved in the circle of Hunt, Millais, Ruskin and Rossetti, and her productive period was the early 1850s. Other Pre-Raphaelite figures recognised her as one of their own, and the critical attention she attracted reflects that acknowledgement.

Born in 1824, Anna Mary was the first child (with five siblings, not all surviving to adulthood) of William and Mary Howitt. Active Nonconformists, both parents became well-known literary figures while Anna Mary was growing up. The family lived in Nottingham until 1836, by which time she had already evinced a 'fine talent' in drawing, according to her mother's diary. It is unlikely that she had any formal training and her mother's correspondence recalled homely beginnings to the activity which she eventually pursued professionally. In 1870 Mary Howitt wrote to her daughter:

> What an age it seems since you were a little child, and used to sit with me in the Nottingham drawing room, and we read the Gospels together, and I used to read you my poems, often written from thoughts suggested by you! I wonder whether you remember

those times, and how you illustrated 'The Seven Temptations' with heads of all the characters? Many other heads you designed, amongst them a Judas, which I thought marvellous . . .[6]

A further picture of Anna Mary's early creativity came in a letter of 1879:

How sorry I am that you destroyed that copy-book full of your early sketches done at Nottingham! There was in it your father standing on the parlour-hearth, with its fine lofty mantelshelf. There was, too, old William Theobald, the Quaker Swedenborgian, once baker at Ackworth School, sitting in his antiquated drab suit, at some meal in the kitchen – a splendid sketch. What a pity it is that precious book is gone![7]

Moving south to Esher in 1836, the Howitts entered a circle of Quakers (with whom they were in a state of happy discord), other Nonconformist social reformers, and especially supporters of women's rights and abolitionists opposing the slave trade. In 1840 this adventurous and unconventional family moved to Germany for the education of the children. They travelled the German states until 1843, their introductions furnished by Anna Jameson, the writer on art and the woman question. Anna Mary, then in her late teens, enjoyed herself in a society which her parents perceived to be very different from early Victorian England. Among the people the Howitts met were the artists Moritz Retsch and Wilhelm von Kaulbach, both of whom made a deep impression on Anna Mary. When her parents returned to Britain in 1843, she remained with her brothers Claude and Alfred to continue at school, but their own return was hastened later that year by the onset of Claude's fatal illness (he died in March 1844).

Living now in north London, the Howitts entertained a varied cultural and political acquaintance, which included the abolitionist leader William Lloyd Garrison, prominent Nonconformists such as the Fox family, the literary figures Alfred Tennyson, Elizabeth Gaskell and Samuel Smiles, and visiting celebrities such as Charlotte Cushman, the American actress and leader of women. William, Mary and Anna Mary resigned their Quaker membership in 1847, although all three remained deeply religious (leading to eventual conversion to Catholicism for mother and both her daughters). This spiritual side of Anna Mary's character gave rise to drawings such as *The End of the Pilgrimage*, illustrating a poem by Christina Rossetti. In this climate she met the social reformer Octavia Hill and also Barbara Leigh Smith, the latter becoming her lifelong friend.

In 1850, according to Mary Howitt's diary:

My eldest daughter, who desired to devote herself to art, had never forgotten the profit and delight which she had derived from our visits to the German capitals and their works of art. Our visit to Munich and the studio of Kaulbach had especially impressed her mind and imagination . . . Anna Mary felt that Munich and Kaulbach would afford her the most consonant instruction, and in May 1850 went thither, accompanied by a fellow-votary, Miss Jane Benham.[8]

Anna Mary studied painting in Munich for two years, during which time Leigh Smith came out for a visit, and Benham gave way to another companion. Howitt's approach was characteristically enthusiastic and intense, as this record shows:

We drew last week, as a refreshment when weary with harder work, a lovely branch of

ELIZABETH E. SIDDAL

1. Clerk Saunders 1857

JOANNA M. BOYCE

2. Elgiva 1854

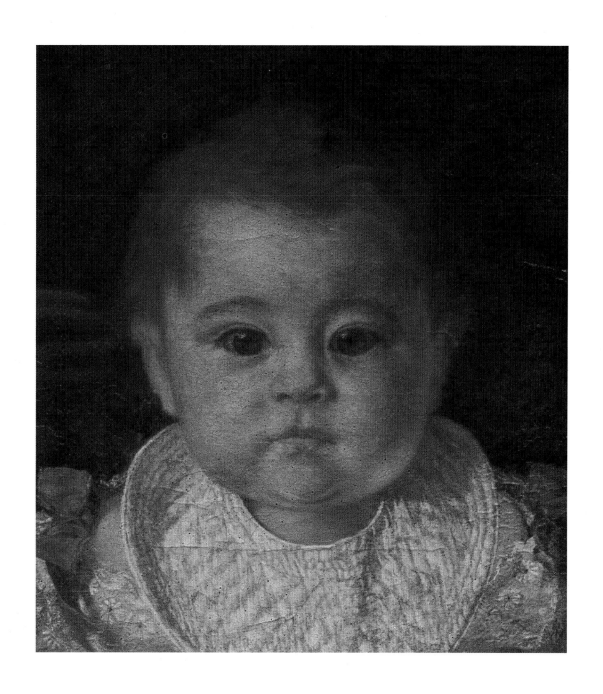

JOANNA M. BOYCE

3. Sidney (the Artist's Son) 1860

LUCY MADOX BROWN

4. Margaret Roper 1873

LUCY MADOX BROWN

5. Ferdinand & Miranda 1873

MARIE SPARTALI

6. The Lady Prays – Desire 1867

EMMA SANDYS

7. Beatrice Blanche Cloakes 1871

ROSA BRETT

8. The Old House, Farleigh 1862

white lily, and became so enamoured of this study that we determined to make another. We resolved to group together the most beautiful flowers growing in the beloved wilderness-field in which the studio stands, and to keep them as memories of this beautiful place, and this no less beautiful passage in our lives. We began, therefore, the other afternoon; and today, being seized with a foreboding that as the field was now again covered with deep grass and flowers it would shortly be mown, we determined to draw flowers from morning to evening . . .[9]

Between sessions in the studio she and her friends saw the sights as well as they could – at the Leuchtenberg Gallery Howitt 'was pleasantly surprised to see the names of three women in the catalogue' – and she sent back several articles on aspects of Munich life and society for publication in the *Ladies' Companion*, *Household Words* and the *Athenaeum*, with each of which journals the Howitt family had connections.

Their friend, the novelist Elizabeth Gaskell, suggested that on her return Howitt should write up her sojourn for publication, and the result was the two-volume *An Art Student in Munich*, which appeared in 1853 to considerable critical praise. Her other writings at this time included a long serial story in the *Illustrated Exhibitor* during 1853, called 'Sisters in Art', also drawing on the author's Munich experience as well as her discussion of women and art with Leigh Smith and others. For this periodical, too, Anna Mary produced a portrait of her father in 1853, and for the *Illustrated Magazine of Art* that year a serial story called 'The House of Life', accompanied by six illustrations [FIG. 5]. Taken together, these published drawings and writings of the early 1850s clearly depict the author's religious feeling and idealism as well as her enthusiasm for women's rights and belief in general social equality.

The Howitt women now moved into a house called the Hermitage in Highgate. William Howitt, like the Pre-Raphaelite Brother Thomas Woolner, had left for the Australian goldfields to see whether his family might make a new life there. Anna Mary, her mother and sister Margaret played host to a steady stream of friends, although Mrs Howitt depicted the three women in her diary as 'alone at the Hermitage, busily occupied in writing, painting and studying'. Regular visitors included Rossetti, Hunt, Millais and the young Irish poet William Allingham.

Howitt made her entrance to the professional art world at this date, already accepted among the Pre-Raphaelites as one of their own. She and Leigh Smith were two of only four women invited to participate in the Portfolio Club set up in the Pre-Raphaelite circle in 1854 for mutual criticism and advice, and from his correspondence it is evident that Rossetti was always ready with comments, if not encouragement, as she prepared for her exhibition debut. This took place in 1854, with *Margaret returning from the Fountain*, a subject from Goethe's *Faust*, at the National Institution (the erstwhile Free Exhibition). Now lost, the painting showed the seduced Margaret 'in a congenial wailing state', according to Rossetti, in an outside setting. The picture had been rejected by the somewhat old-fashioned British Institution before appearing at the more controversial venue, where it was a great success. Sold on private view day to a collector of modern paintings named Herbert, it was rumoured to have had many would-be purchasers, including the Howitts' well-known neighbour, the heiress and philanthropist Angela Burdett-Coutts, whose interest in the subject of the seduced woman harmonised with her concern for the redemption of prostitutes.

ANNA M. HOWITT

5. The House of Life 1853

The *Athenaeum*'s reviewer saw Howitt's image as feminist art, 'tenderly conceived, full of more heart than women usually show to the sorrows of their own sex, and painted by a hand with the firm delicacy of a man's execution',[10] although the point which drew the critics together was the picture's stylistic allegiance to Pre-Raphaelitism, their views of the movement colouring their verdicts. Thus, the *Illustrated London News* came down in the painting's favour, 'though the general treatment of the picture is evidently studied under Pre-Raphaelite influence',[11] while the *Athenaeum* complained about the minuteness of natural detail and vivid colouring, feeling that these qualities betrayed the influence of 'the Pre-Raphaelite school to which Miss Howitt, perhaps unconsciously, inclines', and the *Critic* sniffed grudgingly that it was 'an attempt in the Millais school'.[12]

The next year Howitt's showing at the same venue was a diptych called *The Sensitive Plant*, from Shelley's poem [FIGS 6 & 7]. This shows two scenes, in the first of which the female protagonist moves through the garden and in the second of which she lies dead, garlanded with an array of flowers, plants and insects rendered in vivid and meticulous detail. Although highly individual and worked with conviction, this received markedly less enthusiastic reviews than her debut. Also in this year Howitt made her first and only appearance at the Royal Academy exhibition, with a second picture on the subject of the 'fallen woman', *The Castaway*. Described by Rossetti when he saw it in sketch form to their mutual friend Allingham as 'a rather strong-minded subject, involving a dejected female, mud with lilies lying in it, a dust-heap, and other details; and symbolical of something improper',[13] this painting was bought by Thomas Fairbairn, a consistent patron of Pre-Raphaelitism, and was included in the Art Treasures exhibition of 1857 in his home town of Manchester.

If Howitt was unwavering in her technique, her subjects also maintained her initial vein of intense, melancholic female trial or tragedy. Her close friendship with Leigh Smith, with whom she was involved in the campaign for the married women's property law in the summer of 1855, had as much to do with this predilection as her own egalitarianism, but at least one critic in 1855 found it too onerous. 'We hope Miss Howitt will not confine herself to these heart-broken, tear-stained subjects, but will get out into the sunshine, and show us of what healthy joy the earth is capable,' complained the *Athenaeum*'s reviewer. 'Why will she stand sounding the depths of this salt sea of human tears?'[14] Fault was also found the following year when Howitt showed *Boadicea* at the Crystal Palace exhibition; although recognising it as one of the most promising exhibits from new artists, the same critic called it 'Botany not Art'.[15]

Howitt's professional career came to a sudden end shortly after this. Again her mother's diary provides the commentary:

> Our daughter had, both by her pen and pencil, taken her place amongst the successful artists and writers of the day when, in the spring of 1856, a severe private censure of one of her oil paintings by a king amongst critics so crushed her sensitive nature as to make her yield to her bias for the supernatural and withdraw from the ordinary arena of the fine arts.[16]

Howitt was tempted into exhibition only once more, when in 1857 the Society of Female Artists was set up by friends in the women's movement, and she sent *From a Window* to the second year's exhibition.

The 'king among critics' was John Ruskin, and it is ironic that he should drive a keen Pre-Raphaelite from the field, when he so constantly enjoined any artist who would listen to turn to Pre-Raphaelitism. Howitt, however, had suffered intermittent poor health since 1853 and her abrupt retreat from her chosen profession may well have been a form of nervous exhaustion. Certainly in later years her mother suggested as much when writing to Barbara Leigh Smith (by then Madame Bodichon) about *her* collapse, which had followed a stroke:

> It makes me very sad, for it is another instance in which the noble-minded, energetic woman yields under the force of that mental and physical exertion which her better and

43

ANNA M. HOWITT

6. The Sensitive Plant (i) 1855

ANNA M. HOWITT

7. **The Sensitive Plant (ii)** 1855

larger knowledge and awakened activity have made, as it were, a necessity of her being. That my dear Annie broke down under the strain upon her naturally delicate frame did not seem to me extraordinary; but that you, dear Barbara, should now be ordered into a state of rest does seem very sorrowful.[17]

Even so, Howitt did not wholly cease to exercise her artistic talents nor to support Pre-Raphaelitism. In December 1856 when Thomas Seddon, a Pre-Raphaelite recruit, died in Palestine, Holman Hunt turned to her for a memoir of his protégé, while in June 1861, she and her mother attended 'a great Pre-Raphaelite crush' or soirée, where friends and sympathisers gathered to view recent works and exchange ideas and gossip. This was the last gasp of the Hogarth Club, and it is worth speculating whether Howitt might have maintained her professional career had her Pre-Raphaelite colleagues thought to invite her as a member of the club at its inception.

Howitt married in October 1859, her husband being Alfred Alaric Watts, the son of old family friends. Her great friend Leigh Smith had married, too, in 1857, and thenceforward spent six months of every year in Algeria, her husband's adopted country. Thus the women's friendship was put on a different footing, although the two continued to be close. In 1862 Howitt wrote two articles, entitled 'Unpainted Pictures from an Artist's Diary', which described a stay at Barbara's house Scalands near Hastings, where several years earlier both women had drawn pencil portraits of Elizabeth Siddal on a visit [FIG. 57]. From the articles, it is clear that Howitt still thought of herself as an artist, despite her disappearance from the professional scene. She and Leigh Smith worked in the open air on various natural subjects including a grove of oaks, a cornfield and a secluded plant-filled glade. Interestingly, Howitt introduced into her account two women through whom she mocked the effusive enthusiasm for art widely associated with female artists by conservative or misogynistic critics; clearly she felt herself to be quite a different creature, despite the now private nature of her own art. Indeed, after her marriage her continued love of sketching and drawing took place completely within the private sphere. In 1861 the Swedish author Frederica Bremer, on a visit to Howitt's parents, was observed by her hostess 'looking over Anna Mary's drawings with tears in her eyes'. On a trip to Wales in 1862, Mrs Howitt assured her son Charlton that she would 'get Annie, who is coming to us, to make a sketch of this nice old place for you'.[18]

In 1870, however, William Rossetti observed in his diary that 'she does not now pursue art, except under the form of Spirit Drawing'.[19] Nothing of this survives, but it would have been images conjured up during spiritualist seances, in which Howitt was a firm believer. Her only other public appearance after that date was in writing, not painting, when she was proposed by Christina Rossetti as the best possible author for a memoir of the poet Adelaide Proctor, for the 'Eminent Women' series initiated by John Ingram. This was in 1882, and soon afterwards Howitt's name appeared in print with her husband's, when they published a joint volume of poetry entitled *Aurora*.

Howitt's father had died in 1879 and as a result her mother and sister Margaret moved from Rome, where they had been living, to Germany, where Mrs Howitt expected to live out her days. And it was while visiting her mother in 1884 that Anna Mary Howitt died. Fittingly, since the most important elements in her life had been her art and her family, Mrs Howitt's description of her daughter's death links it with her art:

My dear married daughter, Anna Mary, came to see us at Meran at the beginning of May. It was nearly three years since we had met, and I thought it would probably be our last meeting on earth, I naturally supposing I should be the first summoned hence. She came to Meran at the time of the roses, bringing with her a collection of drawings and sketches, which she had earlier made of her parents' *Homes and Haunts.* She at once began to make sketches of our present surroundings, with a sense of their being needed. Towards the end of June we left for Dietenheim. There too she made many drawings and sketches, as she had always done on her visits to us, for the character of the place was kindred to her spirit. In July the weather was intensely hot. On the night of the 19th, a violent gale came suddenly up from the north. The icy wind seemed to pierce her. She complained of a sore throat, which rapidly developed into diphtheria; and on the night of July 23rd, she passed away. Now the sketches so thoughtfully and lovingly made by her will illustrate the 'Reminiscences' which I have promised to the editor of *Good Words.*[20]

Howitt's brief period of intense commitment to a professional career had been recalled a few years earlier, in 1880, when *An Art Student in Munich* was reissued. Even so, on her death, obituaries were few and slight. For the Quaker paper *The Friend*, an old acquaintance, Alfred Bennett, described her in terms which offer conventional tributes to altruistic womanly self-sacrifice in family and philanthropic causes. 'Her life was devoted to the good of others,' he wrote. 'Of all the women I have known, I think she possessed to the fullest extent the faculty of a loving sympathy for all sorts and conditions of men [sic].'[21] There was no mention of artistic achievement.

Joanna Mary Boyce (1831–61), like Anna Mary Howitt, encountered Pre-Raphaelitism in its earliest days. Her enthusiasm for it was tempered, however, by a different character and a profound ambition to become an independent and self-determined artist.

Joanna Boyce was the third of five children born in London to a middle-class family in which the father was a wine merchant. The oldest of her siblings, George, to whom she was especially close, also became a painter, although he began by training as an architect. By the time Joanna was twelve, both she and George were regular sketchers, with such events as family holidays commemorated in her sketchbooks. Although in 1842 the wine business had

failed, Mr Boyce turned to pawnbroking and the family's comfort increased over the next decade.

In 1849 Boyce was enrolled at Cary's, one of the two private art schools in London with a sound reputation for training students for the Royal Academy. This was not her destination, since the Academy's Schools were still closed to women, but evidently she wished for and was granted more than a young lady's polite instruction in marriageable accomplishments. It was at this time that George gave up his architectural training for fine art, and from family memoirs it is clear that brother and sister supported each other's creative efforts, George suggesting jokingly that Joanna should provide the figures for the landscapes in which he intended to specialise. Together they made useful friends such as the up-and-coming painter William Frith, who came to see their work late in 1849 after meeting the Boyces on summer holiday. Their progress towards professional establishment was interrupted, however, in June 1850, when George fell ill and Joanna 'for five long months sacrificed her own ambitions to devote herself to his care and companionship', as her second child, Alice, wrote in the biography of her mother compiled after her death from letters and diaries. When George recovered, Boyce, 'seeing that her companionship was now no longer required by her brother, whose new friendships with his reviving interests in life would fill any gap made by her own absence, felt herself free again to follow her own destiny. In mid-November after five months of self-negation she returned to her home and again took up her studies at Cary's'.[22]

Boyce eagerly pursued other available forms of education: public lectures (usually in her father's company) and studying works of art in private collections when this could be arranged through a useful acquaintance, as when she visited the Baring family's picture gallery in February 1851. In early 1852, she transferred from Cary's to its only rival, Leigh's.

George was already consolidating his acquaintance with the Pre-Raphaelite circle, which had begun with meeting Tom Seddon in 1849, and both he and Boyce were fast becoming great enthusiasts for Ruskin. Her diaries and notebooks betray an earnestness quite in tune with the moral and devotional attitude to art. On her death, the *Athenaeum* – no friend to Pre-Raphaelitism – remarked that 'at this time she became much impressed with the spirit of the movement in Art, popularly styled Pre-Raphaelite, and by Mr Ruskin's writings. Accordingly, we find in her earlier productions much of the juvenility and not a little of the bizarre earnestness which distinguished the school in question.'[23]

Apart from Ruskin, her reading in the early 1850s included Pascal, Carlyle, Shelley, Hood and the American feminist Margaret Fuller. Her notebooks indicate her interest in the contemporary question of women's rights among other topics. One quotation, probably noted in 1852 with the artist's emphases, reads: 'He saw for *woman* as for *man* no other limits than those which the *intellectual* powers of the individual prescribed.' By this time attending Leigh's three times a week, Boyce was also considering seeking further training in Paris, where a friend of George's, Henry Wells, assured her she would find unparalleled opportunity for developing her talent. In April 1852 she went with her father for a month's stay, and in the round of galleries and exhibitions they visited, she particularly enjoyed the work of Ary Scheffer and Paul Delaroche, respected history painters of the day.

In September 1853 Boyce suffered a setback when her much-loved father died. Of her parents, he had been the one to encourage and support her interest in art, while by contrast her mother was apprehensive about the nature of such an activity for her eldest daughter. When, soon afterwards, Boyce began work on what was to become her first public success, a head of Lizzie Ridley, sister of her brother Mathias's fiancée, she was reluctant to consider entering it for the RA so soon after her father's death, lest this be indecorous. Both George and Henry Wells, now paying court to Boyce, urged her to show the painting, entitled *Elgiva*, when it was completed in 1854, but it was only the following year that she submitted it successfully to the RA exhibition.

Meanwhile Boyce sought further training at one of the government Schools of Design (possibly the Female School), and also worked at home in her own painting room. Among her friends were other young women following the same path, including Bertha Farwell, Jane Todhunter and Anna Mary Howitt, whose book she read with interest but in whose work she privately expressed some disappointment. 'Walked to Portland Gallery,' she wrote in her diary on 4 April 1854. 'Miss Howitt's picture not at all marvellous – very good in feeling – portraits well chosen – painting bad in colour and surface.'[24] This was the otherwise admired picture of Margaret and her companion at the fountain.

In October 1854 the Howitts suggested that Boyce follow Anna Mary's example in going to Germany to study – Düsseldorf was put forward – but it is proof of her independence of mind that she preferred to look to Paris, despite the absence of French examples in the Pre-Raphaelite canon. She had just returned from a short trip to the Netherlands with her family and had already formed decided opinions about the kind of art she wished to follow.

It was Pre-Raphaelite opinion, however, that claimed Boyce when she made her exhibition debut at the RA in spring 1855 with *Elgiva* [PL. 2]. This large female head of an early British queen, who had been the subject of a very different painting by Millais in 1847, was praised both by Ford Madox Brown – who considered it 'the best head in the rooms'[25] – and by Ruskin, who wrote in his influential *Academy Notes* that year:

> If this artist, always looking to Nature and her own thoughts for the thing to be expressed, will strive to express them, with some memory of the great Venetians in her treatment of each separate hue, it seems to me that she might entertain the hope of taking place in the very first rank of painters.[26]

In September, following this auspicious beginning, Boyce achieved her longed-for training in France. With her mother and brother Bob she went to Paris hoping to enrol in the studio of Rosa Bonheur, recently hailed in Britain as the prototype of the modern female artist. In fact, Boyce entered the studio of the much less controversial Thomas Couture, perhaps indicating a compromise reached between the daughter's ambitions and her mother's apprehensions. Mrs Boyce's fears would have been confirmed had she known that part of the curriculum in Couture's classes was study from the nude model, and it was no doubt owing to her mother's concern for the proprieties that Boyce concealed this aspect of her studies in her letters home.

Although in Paris for only three months, Boyce produced during her stay a powerful female figure called *Rowena*, which was submitted but rejected by the 1856 Academy, and a number of studies for other pictures, as well as portraits of her landlady Madame Hereau and others. In addition the editor of the *Saturday Review* asked her to write a review of the Paris exhibitions, which appeared in two parts in December 1855. This exercise was repeated the following spring, when Boyce wrote several articles reviewing the RA show for the paper, in

JOANNA M. BOYCE
9. The Homestead, Mosley Farm *c.1860*

which, giving prominence to Millais and Hunt, she declared that 'the Pre-Raphaelite movement has done good and will do more',[27] adding that it had important lessons to teach more popular but also more insipid painters such as Frost and Pickersgill.

By now Henry Wells was urging Boyce to marry him. She found the whole question irksome, being only too aware of the diminishment that marriage brought to the woman. 'I have so long taught myself to look on engagement and marriage as things to be dreaded and avoided,' she had written to Wells in June 1855 when he first proposed, and she had only consented to become engaged at that point on the condition that they should not marry for at least two or three years, because of her 'intense love of independence'.[28] However, in May 1857 Boyce finally gave in, and it was arranged that she and Wells should marry at the climax of a continental tour which they undertook with friends, travelling through France and Spain to reach Italy in the summer.

While travelling, Boyce sketched and painted enthusiastically in the train, by the roadside and in the streets. She began her next major painting, *The Child's Crusade*, in Rome, since that was the historical location of the twelfth-century incident of her subject. Not finished until 1860, this figure composition was then shown at the RA to considerable praise.

When Boyce returned to Britain in March 1858, she was Mrs H. T. Wells and soon to become a mother. Sidney, born in September 1859, was to be the subject of a tiny immaculate oil portrait [PL. 3], while her second child, Alice, born in 1860, provided the subject of the painting *Peep-bo*, which shows baby, nursemaid and mother in a domestic interior and appeared successfully at the RA in 1861. Also painted during her early married life was *The Outcast*, a treatment of the 'fallen woman' theme bought by Pre-Raphaelite patron Thomas Plint, together with landscapes from the Surrey countryside where the Wellses lived when not in London [FIG. 9], and *The Heather-Gatherer, Hindhead* (1859), a working woman out on the Surrey common land.

Perhaps surprisingly, she was not invited by her male colleagues – who included her brother George – to participate in the Hogarth Club from 1858 to 1861, at a time when Boyce increased her exhibitions to include Manchester and Liverpool as well as the London venues at which she had already had some success, driven by financial need as well as by her own determination not to abandon her profession. In August 1858, she wrote to her best friend Hennie Moore that marriage was not, after all, as terrible as she had imagined. 'Letting you know how happy I am in my married life,' she said, 'and how thankful I am to God for having overruled my wicked selfish purposes as he has.'[29] Her husband was a respected rather than brilliant painter of portraits and miniatures, and evidently both artists had to play a breadwinning role.

By the time the London exhibitions opened in the spring of 1861, Boyce was expecting her third child (Joanna, born in July) but was nevertheless well represented at the Academy. *The Heather-Gatherer* appeared with a small, intense child's head called *Bird of God* and *La Veneziana*, a historical female half-length taken from the artist's friend Charlotte Ridley. [FIG. 55]

When the artist's death was announced, from puerperal fever twelve days after the birth of her daughter, critics and friends alike were shocked and saddened. 'It is indeed a dreadful thing about poor Mrs Wells,' wrote Elizabeth Siddal when she heard. 'All people who are at all happy or useful seem to be taken away. It will be a fearful blow to her husband for she must have been the head of the firm and most useful to him.'[30]

The *Critic*'s reviewer was typical of her obituarists when he wrote that Boyce's 'untimely death is a real loss to the English school'.[31] The attractive and yet controversial power and confidence of the three pictures showing in the RA at that very same time rendered her death even more poignant. The *Spectator* called her 'the Elizabeth Barrett Browning of painting' and 'a genius of extraordinary power'.[32] The projects Boyce had planned to turn to next gave a tantalising glimpse of what she might have achieved further. Apart from unfinished oils of *Gretchen* and *A Sybil*, her list of possible subjects included 'Husband and wife alone together – quiet in the twilight', 'Lady of the Castle', 'London courtship – butcher and maidservant seen at Clifton Road', 'King Cophetua', and portraits of Henry and Alice. She also planned woodcuts including a scene from Barrett Browning's *Aurora Leigh*, a mother and child, and 'The Secret'.

The discrimination with which Boyce had adopted Pre-Raphaelitism was well expressed in the *Critic*'s obituary:

The writings of Mr Ruskin kindled her warmest sympathies and did much in helping to form her taste . . . The example of such men as Millais, D. G. Rossetti and Holman Hunt did more. From their works she derived valuable stimulus, assimilating to herself much that is best in the spirit of them, borrowing nothing of the 'letter' as the common run of so-called pre-Raffaelites do.[33]

Although Boyce's early death and consequently short career may be the main reason why she was forgotten by historians of Pre-Raphaelitism so quickly and completely, hers was a vigorous and creative engagement with the style, which resulted in a varied and vivid body of work no less impressive because of its limited quantity, since one of the artist's most pronounced characteristics was her industry, a fundamental Ruskinian value.

Rosa Brett (1829–82) was, with her brother John, one of the many artists living outside London who became Pre-Raphaelites through their reading of John Ruskin. Their enthusiasm was for the breath of fresh air which the new movement seemed to offer to British art, and in particular for the moral worth and aesthetic dignity which Ruskin's presentation of Pre-Raphaelitism gave to landscape painting, allowing the earnest study of nature to be as important as history painting to the modern artist. Although Rosa Brett continued painting all her life, and remained devoted to Pre-Raphaelitism throughout her career, as with Joanna and George Boyce, it is her brother who has been generally acknowledged and discussed by historians of the movement.

Rosa Brett was one of five children. Her father, an army surgeon, moved the family as his postings dictated. Rosa was born in Camberwell, south London, in 1829, but spent much of her childhood in Dublin, where her father served in the 1830s. The Bretts may also have lived in Manchester for some time during the early 1840s, but by 1850 they were settled in Maidstone, Kent, near Rosa's mother's birthplace and family where they remained for the next twenty-five years.

It is unlikely that Brett had any formal artistic training, although her brother John is known to have had drawing lessons while they lived in Dublin, and their closeness makes it probable that Rosa learned from him. It is clear from family letters and diaries that, as the eldest child and only daughter, Brett was expected to carry a time-consuming burden of housework and quasi-parental responsibilities such as teaching music to her younger brother

Arthur, as well as the social duties which their class demanded of its female members, and that her access to art training and practice was therefore limited.

The few examples of Brett's art that survive from before 1850 – drawings of houses in the Manchester area dated 1843 and 1845 – are very gauche, suggesting enthusiasm but not learning. Her love of art was, however, recognised within the family, and was shared by John, as shown in their father's diary for the summer of 1850, when they were living in Kent. 'We spent all the day on the top of Detling Hills, Rosa and John sketching,' he wrote. 'Started at 10 am and got home at 8 pm, a splendid summer day.'[34]

By this time, John had embarked on a bid to make a career in art by attracting local patrons and pupils. In this it is clear that Rosa was his right-hand woman, and to all intents and purposes his partner in art. Her own diary of 1851 reveals her ambivalent position as a young lady who, as middle-class convention decreed, should have no professional or extra-domestic ambition or identity. 'Mr N. King and his brother called' she wrote:

> they came into the painting room, I had to make my escape not wishing anyone to see me working at the Fungus as the work passes for John's. Mr Dobney called to see John's picture, he brought with him a Mr Batter. Soon after Plomley came and they were all in the Painting room together, and I was listening outside the door.[35]

Her daily timetable included housework, helping to educate her brothers, and administering and assisting John's professional ambitions – stretching paper, keeping the painting room equipped, sending out advertisements for his teaching – in addition to producing drawings and watercolours of her own. Her diary gives a graphic picture:

> Weds. 18th January 1851. In the morning I did the housework, afterwards helped John to pack up his picture. After dinner took a walk and gave Arthur a lesson. Father and the rest of them went out and I spent the evening in talking to Mother. While J. was out I painted for about an hour at the blight . . .[36]

(This was a project they were completing for a local patron, represented to him as the work of John alone.) Rosa and John also managed frequent painting expeditions into the nearby Kent countryside, especially in the summer months, and John's diary for 1852 noted that 'Rosa has lately made a few – first-rate – sketches on Preraffaelite [sic] principles'.[37]

In this same year she fell ill with an unspecified complaint which continued for some while and put paid to the plan for her to go to London to housekeep for John, who was cramming for entry to the Royal Academy Schools, and for Arthur, who was to study music. In the spring of 1853, John's diary noted that she was 'still unwell', and 'very unwell' in the summer. Nevertheless, she continued her drawing and watercolour work, apparently in outdoor locations close to home. Towards the end of the year, when Rosa was 'still dwindling away', according to John, the family considered sending her to Germany for a cure, but money was not available. The family was not wealthy and a large part of its financial resources would have been earmarked for establishing the boys in their professions; while John was prepared for a career in art and Arthur in music, Edwin was sent into the army, only Theodore remaining at home without trade or profession even twenty years later.

In 1854 John entered the RA Schools, and encouraged Rosa too to cultivate aspirations to enter the professional London art world. 'For you I have carved out a membership of the old watercolour society, and *that* once got, your fortune is made,' he wrote. 'I have *no* doubt of your ability to get it, when you shall have got *health*.'[38]

It is doubtful whether there was much substance to this optimism, since the OWS at this time had only five female members, and applications for membership were vetted by a clique which served further to exclude women. Again, when John might have helped his sister in 1858 by urging her membership of the Hogarth Club, of which he was a member, there is no record of his having done so. In any event ill health continued to afflict Brett, although in the spring of 1855 she made a short journey to the Low Countries. While her drawings and watercolours from this trip are mediocre in inspiration and execution, they show that she was evidently not prevented from working by her illness.

However, no work of hers from 1856 survives, and it was not until 1858 that Brett made her exhibition debut, with an oil painting entitled *The Hayloft* [FIG. 11], shown at the RA under the pseudonym Rosarius – despite John's protests at having to hide the identity of this new recruit to the Pre-Raphaelite circle. On receiving the picture at his London lodgings, he wrote to her:

ROSA BRETT
11. The Hayloft 1858

Woolner to whom I spoke of a wonderful picture by an unknown PRB was agonizing in his enquiries – as to how old you were – and whether you were a swell – no suspicion that you were a she. The thing is infinitely laughable in the intensity of its Pre-Raphaelitism.[39]

Priced at £40, the painting, of a cat in the hay of a barn, was eventually sold, although Brett was prepared to send it on to the Liverpool exhibition if it did not find a buyer during its time at the RA. Fred Stephens, PRB, gave it a positive review in the *Spectator*:

> There is an astonishing cat, dozing in tabby comfort, by – Rosarius (a queer name new to the catalogue and to us); how hard she blinks her green eyes, and with what inward satisfaction she tucks up her forepaws upon her litter of hay in the outhouse! For minute picking out of every detail of fur, its softness and its gloss, this little picture is quite a phenomenon; and the same punctilious finish is carried out into each several accessory of bristling straw and the frayed wool waistcoat which the ploughman has left behind him. With such a start, and such a foundation of difficult labour, Rosarius ought to do something very remarkable – and this, we are inclined to think, not only in the way of minuteness, but of characteristic truth of a less special order.[40]

Despite such confirmation, it was not until 1867, on her fourth appearance at the RA and at the age of thirty-eight, that Brett exhibited under her own name. This, together with the fact that her occupation as artist was not entered on the census returns – wives and daughters living at home were not expected to pursue an independent occupation – indicates the ambivalence that middle-class convention gave to her commitment to art.

Brett's exhibition acceptance during the 1860s was very uneven, including a sprinkling of showings in the annual Liverpool and Manchester exhibitions (organised by local art societies) as well as four RA appearances. It is possible that she obtained commissions which were not exhibited, such as *Detling Church* (1858) and the painting now called *Two Ladies* (1864). Landscape remained her chief interest, merging into still life with *Thistles* (1861) and studies of domesticated nature such as *The Artist's Garden, Detling* [FIG. 12]. An oil dated 1860 of her mother sitting in a walled yard shows that Brett's figure painting was still very tentative: the strongest part of this picture is a passage behind the figure where the sun shines through an open door onto flowers in the garden beyond.

She continued to work both in watercolour (for example, *Barming, Kent*, 1869) and in oil (*The Old House at Farleigh*, 1862) [PL. 8], and her subjects were chiefly identifiable locations in the north Kentish countryside. How much rejection from exhibition she experienced is difficult to tell: *The Old House at Farleigh*, for example, a very finished picture, bears an address label that suggests submission to a show, but is not listed as appearing at any of the exhibitions the artist is known to have applied to. While over ninety items from her hand are known at present, she exhibited only sixteen works in her lifetime.

Her subjects indicate the geographical constraints she experienced as a woman, while her brother's career progressed in leaps and bounds, largely through Ruskin's championship, as a painter of Pre-Raphaelite landscapes in Alpine scenes such as the Val d'Aosta and the Rosenlaui glacier. By contrast, there is no evidence that Brett was able to travel for the sake of her art. Nor did Ruskin's patronage benefit her as it did John, who corresponded volumin- ously with Brett on the matter of subjects, techniques and materials, but less successfully in

ROSA BRETT

12. The Artist's Garden *c.*1860s

ROSA BRETT

13. **Page from sketchbook** 1870s

regard to sales. 'I will tell old White [a dealer] to come and see your picture, also everyone else of consequence,' her now famous brother wrote in March 1860. 'I shall hardly have the face to ask Ruskin to come again – I don't think he would.'[41] Brett's home-bound existence brought her into contact with no one influential, and there was no regional exhibiting society or artists' association closer than London. And although by 1861 the Bretts were employing a live-in servant, as the unmarried daughter Brett still had many social and domestic duties.

A brief notice at the RA in 1871 (when she exhibited *A Spring Afternoon*) by the critic of the *Art Journal* illustrates how long-drawn-out the climb up the ladder of success could be: Brett was described as 'worthy of notice and encouragement'. Thirteen years after her first exhibition appearance, this was damningly faint praise.

Brett's Pre-Raphaelitism remained firmly Ruskinian in style, despite the 'second wave' of the movement pivoting on the work of Rossetti and Burne-Jones; in this respect both sister and brother disdained the tides of fashion. Sketchbooks from the 1870s show Brett still studying nature in detail, like a good Pre-Raphaelite, with accompanying notes on colour, tone and weather conditions animating her studies of trees, rocks and local scenes [FIG. 13]. The recorded dates indicate that she went out to sketch frequently but not daily and, especially in the summer months of July, August and September, she covered the locality

again and again. The most distant site noted is the coastal resort of Broadstairs, some forty miles from Maidstone.

By 1871, Brett's father had died and in 1875 the remaining members of the household – Rosa, her mother and unmarried brother Theodore – moved to Rochester, about seven miles away. However, her last exhibition appearances, at the RA and the Society of Lady Artists in 1881, were made from her brother's Harley Street address, and it was with John and his now numerous family, that she travelled to Wales later in this year, going as far north as Snowdon, according to her sketches from the trip.

It was evidently as an aunt that Brett spent her last years, just as it was as a daughter that she spent most of her adult life. She died of cancer in 1882, after three months' suffering, aged forty-two. John's diary recorded her death with the affection he had always felt for her:

> The next family event of importance is of the saddest kind: the loss of my only sister Rosa. She died five days before Gwendolen was born . . . This is a very great loss to our children who were her greatest Pets. Edwin and Alice [her brother and sister-in-law] took care of her during the latter weeks of her life which ended in their little farmstead at Caterham [Surrey] and the grass grows over her in Caterham churchyard.[42]

Like Rosa Brett, Anna Elizabeth Blunden (1829–1915) came to Pre-Raphaelitism through Ruskin, but in her case it was not so much through the critic's writings as through the man himself. While it is difficult to account for Anna Blunden's Pre-Raphaelitism by direct reference to her oeuvre, since the majority of her paintings have been lost or destroyed, it is possible to chart her participation in the movement through critical reaction and correspondence. She was evidently a committed convert and recognised recruit to the controversial style.

Born in London, Blunden grew up in Exeter from 1833, where her mother owned property that housed an artificial-flower and straw-hat manufactory. Two other daughters were born in 1833 and 1834, and it is clear that the family had no great expectations, for after a Quaker schooling Anna was sent to train as a governess. Her sisters Charlotte and Emily went into the retailing of Berlin wool, popular in the mid-century for the pastime of cross-stitch, using their home as a business premises.

ANNA E. BLUNDEN

15. The Song of the Shirt 1854

Blunden served a Torquay family in her first appointment, then moved to a position in Crediton, where she was most unhappy. In later life, she seems to have glamorised her beginnings, drawing a picture of herself as an instinctive artist frustrated by family circumstances. Her mother she portrayed as a figure of some gentility. 'Her talent she inherited partly from her mother who, without ever having had instruction in art, painted figures and flowers in watercolour with considerable taste and delicacy,' recorded the equally snobbish Ellen Clayton in 1876 from the artist's own testimony. [43]

Unsatisfied with the position of governess – as many of her peers would prove to be – Blunden persuaded her parents to let her study art, which she began at Leigh's in London. Although the Devon and Exeter Society for the Study and Encouragement of Art was set up in 1845, there was no local institution of art education until 1854. Her exhibition debut came in 1854, when *The Song of the Shirt* [FIG. 15] was shown at the Society of British Artists, and a picture called *Love* at the Royal Academy. The former, a simple composition on the still topical social issue of garment outworking, was engraved in the *Illustrated London News* shortly after its showing, giving it considerable exposure to a wide audience. The title came from Thomas Hood's famous poem on the sorry position of needlewomen and seamstresses, printed in *Punch* in 1843, which gave rise to numerous treatments of the theme in other forms; in 1854 the *ILN* was running articles on a proposed monument to the poet, who had died in 1845.

These first two exhibited paintings adumbrated the subject matter Blunden concentrated on for the next ten years. Figure paintings on contemporary themes, nearly always with a female protagonist, got her into the RA and the SBA again, the Society of Female Artists and the British Institution. The study at the National Gallery and British Museum with which Blunden had supplemented the classes at Leigh's stood her in good stead in these compositions. *Uncle Tom's Cabin* (1853) [FIG. 4], *The Emigrant* (1855), *A Sister of Mercy* (1856), *The Daguerreotype* (1857), *Hope in Death* (1857) and *The Bride* (1859) tell their own tales by title, although few survive. She supported these exhibits by works of lesser genres such as still life and landscape.

How successful Blunden was in earning a living by this work is hard to say, but that sales did not come easily is indicated by the many cases in which a painting whose first showing was, say, at the SBA or RA was re-exhibited at a lesser venue like the SFA the following season. During these years she would spend some months in London preparing for the spring opening of the exhibition season, then some months in Exeter trying to maintain a portrait-painting and art-teaching practice. Advertisements and 'puffs' in the local papers of Exeter and the surrounding district indicate a determined attempt on Blunden's part to persist in her chosen profession in all ways open to her. She persuaded the reporter from the *Western Times* to give her a plug, for instance, when the *ILN* engraving of *The Song of the Shirt* came out. Under the heading 'A lady artist', it reported:

In connection with its illustrations to the monument to Thomas Hood, the *ILN* gives a print from the picture of The Song of the Shirt, by Miss Anna E. Blunden – a lady artist, and an Exonian. The picture evinces high talent, and our illustrious contemporary describes it as 'embodying, in a very forcible manner, the sentiment of the famous song'. Miss Blunden is, we believe, on a visit to her family in Exeter, whom we congratulate upon the talent she displays, and the good example which her energy gives to young ladies generally, not to sit down idle when they can find work to do. [44]

Surely in the same spirit of businesslike self-promotion, in the autumn of 1855 Blunden wrote to the patron saint of young artists, John Ruskin. Her letters have not survived, but it can be inferred from Ruskin's side of the correspondence that her approach was intended to seize whatever advantage the great man might be willing to give. The acquaintance – conducted mostly by correspondence, despite Blunden's evident desire to become an intimate of Ruskin's – lasted for the better part of seven years, and was a curious affair.

To begin with, Blunden seems to have concealed the fact that she was a woman, writing to Ruskin on the pretext that she intended to try to publish her poetry, and requesting his opinion. But like any artist who petitioned Ruskin, she most keenly wished him to notice her pictures in the London shows, since he might then mention them in his influential reviews or among his wide (and relatively moneyed) acquaintance. In the event, replying in June 1856 to Blunden's revelations of her artistic ambitions, Ruskin was far from encouraging; he wrote:

> What you tell me of yourself may be indicative either of real talent, or of overtaxed nervous temperament. I dare not encourage – I would not willingly discourage you. I say to all my friends who are unprosperous in the Arts: Try to find some simple means of livelihood – however humble. Don't depend on your Art; or depend on it only in some mechanical way – till you can command an income. Don't let your feelings or aspirations come in the way of any available means of independence. As to what you say of your Master's teaching, it cannot *but* be inconsistent with mine, unless he be a Pre-Raphaelite. [45]

In fairness to Ruskin, he was probably unaware that this advice would put Blunden right back in the very position she was trying to transcend.

Embarrassing and foolish though the connection was in some ways – at one stage Blunden evidently entertained the hope that Ruskin might marry her – through it she formed herself as an artist. She determined to be what Ruskin could admire and endorse.

By 1858, her mention in the Devon press was enhanced by his famous name:

> The admirers of native talent, if there be any such in this district, may gratify their taste by visiting the studio of Miss Blunden, Cathedral yard. This fair young artist exhibited several pictures of the genre class at the Royal Academy. They secured flattering notices in several journals of London, and one of them especial commendation by the great critic Mr Ruskin, in his Notes, which the young lady, we are told, rejoices over more than all the rest. She is a diligent, enthusiastic young artist with considerable powers of imagination, well directed by a good technical knowledge of her art. [46]

The picture which Ruskin had especially praised, and the mention of which in his *Academy Notes* brought Blunden considerable attention, was *Past and Present*, an oil composition of a ruin representing the past, with two children gathering flowers before it to represent the present. Its success was followed the next year by *God's Gothic*, which was bought from the RA exhibition by the painter David Roberts.

Blunden now began to specialise in landscape, although she still retained a portrait practice in Exeter to help her earn a living. Her acquaintance with Ruskin almost broke up at this point over her attempts to lay emotional claims on him, but she persisted in their correspondence, and he continued to help her out with commissions for copying and with references in her search for teaching or governessing posts to which she considered returning. Her range of landscape subjects at the exhibitions throughout the next decade – Wales, Devon, Cornwall, the Lake District, Ireland – may derive from journeys undertaken in search of employment, not simply subject matter. Ruskin remained willing to help with sales, although it is unclear how successful this avenue was to her. In August 1859, his verdict on her vocation was: 'You will probably paint, ultimately, in a way calculated to be of great use and give great pleasure – although you will never be a great painter' – a judgement tempered by the consolation that 'no woman has ever been a great painter yet'.[47]

Greatness, it may be guessed, was not Blunden's ambition, but rather sufficient success to gain security with the galleries, critics and patrons. A further stricture from Ruskin was that she should give up figure painting, since she 'had no feeling for it' and so would never sell anything in this line. This came in 1862, almost his last words to her, and it was perhaps this kind of withering honesty in reply to her variously coy and desperate requests for guidance that led Blunden to break off the correspondence at this point. Certainly other critics were less dismissive of her sensibility. Two now unknown paintings of 1861 attracted favourable verdicts from the *Spectator*'s reviewer. *Passing through the Cornfields on the Sabbath Day* at the SBA was thus described:

> A rustic boy is holding open a gate through which two female figures have passed on their way to the church that may be seen in the distance above the waving corn. As a work of art it is deficient in many respects, but the feeling of calm quietude which characterises a sunny Sunday morning in the country has seldom been better expressed.[48]

Of *The Penitent* at the City Exhibition, the same critic remarked: 'A wayward but subdued child praying at its mother's knee [is] tender and quiet in feeling.'[49]

Nevertheless, Ruskin's advice swayed Blunden, and she became established during the 1860s as a landscapist [see FIG. 16]. She continued to be accepted at the RA, while showing also at the Suffolk Street Gallery, London, the Birmingham municipal exhibition, and at the Dudley Gallery, which from 1865 gave watercolourists a new venue in London. *Kynance Cove* at the 1863 RA, and *Marsden Rocks* at the same venue three years later, were especial successes with the critics, and by 1864 her membership of the Pre-Raphaelite school was established. Discussing John Brett, Ruskin's most sensational protégé of the moment, the *Spectator* commented: 'In his own peculiar line Miss Blunden comes not far behind him.'[50]

This stylistic affinity was not, however, something which would commend an artist to all critics; in 1867 the *Art Journal* reviewer noted somewhat piously of Blunden's *Tintagel*: 'At one time it was feared that this artist was going the way of all Pre-Raphaelites. Mannerism, however, has been corrected in time, and now this little picture, which for harmony of colour is a perfect delight, shows the reward of faithful study.'[51]

Although now receiving regular critical attention, Blunden was still not able to support herself fully by sales and commissions in London, and until 1866 continued to shuttle between London and Exeter, maintaining a teaching and portrait practice in Devon while

ANNA E. BLUNDEN
16. Lake Killarney undated

exhibiting and making copies for Ruskin in the capital. She was also still evidently prepared to return to governessing. In the event, however, she lighted on the idea of going abroad, perhaps in emulation of John Brett, who had made his name on his return from Switzerland in 1858 and with whom she corresponded in the 1860s. In Blunden's own words, 'I had myself no wish to go abroad, but I was strongly persuaded to leave England by some friends, who thought the change would be likely to relieve or cure a nervous illness from which I suffered.'[52] This may have been a retrospective attempt to endow her travels with some romance, or a euphemistic reference to a nervous breakdown. However, with introductions to assist her through Europe, Blunden evidently survived her travels. In 1867 she left for Switzerland, moving on to Germany and then settling in Rome, where she stayed until 1872. She seems to have embarked on this venture alone and, in Ellen Clayton's romantic version, 'in watching and striving faithfully to depict the sunshine and clear days she became more and more enamoured of sweet, radiant Italy . . .'.

There was a brisk market in local views within the holidaying and expatriate British communities abroad, and a roving reporter for the *Art Journal* went as far in 1870 as to report, in an article on the British artist in Rome, that 'there are those here who do not hesitate to pronounce her to be the greatest genius in Rome'.[53] During her time away from Britain, Blunden sent back French, Swiss and Italian views in oil and watercolour to the various London and provincial shows at which she was a regular exhibitor. Reviews suggest that her devotion to the Pre-Raphaelite approach remained constant, minute and lacking in subtlety.

By this time, of course, Ruskinian Pre-Raphaelitism seemed passé in Britain, and the

second phase of the movement, under the Rossettian banner of controlled fantasy, commanded more critical and popular attention. Whether or not Blunden found exhibition outlets in Rome is unknown; it may be supposed that, despite her evident industry, she had a difficult time in Italy as a single foreign woman of limited financial resources. The only identifiable associate of her foreign years (whom she mentioned in her submission for Clayton's *English Female Artists*) was the painter Elisabeth Jerichau, and even Blunden's genteel language conveys what a lifeline such acquaintance was for her in that situation. She wrote:

> One of the most kind friends I met in Rome was a Danish lady artist, well known for her bright, genial cordiality and hospitality to many people of all nationalities. She speaks various languages with fluency. For many pleasant evenings, and still happier hours, spent with her family, I was indebted to this gifted and charming lady . . .[54]

Elisabeth Jerichau, née Baumann, was a Polish painter who, marrying a Danish sculptor in 1845, became famous in Scandinavia, Britain and other European countries.

In 1872 family matters recalled Blunden to Britain. Her younger sister Emily, having married Francis Richard Martino, a widower of Italian descent, two years before, had now died, leaving a baby and a stepchild. Her other sister Charlotte died in 1872, and Anna stepped in, to marry Martino and take on the care of his two children. This was despite being his deceased wife's sister, a relation that still precluded marriage in English law, and the wedding therefore took place near Hamburg. The Martino household then established itself in Birmingham, where Blunden's new husband ran an engineering business. It is not known whether Blunden's motive for marrying her brother-in-law was family duty, the desire for the status and title of a married woman, or genuine affection.

Her absence from the major exhibition venues from 1872 onwards suggests either that at last Blunden could relax her efforts to support herself or that Mr Martino disapproved of working wives; whichever was the case, she could now approach art with a more leisurely and ladylike attitude. From this date she showed work only at the Birmingham exhibitions, where she was a regular exhibitor until her death in 1915. These works were nearly all landscapes, in oil and watercolour, their subjects drawn from various parts of Britain and the European countries she had lived in.

Blunden gave birth to a daughter, Violet, in 1874, thus becoming a mother at the age of forty-five. In the later 1870s she extended her activities further when she began to write and publish pamphlets on social questions, suggesting that she kept in touch with Ruskin's published works; one from 1877 tackled the subject of industrial pollution in urban areas and its effects on working people, while another, written ten years later, addressed the Irish question. She intended, too, to publish autobiographical memoirs, but found no publisher. The proposed title – 'The Romance of a Life – the forbidden letters of John Ruskin' – suggests a rather desperate attempt to capitalise on her earlier connection. Even in her will, Ruskin was remembered: she wished her letters from him to be sold to establish a cemetery in Birmingham whose design should accord with Ruskinian principles.

While Blunden's descendants recall her as a grudging and ungracious woman, she was anxious to the last to establish herself in her eventual milieu as a respectable, even benevolent lady. An article in the local magazine, *Edgbastonia*, devoted to the fashionable suburb of

Birmingham in which the artist lived, described her in 1898 as 'well-known in the neighbourhood as an accomplished artist and littérateur', who was keen to sell her remaining works 'in order that the proceeds may be devoted to charitable institutions'.[55]

She died in December 1915 at the age of eighty-six, described in the *Birmingham Post* obituary as 'a lady who for a great many years had been well-known to the artistic world', citing the names of John Ruskin and Holman Hunt.[56] These venerable persons, however, evoked an era long gone for the early twentieth-century reader, and it is no surprise that the art press quite failed to note the passing of this forgotten Pre-Raphaelite.

Ever since the death of her husband D. G. Rossetti in 1882 and the revelation that her coffin had been exhumed to retrieve his poetic notebook, Elizabeth Eleanor Siddal (1829–62), despite retaining her own name in the histories, has been seen and described almost exclusively in relation to her role as Pre-Raphaelite model and muse. Unlike that of the other artists in this book, her own artistic work has been eclipsed by the often fanciful legends that have accrued to her story; until recently, most people were unaware that she was also a Pre-Raphaelite painter as well as the movement's chief victim. Believing that the latter aspect of her life story is well known, we here concentrate on her career as artist, for while her name is among the most famous in the whole Pre-Raphaelite circle, her work is still barely known.

She was born in 1829, daughter of Charles Siddall, a Sheffield-born cutler who ran an ironmongery business in Southwark, and his London-born wife, Elizabeth Eleanor Evans, of petit-bourgeois origin. Although not as unequivocally 'working class' as later accounts have sometimes suggested, Elizabeth Siddal (as the artist spelt her name) came from a lower social grade than most of the other artists in this book; she had no money of her own, and no family connections with painting, and her entry into the artistic world was therefore somewhat unorthodox.

The third of seven children, Elizabeth, like her sisters, became a dressmaker. In this capacity she was introduced, at the age of twenty, to the family of Mr Deverell, principal of the government School of Design in London. His son, Walter Deverell junior, assistant master at the School of Design was an honorary member of the Pre-Raphaelite Brotherhood and a contributor to *The Germ*.

Nearly all our information about Siddal comes from the recollections of the PRBs, except for one hitherto unnoticed obituary, which appears to derive in part from her own testimony. According to this, she showed 'some designs of her own leisure hours' to Mr Deverell senior, 'and he, much pleased with them', showed the drawings to his son and the other young artists, who then encouraged Miss Siddal to practise. They also welcomed her into their studios as an occasional model (although this was not mentioned in the obituary, modelling not being considered respectable) where she first sat to Walter Deverell, then to Hunt and also to Millais, for the celebrated *Ophelia*. Towards the end of 1852 she became Rossetti's pupil; according to the obituary, she herself 'selected as her instructor Mr Rossetti, father of the Pre-Raphaelite school', in preference to Hunt;[57] at this date, there was no public acknowledgement of any romantic attachment.

The tuition appears to have been minimal, in line with Pre-Raphaelite iconoclasm that saw conventional art training as stale and stultifying. Rossetti, whose own response to formal training had been impatient, tended to insist that anyone with imagination could paint, and his instruction seems to have consisted chiefly in allowing his pupil to create her own compositions rather than make painstaking studies of casts, still life and drapery; she thus remained uncontaminated by the curse of academicism but therefore essentially untaught.

Siddal's first productions within this Pre-Raphaelite mode were commended for their 'freshness of invention' or imaginative originality. The figures tend to be stiff and anatomically awkward and the drawing technique rather primitive. Her subjects, however, were ambitiously literary and poetic. At the beginning of 1853, she was at work on a subject from Tennyson which Rossetti hoped she would send to the Royal Academy – probably the first version of her *Lady of Shalott* – and on a watercolour illustration to Wordsworth's poem in praise of simplicity, *We Are Seven*, showing a girl grieving in a churchyard among mountains. Later the same year she was engaged on a self-portrait in oils. This at least was a standard task set to students, especially those who could not afford models, but it was unusual for students to be encouraged to work in oils at such an early stage; conventionally, years of patient drawing preceded such work. It appears to have presented difficulties and was several months in progress; the artist received helpful advice from Madox Brown, and was then able to 'improve it greatly' according to Rossetti.[58] Several drawings and sketches of Siddal done by Rossetti at this time show her drawing and painting, seated with drawing board or easel, concentrating intently on her work, and all the evidence is of a strong desire to succeed.

Through Rossetti she met Howitt and Leigh Smith; the latter took an immediate interest, declaring that Miss Siddal

> is a genius and will, if she lives, be a great artist, her gift discovered by a strange accident such as rarely befalls woman. Alas! her life has been hard and full of trials, her home unhappy and her whole fate hard. D.G.R. has been an honourable friend to her and I do not doubt if circumstances were favourable would marry her. She is of course under a ban having been a model (tho' only to two PRBs).[59]

This response accurately conveys the social difficulties of Siddal's position at this date, studying art under the personal tuition of a man whom convention decreed she could not marry, but unable as yet to support herself independently in her professional career.

ELIZABETH E. SIDDAL

18. Clerk Saunders 1854

By the spring of 1854, Siddal was preparing a sequence of illustrations to a book of ballads to be edited by William Allingham. Two volumes of Siddal's own copy of Sir Walter Scott's *Border Minstrelsy* survive, showing seventeen texts marked, of which at least four were begun: *The Gay Goshawk*, *The Lass o'Lochroyan*, *Sir Patrick Spens*, and *Clerk Saunders*. Only the last of these seems to have been fully completed for woodblock engraving [see FIG. 18], while all except *The Gay Goshawk* were later reworked in watercolour.

Other early work includes an illustration of *Pippa and the Women of Loose Life* from Browning's dramatic poem, which is her version of the 'fallen woman' theme treated by Howitt at the same date, and an original composition now known as *Lovers Listening to Music* [FIG. 19), in which the male figure is a portrait of Rossetti. The whole drawing can be read as an imaginative representation of the artist and her beloved, the background landscape probably inspired by the romantic spot known as Lovers' Seat on the cliff walk between Fairlight and Hastings, where Siddal and Rossetti were together in the early summer of 1854. (A companion piece, incidentally, is Rossetti's own *Writing on the Sand*, showing a couple on a windy beach, the man drawing his beloved's profile in wet sand). In *Lovers Listening to Music* the oriental girls making music perhaps represent the 'song of love', and Love is probably the identity of the small, childlike cupid attending the couple.

This combination of conceptual sophistication and naive handling is characteristic of Siddal's work, and some part of her tuition may also have involved study of two early Pre-Raphaelite enthusiasms. Echoes of the work of William Blake (then generally neglected) and of late-medieval manuscript illumination are seen in her images, one striking example being her 1853 illustration to Tennyson's *Lady of Shalott*, which is similar in mood and composition, though not in detail, to a fifteenth-century illumination to Christine de Pisan's *Cité des Dames* in the British Museum.

By 1855 Siddal was occupied with a series of illustrations to Tennyson's poems, apparently in response to Rossetti's suggestion that she be included in the contributors to Edward Moxon's illustrated edition, alongside himself, Millais and Hunt. He urged this opinion on the author, and claimed triumphantly (but vainly) that 'Mrs T[ennyson] wrote immediately to Moxon about it, declaring that she would rather pay for Miss S's designs herself than not have them in the book'.[60] Although not commissioned, Siddal prepared illustrations to six Tennyson poems; that for *The Palace of Art*, depicting St Cecilia, was taken by Rossetti as the basis for his own illustration in the Moxon edition. 'In the wonderful illustration to the "Palace of Art",' wrote H. C. Marillier in 1899, 'Rossetti availed himself of a design by Miss Siddal.'[61]

This concentration on illustrative subjects suggests a careful assessment of commercial possibilities, as well as the constraints of her situation. Unable to afford studio space or materials of her own, Siddal's work remained generally small in scale and conventional in theme if not in treatment. At this time she was also engaged on a series of religious subjects which may have been intended as a sequence for the life of Christ, such as formed a staple theme in the work of early Italian art, and which was also in keeping with the mood of the Anglo-Catholic revival of the 1850s. Among these subjects are a stable scene *Nativity*, with Virgin and Child and attendant angel, several other Nativity sketches (including one with lamb and donkey), a watercolour version of the Madonna and Child, showing Christ as an active infant rather than swaddled babe, a Deposition, and a sketch for the Maries at the

ELIZABETH E. SIDDAL
19. Lovers Listening to Music 1854

Sepulchre, inscribed 'St John Chapter 20'. She also produced several designs showing angels, evidently intended for a carved capital.

Such subjects do not prove that the artist was a religious believer, although there is other evidence of her membership of the Congregational Church, but they accord with and amplify the commitment to Christian themes which forms a major strand in the story of Pre-Raphaelitism as a whole, and one to which a number of the female artists were especially drawn. The subjects may also have been calculated to appeal to Ruskin, and when the author of *On the Nature of Gothic* was shown Siddal's work in the spring of 1855 he responded by offering to buy her entire output, and pressed her to accept a regular allowance in exchange for whatever works she produced. Although this has been interpreted as a move designed to secure Rossetti's gratitude, it was consistent with Ruskin's habit of offering financial patronage to other artists, male and female, whom he believed to be needy and in sympathy

with his own ideas. He was given a carefully tailored account of her history, in which Rossetti had been responsible for discovering her talent for drawing, and her parents hostile to her ambitions; as a result, Ruskin reported:

> she is uncomfortable in her family who, although kind enough in other matters, set their faces steadily against all her artist's feelings – and have in no wise any sympathy with her, so that she goes up to her room without fire in the winter to hide herself while she draws.[62]

The qualities of Siddal's work at this date were comparable to those which Ruskin admired in medieval art, as he praised the awkward, expressive aspects of Gothic, and hailed the work of Rossetti and other Pre-Raphaelites as 'the dawn of a new era in art, in a true unison of the grotesque with the realistic power'. At this date, Rossetti sold several small pictures of his own to his patron, which seem indebted to the grotesque or 'Siddal' style of composition. The cramped, ill-drawn *Arthur's Tomb*, of which Ruskin wrote, 'I dare not show it to any anti-P[re] R[aphaelite]s but I value it intensely myself,'[63] is indeed so like a parody of Siddal's technical deficiencies in drawing that it has sometimes been attributed to her, to excuse Rossetti's 'failure'. This indicates how close Siddal's alleged incompetence was to the deliberate primitivism of the Pre-Raphaelites at this date.

Reluctant to accept the terms offered – she preferred to sell her work as it was produced – Siddal was 'coerced' (in Rossetti's words) into taking Ruskin's allowance. Her first purchase with the money was her own supply of brushes and paints. With the allowance (which in the event lasted only a year) came Ruskin's advice on how she should paint. He wished her to stop drawing 'fancies' or imaginative scenes, saying she should 'be made to draw in a dull way sometimes from dull things' – his own favoured subjects: stones, leaves, rock. Having also been told that she was grievously ill and 'probably dying', Ruskin sent her to an eminent physician, who found no traces of disease but pronounced her symptoms to be the result of 'mental power long pent up and lately overtaxed'. In one form or another this diagnosis – that the artistic and social intensity of the Pre-Raphaelite world was too great for her weak, female constitution – was to be repeated throughout her life and beyond, as if in justification of her failures. In the short term the result of Ruskin's well-meaning intervention was that Siddal was advised to be 'absolutely idle' in a warm climate, and not to exert herself with painting. She therefore spent the winter of 1855–56 on the Mediterranean coast at Nice, without congenial company, but still attempting to pursue her artistic studies. At Christmas she agreed with her patron on the 'vapid colour' of the local landscape, and he advised her to try the Italian Alps.

But she preferred to return to London, where she found Rossetti's affections were faltering. The following twelve months were emotionally stormy. But it was one of her most productive artistic seasons, during which she completed several watercolour compositions including the *Ladies' Lament* from Sir Patrick Spens, a watercolour of *The Lass of Lochroyan*, and one of *Clerk Saunders* [PL. 1], together with a finished version of *Lady Clare* in watercolour and bodycolour, inscribed with a new monogram and dated 1857.

In June of this year Siddal was among the contributors to the Pre-Raphaelite exhibition mounted at Russell Place in Fitzroy Street, where her work was shown alongside that of Madox Brown, Millais, Rossetti, Hunt and others. She exhibited three subject pictures: *We Are Seven*, *The Haunted Tree*, *Clerk Saunders* (sold to Charles Eliot Norton of Harvard for forty guineas), two drawings from Browning and Tennyson, and a *Study of a Head* – her self-portrait. In general the exhibition was accorded a muted reception; in particular Miss Siddal's work was mentioned by the *Saturday Review* and by William Rossetti in the *Spectator*, who remarked that it was 'quite unlike anything which the manner of lady artists has accustomed us to' – which was intended as a compliment.[64] Hunt recalled being favourably impressed, remarking that Siddal's works reminded him of Deverell's. *Clerk Saunders* was then included in an American Exhibition of British Art shown in New York, Philadelphia and Boston at the end of the year, where it was seen alongside work by many established artists and members of the RA and described as 'sketch for a picture', suggesting that a larger oil painting of the same subject was proposed. These were the only occasions on which her work was shown publicly.

In the summer of 1857, Siddal left London for Sheffield, where she visited family and friends, rented a house, and enrolled in the ladies' class at Sheffield Art School, then run by the energetic principal Young Mitchell. A contemporary student recalled:

> She attended the school regularly, and worked in the 'Figure Room'. She remained after class hours [11–1 on Wednesdays and Saturdays, advanced pupils having 'the privilege of studying till four in the afternoon']; so did I, and as I ate my luncheon and wandered through the rooms, I met with her and we talked sometimes, or if Mr Young Mitchell joined us, I listened to them, and it was then I first heard of Ruskin and the Pre-Raphaelites.[65]

The female class, according to the school's annual report, offered the kind of tuition Siddal lacked – basic instruction in outline drawing (figure, ornament, fruit, flowers and landscape), shading from the flat and the round, painting in oil and watercolour 'from Copies and Still Life. Fruits and Flowers from Nature etc.', and modelling from fruit, flowers and casts. The life class, with its studies from the human figure, was open to male students only.

From around 1856, with the new enthusiasm for late-medieval chronicles and tales by Froissart, Malory and Chrétien de Troyes, Pre-Raphaelitism became infected, as some regarded it, by archaism in painting and poetry. Siddal's work, already inspired by ancient narratives from border balladry, also reflected this new medievalism, as in her watercolour of the popular chivalric theme *Before the Battle* showing a knight and lady engaged in fixing a red pennon to the knight's lance, while outside squire and horse await his departure. A tournament scene entitled *The Woeful Victory* was more complex, with a young princess seeing the knight she loves vanquished and killed by the knight she must now marry. This subject, according to William Rossetti, was 'wholly her own invention' and was later used by Rossetti as the projected ending to his unfinished long poem *The Bride's Prelude*.

In the spring of 1858 the unofficial engagement between Siddal and Rossetti was broken off, he having repeatedly failed to honour his promises of marriage. It is not known where Siddal spent the subsequent months but it was probably during this period that she became severely addicted to the opiate drug laudanum. Her father died in the summer of 1859, leaving the cutlery business in the hands of his widow. In the spring of 1860, through Ruskin's intervention, Siddal was reunited with Rossetti, who, believing she was dying, finally arranged their wedding in Hastings and honeymoon in Paris. On returning to London

the couple settled in Gabriel's studio near Blackfriars Bridge, taking extra rooms to enlarge the apartment.

'Indeed and of course my wife *does* draw still,' Gabriel told Professor Norton early in 1861, adding:

> Her last designs would I am sure surprise and delight you . . . she has real genius – none of your make-believe – in conception and colour, and if she can only add a little more of the precision in carrying out which it so much needs health and strength to attain, she will, I am sure, paint such pictures as no woman has painted yet.[66]

This optimism was misplaced, although in the census return of 1861, Mrs Rossetti's occupation was listed, like that of her husband, as 'Artist: Painter' – a deliberate assertion, since married women's occupations were seldom given. She attempted to continue painting – while visiting Brighton with her sister she wrote for her paintbox 'as a means of keeping myself alive'. She participated in the mural-painting endeavours at the Morrises' new home Red House in Kent, and planned with Georgie Burne-Jones to illustrate a book of fairy tales. But addiction and then pregnancy inhibited artistic production. When her baby daughter was stillborn in May 1861, the balance of Siddal's mind was disturbed and her dependence on laudanum increased. In February 1862 she died of a massive overdose, which the coroner judged accidental.

Subsequently Rossetti collected together all Siddal's works, hanging her watercolours in his new home and having her drawings and sketches photographed for a memorial portfolio compiled in 1867. At his own death in 1882 a number of her works were sold as mementoes while most remained within the family, Christina Rossetti for example choosing to keep *St Agnes Eve* with its image of a novice nun. Few, if any, works were exhibited, but around the turn of the century several were reproduced in books about the PRBs and their associates. *Lovers Listening to Music* was reproduced in 1897, *The Woeful Victory* in 1899, *Lady Clare* in Percy Bate's book (1899) and *Galahad and the Holy Grail* in Ruskin's *Letters* (1912).

The glamour that surrounded the story of the original PRB led to a subsidiary cult of their model 'Lizzie', and in 1903 William Rossetti published a memoir of his late sister-in-law in the *Burlington Magazine*, giving a summary of her artistic career and listing twenty-three subjects. He commended her self-portrait as 'the most competent piece of execution that she ever produced, an excellent and graceful likeness and truly good: it is her very self', and defended her apparent lack of skill against the sneers of 'the present day, when vigorous brushwork and calculated "values"' were admired more than imagination and feeling. 'In those early "Pre-Raphaelite" days,' he wrote,

> and in the 'Pre-Raphaelite' environment, which was small and ringed round with hostile forces, things were estimated differently. The first question which my brother would have put to an aspirant is 'Have you an idea in your head?' This would have been followed by other questions, such as 'Is it an idea which can be expressed in the shape of a design? Can you express it with refinement, and with a sentiment of nature, even if not with searching realism?' He must have put these queries to Miss Siddal practically if not viva voce; and he found the response on her part to be such as to qualify her to begin, with a good prospect of her progressing.

He excused her weaknesses on the grounds that her health was 'so extremely bad that she was really not capable of going through the toils of a thorough artist student', and concluded that, 'without overrating her actual performances', she was 'a woman of unusual capacities, and worthy of being espoused to a painter and poet'.[67]

We need not linger over this assessment of woman's highest destiny, except to note that as a consequence of William Rossetti's account of Siddal's career and his insistence on her dependence on his brother (when her attendance at Sheffield Art School was revealed in 1911, William denied that Siddal had ever received any such formal training), her pictures have always been viewed as pale and incompetent imitations of her spouse's work. Several writers have indeed stated authoritatively that Rossetti worked on and was responsible for Siddal's more successful productions. 'There is no doubt that Gabriel Rossetti himself worked on this picture, as was customary with him,' noted the collector Fairfax Murray of *Clerk Saunders* (perhaps thereby hoping to raise its value), adding unjustly that 'much of the merit her works have belongs to him, and his aid is frequently visible in the preliminary drawings'.[68] Thus Elizabeth Siddal has been denied the credit for her own achievements as well as being sometimes blamed for Rossetti's failures.

Our summary of Siddal's short career has attempted at least a partial disentangling of her work from that of her husband. In this context, her display of drawings to Mr Deverell, her persistence in the face of family indifference, her work as a model to the PRB (possibly her only access to the studio), her choice of Rossetti as instructor, her acceptance of Ruskin's allowance, her participation in the Russell Place exhibition and her attendance at Sheffield Art School, should all be interpreted as the actions of an artist aspiring to professional status. And it is appropriate that her death in 1862 marked the closing of the first, intense, naive and perhaps most adventurous phase of the Pre-Raphaelite movement.

THE

SECOND

GENERATION

1865–80

etween the mid-1860s and the end of the 1870s, Pre-Raphaelitism was in its second phase, and by this time women artists had become a fixed feature of British culture. Census returns in 1861 and 1871 showed a continuing rise in numbers nationally, from 853 to 1069 respectively, and exhibitions testified to the overall acceptance of the female artist as a phenomenon that had proved itself a fact of life. The publication in 1876 of Ellen Clayton's two-volume *English Female Artists* was a sign, too, that this creature had entered the ranks of social types, numerous enough to attract the attention of the encyclopaedist and her audience.

Although the number of women in the annual Royal Academy exhibitions of the later 1860s and early 1870s stayed below a hundred, this small proportion of the total exhibitors was now routinely noticed by reviewers, only a few of whom found it still necessary to approach their works with a display of basic prejudice or defensive argument. At other London venues, such as the Society of British Artists or the British Institution, numbers of female exhibitors rose steadily throughout this period. The opening of the Dudley Gallery in 1865, first as a watercolour venue but soon adding an oil show, provided women artists with a new exhibition forum in which they quickly became a feature. The establishment of the Grosvenor Gallery in 1877 as a showplace for Pre-Raphaelite and Aesthetic art indicated that the range of venues would expand even further for the next generation, although here exhibition was by invitation only of the founder, Sir Coutts Lindsay.

Perhaps because of this acceptance, the Society of Female Artists, established in 1857 to publicise the fact of women artists' existence and provide them with an unprejudiced arena for their works, suffered a decline during the 1860s. It reoriented itself in 1865 from an exhibiting body with an annual show based on jury selection and commissions on sales, to a quasi-charitable institution with patrons and patronesses (sic) who could guarantee financial survival. To secure artists' commitment, a subscriber system was created as a further precaution. Between the mid-1860s and mid-1870s the SFA still exhibited an average of nearly two hundred women artists – twice that of the RA – but its claim to artistic status declined further. In 1872 it changed its name to the Society of Lady Artists, and this slight but eloquent alteration signified the society's abandonment of any feminist stance with which it might be said to have started out, and indicated its belief that the female artist was now an undisturbing fixture in a comfortable niche of her own.

But a niche it was, and no more, as far as the Royal Academy was concerned. Although there was journalistic pressure throughout the 1860s to open the RA to women on equal terms with men, both in the Schools and in membership, the Academy resisted any encroachment on its privilege by women artists. Despite being forced in 1867 to repeal its quota for female students, membership in the RA continued to be fiercely guarded by Academicians for men alone. 'Where then is the woman who is entitled to put those coveted letters of RA after her name?' enquired a reader of the *Examiner* in 1871 and, recognising that it wasn't a simple matter of aesthetic affinity which made membership desirable, went on: 'everyone well knows the *money* value (to mention no others) of the magic letters.'[1] The death of Margaret Carpenter in 1872 kept the matter in circulation; typically, the *Art Journal*'s obituary concluded:

> Had the Royal Academy abrogated the law which denies a female admission to its ranks, Mrs Carpenter would most assuredly have gained, as she merited, a place in them; but we despair of ever living to see the 'rights of women' vindicated in this respect: the doors of the institution are yet too narrow for such to find entrance.[2]

Then in 1874 the sudden success of the young artist Elizabeth Thompson with her painting *The Calling of the Roll after the Crimea*, selected as the RA exhibition's 'picture of the year', gave further impetus to the argument for female admission to Academy membership. Since Thompson's large and stark picture was praised largely for its perceived lack of feminine weakness and therefore its supposed achievement of masculine strength, a ban based purely on gender seemed all at once to many more people a poor rationale on which to base the recognition of excellence. Accordingly, a covert campaign for the admission of women began in 1875 with the putting forward of female names by sympathetic Academicians, hoping to force a change in the rules. It was not successful, although it kept the Academy's mind focused on the question for the rest of the decade.

The Academy's importance was steadily declining in other respects, however: most obviously in education. A significant development in art education for women occurred in 1871 with the establishment of the Slade School of Art as part of University College London. Its first director, Edward Poynter, claimed from the outset to recognise women's equal claim to art education. In his opening address he acknowledged the hindrance which female art students had suffered in the areas of anatomical study and life study, promising to supply that deficiency. Further encouragement might be required, however; in 1874 the daughter of John Marshall, the Pre-Raphaelites' physician, enrolled in a weekly class at the Slade. On the first day she saw 'an Indian *all but* unclothed . . . being drawn by men and women together' and was forbidden by her father to continue.[3] In proof of Poynter's good intentions, the Slade's medals and scholarships were also open equally to female candidates, and indeed many of these rewards were won by girls and women in the Slade's first five years. As the critic Charlotte Weeks recalled a decade later when writing about women at the Slade:

> Here, for the first time in England, indeed in Europe, a public Fine Art school was thrown open to male and female students on precisely the same terms, and giving to both sexes fair and equal opportunities. And it is to the precedent then established that ladies have since elsewhere had the necessary advantages for study placed within their reach.[4]

It was as well for potential artists of the female sex that the Slade did offer such opportunities, for the Female School in the government system had been allowed to decline by the mid-1860s into an institution relying on charitable support and royal patronage.

Broadly speaking, the government system of schools of design had a low reputation among women studying for fine art in the 1870s, since those institutions still offered basically a design and not a fine-art training. As Barbara Bodichon's niece Amy Leigh Smith was advised by her aunt's friends in 1878, not only were the students at the Slade of a higher social class, but 'the teaching is much more what you want at the first than at the second. The South Kensington is a *school of design*, you want to learn to be an artist, not a designer, don't you?'[5] This, it should be noted, was the 'strong-minded' approach to the question, for the South Kensington School of Design had received quite a fillip among many aspiring students and their parents when it became known that Elizabeth Thompson had studied there.

For the second generation of Pre-Raphaelites, the creative field had not only opened but opened up, to include in its spectrum other arts such as photography – 'few professional photographers have gained as much fame, or more honours, than Mrs Cameron,' *The English Woman's Review* tempted its readers in 1867 in an article on 'Photography as an Employment for Women'[6] – as well as illustration, engraving for the press, and drawing for the fashion industry. Although there were still obstacles to overcome, the general perception was that the woman and art question was being won by the liberalising forces. The general debate about women in British society was by no means settled, however; if anything, it was escalating, with the publication in 1869 of J. S. Mill's *On the Subjection of Women* and the vivid and heated debate over the Contagious Diseases Act governing prostitution, which began on the first day of 1870. But within this general perspective, the female artist was now a matter of fact. In the would-be liberal voice of the *Art Journal*, reviewing the Academy exhibition of 1870, one hears how emphatically the female artist was now established, but also how unresolved were the basic arguments affecting her acceptance. In remarking on the picture *Lost* by Emily Osborn, one of the painters then seen as typical of the rise of women artists, the *Art Journal* said it was 'worthy, we will not say, of a "female artist" – now a term of contempt – it holds its place strongly by its genuine pictorial merits'.[7]

Lucy Madox Brown (1843–94) and her half-sister Catherine inherited Pre-Raphaelitism more literally than any other artists studied here. As painters, their Pre-Raphaelitism seems to have been assumed from the start, and certainly the first historians of the movement automatically included the two women as successors to their father – although more to his credit than their own. Thus Percy Bate mentioned the sisters under their married names as a coda to his account of their father, along with their brother:

> No notice of Madox Brown, however brief, would be complete which did not include an allusion to the accomplished attainments of his daughters, Mrs Hueffer and Mrs W. M. Rossetti, and the dawning genius of his son Oliver. The work of both Mrs Hueffer and Mrs Rossetti is notable for charm and distinction, the portraits and fancy heads of the former, and especially the subject pictures of the latter, being remarkable in a high degree.[8]

Lucy was the eldest of Madox Brown's children, born in Paris to his first wife, Elizabeth Bromley. Her mother died in 1845, while the young couple were returning to Britain, and her distraught father, whose career was only at its beginning, placed his child in the care of her aunt, Helen Bromley, in Kent, who was later said to have been the greatest friend of her childhood. Indeed, Lucy saw her father only on visits over the next few years. His life, meanwhile, developed in ways that shaped Lucy's later life considerably: he became a father for the second time in 1850, when Catherine was born to him and Emma Hill, a young woman whom he was employing as a model. Brown married Emma in 1853, and from then on Lucy spent her school holidays with her father and his new family in Finchley. Another child, Oliver, who became their father's favourite, was born in 1855, followed by a second son, Arthur, who was born in 1856 and died in infancy.

One of Catherine's sons, later the author Ford Madox Ford, writing in 1897 of his mother and aunt, said that Lucy 'was a quick learner, and retained to the end of her life sufficient scholastic and classical knowledge to render her conversation brilliant, and well grounded'.[9] This was a tribute to her aunt Helen as well as herself, and also to Frances Rossetti and her daughters Maria and Christina, who took over Lucy's education in 1856, when she came to live in London with her father's family, now resident in Kentish Town. In 1865 they moved to a large house in Fitzroy Square.

Madox Brown used Lucy extensively as a model over the years and, as she grew older, also as a studio assistant. His diary gives vivid glimpses of the trials this industry brought his young helper. 'Drew at the man's hand again, then painted in the woman's glove from Lucy holding the Nurse's hand,' he recorded in March 1855 while working on *The Last of England*; 'dined, then at 4 p.m. out into back yard and painted the man's hand from my own with Lucy holding it (in a Glass). Snow on the ground and very cold.' In the summer, work was still in progress: 'All day after at the hand of the scoundrel in the picture trying to make him with a glass of brandy and water in it. Lucy sitting for it with a glass of beer spilt the whole in her lap being asleep.'[10] She was twelve years old, and for that day her father noted a total of eight hours spent at his easel.

Her graduation from model to apprentice artist seems to have come relatively late. The account given in 1876 by Ellen Clayton, which was repeated by later commentators, suggests a dramatic and, more curiously, unexpected entrance into the role of potential artist:

> Miss Lucy Madox Brown's early art education was a peculiar one, and might be said to have consisted in a special kind of mental development. With the exception of drawing for two or three months, at the age of eight or nine, she made no practical attempt till a casual necessity suddenly revealed her innate ability. It was about the beginning of 1868: one of her father's assistants failed to do some routine work, and she boldly volunteered to supply the defaulter's place. So well did she carry out this task that she was encouraged to begin studying in earnest.[11]

She probably went to study part time at the government School of Design while receiving more important guidance from Madox Brown himself. Certainly Lucy's nephew recalled her energies being no less bound up with her father's as she reached adulthood:

> Later, both Lucy and Cathie assisted their father in his studio – arranging lay figures, drawing from his models, and occasionally doing a little work on his replicas. Lucy also acted as her father's amanuensis. I have in my possession hundreds – I had almost said thousands – of copies of Madox Brown's carefully studied business letters in the handwriting of his eldest daughter.[12]

Even so, in the 1871 census both daughters were listed as 'students' rather than artists, although by the late 1860s all three of Madox Brown's children had attained an exhibitable and saleable level of skill and were regarded by their proud father as forming, with him, a veritable family firm. In May 1869, Madox Brown wrote to fellow painter Frederick Shields:

> Other commissions will follow this one, I feel. This has been the first one I have had this year, indeed, since June, I think, of last year. However, Lucy, Cathy and Nolly selling four pictures for small sums have helped to keep things square.[13]

Lucy's public debut came only a year after she began painting seriously, at the Dudley Gallery watercolour show of 1869, with *Painting*, taken from her sister Cathy at work in the studio. Its reception was mixed, but the critics certainly noticed it. Of the more favourable reviews, the *Athenaeum* bracketed it with Marie Spartali's *Nerea Foscari*:

Miss Brown makes her first appearance this year; yet, by her work alone, we should conclude that she has practised long and well. So far, however, would this conclusion be from the truth, that we have now to commend Miss Brown's first picture in 'Painting', no. 239, which represents a student seated at work at her easel, and surrounded by studio properties. It is seldom that so deeply-toned and soberly-coloured a picture comes from the hands of a lady; rarely have we seen an example of such high technical merit from those of a tyro. Miss Spartali's key of colour and pitch of tone differ widely from those which Miss Brown employs: she deals with the richer and more luminous development of these elements of art; the other lady is successful in graver, if not broader, and more sober, if not more potent appearances than those which her companion here affects. Both artists lack the fruits of severe study, this is made evident by their common shortcomings in respect to the representing of form by drawing outlines and modelling contours . . .[14]

Although Lucy was seven years older than Cathy and twelve years older than Oliver, the three emerged on the scene at the same time, and the extended Pre-Raphaelite family was quick to claim them as its own. William Rossetti, writing an essay in 1871 for a survey of contemporary British artists, took care to include a section with the heading 'Miss Spartali [and] the Junior Madox Browns'. Here he recognised that while the day of Pre-Raphaelitism was over, coming artists such as these could yet be seen as Pre-Raphaelites:

We have got clear out of the era of Pre-Raphaelitism, and are only attached to it by a link of connexion and tradition. Mr Madox Brown had distinguished himself as a painter and designer before Pre-Raphaelitism existed [and] as the Pre-Raphaelite movement expanded, he lent it his powerful but independent support. Of late years, our exhibitions have been conscious of his influence, not only in the original works which he continues from time to time to contribute, but also in the production of a small knot of painters formed under his immediate training. The fact that all his own children – three in number – are among these, lends an exceptional interest to the case.[15]

At the time this was written, Lucy was showing another watercolour, *Après le bal*, at the Dudley, and an oil entitled *The Duet* at the Royal Academy. These were followed at the Dudley in 1871 by *Romeo and Juliet*, generally agreed to be her finest work [FIG. 23]. She was also successful in provincial centres of Pre-Raphaelitism such as Liverpool (exhibiting there 1871–73), Manchester (1870–75) and Birmingham (1874–79), although her work was never accepted again at the RA. Her subjects were varied, and always ambitious in their presentation of figural relationships. *The Fair Geraldine and the Earl of Surrey* followed at the Dudley in 1872, together with an oil in the Dudley's painting show the same year of a second Shakespearian subject, *Ferdinand and Miranda*, from *The Tempest* [PL. 5]. In 1873, the grim but dramatic scene of *Margaret Roper*, retrieving the head of her executed father Thomas More from London Bridge, was rejected by the RA [PL. 4].

In 1869, Lucy had travelled briefly in Belgium and Germany with Jane and William Morris, and in 1873 she was invited to join the artist William Bell Scott, his wife Letitia, the painter Alice Boyd and William Rossetti on a trip to Italy. On her return, at the age of twenty-nine, she became engaged to William Rossetti, fourteen years her senior, and they married in the spring of 1874.

After her marriage, Lucy's artistic activity was reduced to a desultory affair, despite her husband's professed support for her painting, and her only exhibition appearances after 1874 were with earlier works sent to the Birmingham exhibitions of 1878 and 1879. She became pregnant soon after marrying, although it is said by descendants that the stress of living in the Rossetti family home with her husband's mother and sister – whose position in the household was displaced by what her husband called Lucy's 'enthronement as bride' – caused her to suffer a miscarriage late in 1874. As recorded in her brother-in-law's letters to his aunt, 'poor Lucy's health seems still further seriously affected by her pain of mind and exertions as a nurse'.[16] This was in November 1874, the month that her half-brother Oliver died of a sudden and unexpected illness.

The first of Lucy's five children was born in September 1875 and named Olivia. Lucy's health had never been strong and she suffered frequently from minor but debilitating colds and failures of strength. All parties acknowledging the difficulties of living together, Mrs Rossetti and Christina moved out of the Rossetti home in 1876. In the absence of her own

LUCY MADOX BROWN

22. Romeo & Juliet in the Tomb 1871

testimony, Lucy's creative decline can be gathered from her husband's later recollection of this period:

> After our marriage she tried more than once to set resolutely to work again; but the cares of a growing family, delicate health, and a thousand constant interruptions which are not the less real at the time for being dim in the after-memory, always impeded her and very much to her disappointment and vexation she did not succeed in producing any more work adapted for exhibition.[17]

The births of a son, Arthur, a second daughter, Helen, and in 1881 twins, Michael (who died in infancy) and Mary, were no doubt, with ill health, major impediments to painting. Lucy undertook her children's early education – their aunt Christina noting how she was training their intellects while her sister Cathy supplied their musical education – and also took care of Cathy's daughter Juliet in 1889, when after her husband's death Cathy's own health broke down.

In 1885, after contracting pneumonia, Lucy showed symptoms of the tuberculosis that would eventually cause her death. At the same time, her identification with art was seen in several pieces of writing, among them a long article on her father for the *Magazine of Art* in 1889 and a biography of Mary Wollstonecraft Shelley in 1890. Despite extended stays in warmer climates in the late 1880s – San Remo in 1886, Pau and Biarritz in 1888 – her health declined inexorably, especially after 1892. Her stepmother died in 1890, her father in 1893 and Lucy herself lasted only until 12 April 1894, when she died in San Remo aged fifty.

Unsurprisingly, the career of Catherine Madox Brown (1850–1927, known within the family variously as Cathie, Cathy and Katty) had close parallels with that of her half-sister. As clear as their common bond to the Pre-Raphaelite movement is their position as artists *manquées*, torn from their professional potential and ambitions by octopuslike domestic demands. In 1921, Cathy's daughter Juliet wrote of her mother:

When she was a girl she had painted some very beautiful pictures which had been admired by famous artists, and placed in exhibitions, and nearly always sold. But she couldn't give much time to painting because there was always someone ill or in trouble, or who wanted taking care of. At first she took care of her father and mother and her brother Oliver, who was said to be a genius. When she was married she took care of my father and her children and her house and servants and a lot of other people besides, and then she gave up painting altogether. Sometimes when she was telling me about it her face would look wistful and she'd sigh and say, 'It *did* seem a pity!' But then she'd correct herself immediately afterwards and say she thought perhaps she had been happier taking care of other people than painting pictures.[18]

Sharing the financially hard-pressed early life of Lucy, Cathy was, in addition, an illegitimate child only officially acknowledged two years after her birth, when her parents married; her birth date was conveniently obscured to conceal this irregularity. Throughout her childhood, she too was used as an artist's model, and by the time she was thirteen, her father sometimes took up her time for as long as seven or eight hours a day. Probably soon after this she was enrolled at Queen's College, Harley Street, conveniently close to Fitzroy Square, the first of the new day schools offering a serious academic education to girls rather than the social accomplishments taught in most finishing schools for young ladies. Here Cathy studied with other young women keen to become artists or, like her, from artistic families.

By the late 1860s she was being instructed by her father, and emerged onto the exhibition scene at the Royal Academy in 1869, with *At the Opera*, a head and shoulders which was brought to critical attention by being hung 'on the line', in the most favoured position, at eye-level. In the same season the Dudley exhibition included her portrait of fellow student Ellen (Nellie) Epps, who became another pupil of Madox Brown. Cathy's subsequent work was almost all in portraiture, although she also produced an occasional landscape or fancy head. Her son Ford Madox Ford, writing at the end of the century, characterised her oeuvre with the words 'Catherine Madox Brown was – and remains – essentially a portrait painter'.[19] In September 1869 her father told Lucy that Cathy was planning portraits of both her parents, depicting her mother 'in the black flame-powdered grenadine [dress] sitting near to the window in the drawing room at needlework, but *musing*, it looks most lovely in nature, so I hope may turn out well' [FIG. 26].[20] This was exhibited at the RA in 1870 under the title *Thinking*, and complements her portrait of her father done in the same period [FIG. 25].

Her other exhibition appearances make a short list, since marriage in 1872 virtually put an end to her professional life. *Thinking* appeared again at the Manchester exhibition later the same year; in 1872 her portrait of Nellie's sister Laura Epps, recently married to the academic painter Laurens Alma-Tadema (and herself an artist who exhibited regularly) was shown at the RA, and her full-length portrait of Madox Brown was shown at the Liverpool exhibition; and in 1874 she showed a fancy head of a small girl called *M'liss* at the Manchester show. A sequel, *A Deep Problem*, was shown at the same venue the following year, together with a landscape, *Cromer* [FIG. 27]. Mostly watercolour, her work was unusually substantial for the medium and remarked upon, where it was noticed, for richness of colour and solidity of form.

In 1872 Catherine Madox Brown married the German-born musicologist Franz (Francis)

CATHERINE MADOX BROWN
24. Ford Madox Brown (the Artist's Father) 1870

CATHERINE MADOX BROWN
25. Thinking (the Artist's Mother) 1870

Hueffer, the ceremony taking place in a registry office in keeping with the Brown family's 'advanced' views, which included atheism, republicanism and in the 1890s even – among Lucy's children – anarchism. The honeymoon took Cathy and her husband to France and Italy. In 1873 she became a mother, her first son Ford being followed by a second, Oliver, and then by a daughter, Juliet, in 1879. In 1874 she was much distressed by the sudden death of her brother Oliver at the age of nineteen. She continued to paint occasionally, for her own pleasure; there is, for instance, an oil sketch of her two boys when young. But her life was further assailed when her husband died suddenly of heart failure in 1889.

Although Cathy belonged to a so-called advanced circle, her family friend and solicitor Theodore Watts Dunton was placed in charge of her financial affairs, becoming her trustee and her sons' guardian. When Cathy's health broke down after her husband's death, Lucy looked after little Juliet while she convalesced. She was offered a pension from the Privy Purse in recognition of Hueffer's achievements, but Madox Brown's political views led him to reject it on her behalf. Subsequently he became the small family's chief financial support, and Cathy and the boys moved to live with him. She was thus in straitened and dependent circumstances, and had for example to go regularly to collect her allowance from Watts Dunton, as if on charity. In desperation she took her elder son to ingratiate himself with his German relatives in the early 1890s, hoping to ensure a share of the sizeable wealth which their unconventional English relatives hoped these successful business people would leave.

CATHERINE MADOX BROWN

26. Cromer 1875

Cathy nursed her mother until her death in 1890, which was followed by the death of her father in 1893 and that of her half-sister in 1894. These sad events seem to have brought down a veil of melancholy over the rest of her life, as her daughter later described:

So many people she had loved had died within the past few years: my father and my grandfather, who was her father, and my grandmother, who was her mother, and my aunt, who was her half-sister; and she always seemed to be afraid that other people were going to die . . .[21]

Both her sons proved difficult and wayward: Ford, a precocious author, eloped in 1894 with a teenage girl, and sponged off his mother and her family for the rest of the decade, while Oliver became a gambler and spendthrift who had debts of £200 by the age of seventeen. Over the next twenty years, Cathy often travelled to the Continent, as and when Ford's erratic habits dictated; in 1904 she nursed him through a nervous breakdown and then accompanied him to Germany to recuperate. In 1905 she went to France with his estranged wife and children, and in 1911 made another trip to Germany with her errant son, who was claiming to be married to a second woman, although not divorced. In 1924, Catherine Madox Brown contracted diabetes and died three years later in London. As an artist, the last the public had seen of her work was in 1901 when the earlier landscape *Cromer* appeared in an exhibition at the Whitechapel Gallery, London, as a companion to her father's paintings.

Emma Sandys (1843–77) was also the daughter and sister of artists, but very little is now known about her life and work. She was born in Norwich to a textile-worker mother and a father who had turned from the dyeing trade to portrait painting. She was named for the former, Mary Ann Emma Negus Sandys. Her brother, named Anthony Frederick for their father, was fourteen years older. This age difference is emphasised by the existence of portraits of Emma by Frederick, showing that she was still a child when he had already attained a marketable level of painterly proficiency. She lived always in his shadow: although Frederick made his name in the art world of London, Emma stayed in Norwich, at the same address, all her life.

Emma Sandys was sent to school as a girl and was later taught art by her father, just as her brother had been. Even so, at the age of nineteen she was not entered in the 1861 census as an artist. It is evident, however, that she became a professional artist soon after this, since one of her earliest exhibited works, *Girl with a Butterfly*, shown at the Norwich and Eastern Counties Working Classes Industrial Exhibition in 1867, was listed as the property of William Dixon, a local collector who later owned at least two other pictures by the artist, *Pleasant Dreams* and *Devotion* (currently unlocated). Sandys's other exhibit at this, her first show, was *Preparing for the Ball*, sometimes erroneously called 'The Lady of Shalott'. Other early works, not apparently exhibited, include *Portrait of a Saxon Princess* (1863), *Adeline* (1864), and the female head which appeared engraved in *London Society* in 1865 as 'A Maid of Athens'. These are medium-sized oil heads, typical of what she was to make her speciality.

The year after her exhibition debut Sandys again exhibited locally, at the Norwich Fine Arts Association, but also at the Royal Academy, with *Enid*. This was the first of her four appearances at the Academy: in 1870 she showed two child portraits; in 1873 another literary

fancy, *Undine*; and in 1874 a chalk head of the *Duchess of St Albans*. Her only other London exhibition appearance was at the Society of Lady Artists in 1874, with *Fair Rosamund*.

Although Sandys's work has been confused with her brother's since his death, there are sufficient pictures surviving that are demonstrably by her for some characteristics of her output to be clear. She evidently worked in the same vein of literary or fancy heads as Frederick began in and which was in the 1860s especially dependent on Shakespearian and Tennysonian references. Frederick had entered Pre-Raphaelite circles in 1857 and doubtless brought that influence back to his sister in Norwich. Her heads of *Adeline, Enid, Elaine* (undated, exhibited 1885), *Ophelia* (undated, sold 1910) and *Viola* (undated, presented to the Walker Art Gallery 1908) [FIG. 2] are obviously part of the second generation Pre-Raphaelite preoccupation with woman as icon, vividly costumed and richly coloured, and extracted from their literary narratives to represent the drama of womanhood.

Pictorial evidence indicates brother and sister working closely together, both under the spell of Rossettian Pre-Raphaelitism. Shared subjects – for example, *Onora*, painted by Fred in 1861 and Emma in 1867 – and a shared stock of studio props – the cloak worn in Fred's *Vivien* of 1863 and Emma's anonymous female head of 1866, or the shell in Fred's *Medea* of 1868 and Emma's so-called *The Shell* drawing of 1873 – suggest a close, businesslike partnership, in which Emma may have acted as Fred's unacknowledged assistant as well as producing her own work. Emma being considerably younger and single, this situation would have seemed natural to many. A notable characteristic of the paintings known to be by Emma is the variety of her models. In some cases she evidently took her lead from a Rossettian type but elsewhere her women – whether actual individuals or imaginary figures taken from employed models – remain various and individualised.

Emma Sandys became a skilled and valued portrait painter, particularly of children [FIG. 28], equally capable in oils and chalks [FIG. 20], and attracting a variety of sitters within the Norfolk region and beyond. Evidently some portrait commissions led to other figure work. Thus a vivid and charming oil portrait of a child called *Beatrice Blanche Cloakes* [PL. 7] which, although not apparently exhibited, is dated 1871, is presumably related to the presence of Sandys's *Ophelia* in the sale of I. B. Cloakes of Norwich in 1910.

During her short career, Sandys attracted very little critical attention, in contrast to the somewhat scandalous reputation her brother gained in the 1860s, not only for his irregular private life (a wife in Norwich and a subsequent common-law wife and family in London) and irresponsibility, but also for his plagiarism of other artists' ideas (notably Rossetti's). Even in accounts of her brother's work she gets short shrift. J. M. Gray, writing on Frederick in the *Art Journal* in 1884, merely remarked on 'a sister, Miss E. Sandys, who died recently after having produced much interesting though far from perfect work'.[22] Indeed, perhaps her evident unevenness is a significant factor: of the twenty or so verified works currently known, some are precise, confident, sophisticated, beautiful and compelling, while others are more like hack work, inept, unsubtle and crude. It is impossible to explain this aspect of her oeuvre without more knowledge of her life. Her early death at the age of thirty-four aroused little press interest. The local paper carried a mere notification of her demise in 1877, from congestion of the lungs, although in later times local people remembered her and her brother vividly, recalling being asked to sit for both artists in the studio in Grapes Hill, Norwich, Emma Sandys's lifelong residence.

EMMA SANDYS

27. Lady Winifred Herbert 1870

Julia Margaret Cameron, née Pattle (1815–79), is in many ways an anomalous figure in this study of Pre-Raphaelitism, yet provides an eloquent example of the popularity and potential the movement had for both amateur and professional artists and its extension to the pictorial art of photography. She is placed here as a member of the second generation, since her enthusiastic engagement with Pre-Raphaelitism began only in 1864, and her understanding of it was not so much Ruskinian as Rossettian.

Julia Pattle was born in Calcutta, where her father enjoyed a high position in the civil service by which Britain administered its large colony. Her mother was French, with one daughter already; there were to be seven more, and a son. As girls, Julia and her sisters were educated in England and France, shuttling back and forth between India and Europe where their maternal grandmother brought them up with ladylike accomplishments and European sophistication. The Pattle sisters became celebrated amongst their kind for their beauty, wit and intelligence. In British India the family enjoyed the importance of the large fish in a small pool: according to one visitor of 1850, 'You must know that wherever you go in India, you meet with some member of this family. Every other man has married, and every other woman has been, a Miss Pattle.'[23] Julia, however, was considered something of the ugly duckling, and in 1838, at the age of twenty-three, found a respected rather than dashing husband in Charles Hay Cameron, a liberal scholar and legal man, and a widower twenty years her senior.

The next ten years were hectic for Julia Cameron. Not only was she expected to take a prominent part in the expatriate community, since her husband's rank was one of the highest in that society, but she became a mother six times over between 1839 and 1848. Since the death of her eldest sister Adeline in 1836, Julia had been the senior daughter and so on her parents' deaths in 1845 she became the head of the family. Additionally, she took on the role of unofficial wife to Governor-General Hardinge, who as a bachelor needed a 'right-hand woman' to organise the British community's social functions as well as the women's philanthropic work. By the time Julia's husband retired in 1848 and the Camerons returned to Britain, most of the other sisters, with their families, were also back in the old country.

The family settled in Tunbridge Wells but rapidly established an acquaintance among the cultural figures who peopled the salon of Julia's sister Sara Prinsep in Kensington. Already in 1847, Julia had tried her hand at an activity independent of marriage and the home, when her translation of the popular German writer Gottfried August Bürger's ballad 'Lenore' was published with illustrations by Daniel Maclise.

The most influential friend Julia made in her sister's home, from an artistic circle including Holman Hunt, Rossetti and Millais, was the painter George Frederick Watts, whose classically derived imagery was presented in a painterly style which she later tried to emulate in photography. Watts was joined in her estimation by the Poet Laureate Alfred Tennyson, whose acquaintance she made in 1850 when she moved to the Surrey suburbs of London. Within the fashionable indulgence of hero worship, Cameron became fanatical in her devotion to these two cultural lions of the day, especially Tennyson. In 1860, she moved her family home to the Isle of Wight in emulation of the poet, joining other upper-middle-class households in imitating the royal couple who had set up a holiday home at Osborne, where the widowed Queen Victoria spent much of her time.

Cameron's role in the world of culture was that of organiser, benefactor and fan until 1863, when her daughter Julia gave her a camera, as a novelty that might divert some of her mother's redoubtable energies. With this apparatus, the art lover and the artist became combined in one.

Characteristically, once she began photography her enthusiasm rapidly became a commitment which others might easily call an obsession. As her biographer Amanda Hopkinson put it: 'All the abundant energy and much of the enthusiasm she had poured into her family, house-guests and friends, her cookery and home entertainments, her sporadic bouts of gardening and home-decorating, was now redirected.'[24] The energetic, uninhibited woman who tended to smother the people and projects she took on, now let herself be taken over by photography. Visitors and local residents pressed into service as models or assistants testified to the intensity of Cameron's new-found creativity, which was, of course, paralleled by the enthusiasms of many more novice photographers up and down the country, many of whom also tried to imitate painterly Pre-Raphaelitism in photography.

Lacking neither leisure nor means, she set herself to learn a relatively new, very messy and culturally controversial métier. Intending to function as more than an amateur, she enlisted in the Photographic Society of Great Britain in 1864, presenting Watts, whom she credited as her mentor, with an album of her work. She immediately began registering her photographs with the Fine Arts Register of the Public Record Office, and entered into an arrangement with the art dealers Colnaghi in London for sale of her work. This was the venue of her first solo show in 1865, a year in which she also exhibited in Berlin and at the International Exhibition in Dublin, as well as in Scotland and in London.

Her favourite genres were soon established: portraiture, imaginative figure compositions and fancy heads. Her pictures included images of her now famous friends and of her relatives and servants, sometimes presented in fancy guise, such as *Paul and Virginia* (1865) or *The Annunciation* (1865), and sometimes as straightforward likenesses. Her photographs excited criticism for their technical idiosyncrasies and effusive sentiment, but they attracted a bronze medal in Berlin in 1865 and a gold from the same exhibition the following year. Of her initial public reception, Cameron later wrote:

The Photographic Society of London in the Journal would have dispirited me very much

JULIA M. CAMERON

29. Mariana 1874

had I not valued that criticism at its worth. It was unsparing and too manifestly unjust for me to attend to it. The more lenient and discerning judges gave me larger spaces upon their walls, which seemed to invite the irony and spleen of the printed notice.[25]

As one of her recent biographers has put it: 'She was severely criticised by contemporary photographic practitioners for her careless technique, but lavishly praised by artists and art critics for the pictures she produced.'[26]

In 1867, the year in which she produced some of her most enduring and least self-indulgent work, she gained an honourable mention at the International Exhibition in Paris. To follow this up, she paid for a one-woman show in January 1868 at the German Gallery in London. Her assiduity in distributing her work had as much to do with financial need as with the seriousness with which she took herself and her new-found vocation, for the Camerons' income from their coffee and rubber plantations became less secure and less adequate as the 1860s progressed and in one year the coffee crop failed entirely.

Cameron produced a range of work, all inspired by painterly examples. This tendency in photographers of the 1850s and 1860s to emulate painting was widespread and most popular in the work of Henry Peach Robinson and Oscar Reilander before Cameron's own pictures became well known. Her characteristic products were informed by admiration for the early-Renaissance piety which Ruskin and the first generation of Pre-Raphaelites professed to see in painters like Perugino, whose Madonnas are echoed by Cameron's, but also by the fervent love of physical beauty which Rossetti's work and ideas led the second generation to make a priority. Cameron's favourite painting was reportedly Arthur Hughes's *April Love* (1856), which indicates very well her position vis-à-vis Pre-Raphaelitism. For Hughes, a follower of Millais, whose standing figures against a wall, hedge or leaf-covered background he often imitated, made sentiment the chief subject of his pictures and literature their backbone. Similarly, although Cameron often posed figures out of doors [FIG. 31] or suggested a natural environment through such accessories as branches and flowers, hers was not a Ruskinian love of nature but a Rossettian celebration of the sources of passion and poetry. Hence her numerous allegories, Shakespearian [FIG. 30] and Tennysonian groups, and generalised vehicles of sentiment like *The Kiss of Peace* (1869) and *The Dream* (1869). Although Cameron wrote to Ruskin in 1868 for an opinion of her work, it was not his exactitude and submission of imagination to facts which she followed but rather his belief in a moral visual world. In appearance, her images evoke the female icons of Dante Gabriel Rossetti and the catalogue of Pre-Raphaelite historico-literary enthusiasms, and in theme the idealism of G. F. Watts. Even so, many of Cameron's specific subjects were original to her, her vision and range of represented womanhood far wider than the repetitive mythology celebrated by her two male mentors.

Her most emphatic works were those in which the photographer's instinct to ornament the fact in order to achieve greater beauty is at its most restrained, placing the work more within the imitative genre of portraiture than in the inventive ones of literary or religious art. Among the examples which increased Cameron's fame and success were the likenesses of prominent men that she made between 1867 and 1870. They included not only Tennyson and Watts, but also Thomas Carlyle, the astronomer Sir John Herschel, Charles Darwin, the poets Henry Longfellow and Robert Browning, the men of letters Sir Henry Layard and Sir

Henry Taylor, as well as Holman Hunt and William Rossetti [FIG. 3]. Her female sitters, by contrast, tended to be women who were not well known, and whom she represented in fictional guise, as 'Spring' or the Madonna, suggesting that, in Cameron's mind, beauty distinguished a woman as intellect did a man.

During the 1870s she developed a range of figure compositions drawn from Shakespeare, the Bible and Tennyson, all to some degree studied from the work of the Pre-Raphaelites. Single figures embodied characters from an eclectic reading of literature ancient and modern, as in *King Lear allotting his Kingdom to his three Daughters* (1872) or *Ophelia* (1875). And, as in *Zuleika* (1864), *Pharaoh's Daughter* (1866), and *Rebecca* (1870), different subjects might be all personified by the same model, recognisable in spite of costume changes.

In 1873, Cameron's only daughter Julia died in childbirth, an event which sapped the artist's spirit and energy. But family fortunes, if nothing else, forbade her grief subduing her art, and although she more or less gave up exhibiting, she continued to press forward as hard as she could on sales of her pictures. She also began to write her autobiography at this time, a project which remained unfinished at her death, despite its confident beginning:

> 'Mrs Cameron's Photography', now ten years old, has passed the age of lisping and stammering, and may speak for itself, having travelled over Europe, America and Australia, and met with a welcome which has given it confidence and power. Therefore I think that the 'Annals of my Glass House' will be welcome to the public . . .[27]

Another major project started at this point was a new edition of Tennyson's *Idylls of the King*, in twelve volumes, with the pictures in the books in the form of engravings from her photographs. In the event, Cameron was so disappointed with the resulting publication – her images reduced far below their original scale – that she had the illustrations published separately with the verses to which they referred copied out in her own hand. As she wrote to a friend, in this venture she hoped 'to get one single grain of the momentous mountain heap of profits the poetical part of the work brings in to Alfred'.[28] While photographs such as *King Arthur*, *The Parting of Sir Lancelot and Queen Guinevere*, and *Sir Galahad and the pale Nun* inevitably owe a debt to the Pre-Raphaelite tradition, the subjects are cast in a colloquial compositional vein which is quite Cameron's own.

Although the Camerons' home life had been enriched by the removal to the Isle of Wight in 1874 of Watts and the Prinseps, Cameron's husband was anxious to spend the rest of his life with his sons, out in Ceylon. Thus, despite Julia's private reluctance, they left Britain in 1875 for Colombo. In this new context, Cameron's art had no purchase and therefore no purpose. She tried to find a fresh repertoire in the landscape and local inhabitants, attempting to mould the servants here into her dramatis personae as she had her employees on the Isle of Wight. The results were desultory: a mere dozen or so pictures remain from this period. A short burst of the old creative stimulus occurred when the artist Marianne North paid a visit to Colombo on one of her voyages, and Cameron had her posing in a variety of imaginary situations and settings on the verandah of the Cameron home. Had she been younger and still energetic, Cameron might well have generated another stage of work, learning to draw from the Sinhalese community a new sequence of subjects. As it was, after an unsatisfactory trip back to England in 1878, Julia Margaret Cameron died in Ceylon quite suddenly, at the age of sixty-three, in January 1879.

JULIA M. CAMERON

30. Mrs Herbert Duckworth (the Artist's Niece) 1872

Marie Spartali (1843–1927), hitherto known chiefly as a model to Cameron, Rossetti and others, had close professional and personal links with the Pre-Raphaelite circle; as an artist she became a prominent exponent of the style in the 1870s and 1880s, with a total of over a hundred works to her credit. As Henry James noted in 1875, she

> inherited the traditions and the temper of the original Pre-Raphaelites, about whom we hear nowadays so much less than we used to; but she has come into her heritage by virtue of natural relationship. She is a spontaneous, sincere, naive Pre-Raphaelite.[29]

From family correspondence, the Delaware Art Museum catalogue noted that 'she was a very serious artist, working regularly every day in a very disciplined way until her death in 1927 at the age of eighty-three'.[30] Her obituary referred to 'a strenuous and arduous life' which involved many changes of residence between Britain and Italy, during which 'she went on painting steadily' and exhibiting.[31] With Pre-Raphaelitism's decline in critical favour in the twentieth century, followed by the reinvention of the Pre-Raphaelite Brotherhood as a masculine movement of virile painters pursuing pretty women, Spartali's work slipped from view and is only now being recovered.

Marie Spartali was born in Tottenham, Middlesex, the elder daughter of the Greek-born businessman Michael Spartali and his wife Euphrosyne, and brought up in a large house in Clapham with her sister Christine and brother Demetrius. The Spartalis were members of the naturalised Anglo-Greek community in London that included the Ionides, a wealthy, cosmopolitan and cultured group who became important Pre-Raphaelite patrons. This has been perceived as a community in which social relations were relaxed in comparison with the prim conventionalities of the British bourgeoisie – the writer George du Maurier noted that 'girls would sometimes take one's hands in talking to one, or put their arm round the back of one's chair at dinner'.[32] But this impression was exaggerated; the carefully chaperoned young women were expected to marry only approved suitors.

Nevertheless, myths proliferated in the memoirs of their male contemporaries, who claimed that the Misses Spartali were hailed as ravishing beauties (who also happened to be wealthy). One tale tells of a cabload of artists meeting Marie and Christine at a garden party; 'we were all à genoux before them,' recalled the author, 'and of course every one of us burned with a desire to paint them.' Swinburne was said to have exclaimed that Marie was 'so beautiful I feel as if I could sit down and cry',[33] but in old age Marie called this account a fanciful story; her own recollection was of seeing Swinburne present *Songs before Sunrise* to the Italian nationalist leader Mazzini, and this political emphasis was in keeping with her own sense of values.[34]

Christine Spartali sat to Whistler for his *Princesse du Pays de la Porcelaine* (1864) before marrying into the European aristocracy, and a similar future was envisaged for Marie, but she had other aspirations. Already well educated in languages and other accomplishments, according to Clayton's *English Female Artists* (1876),

> with Marie Spartali the love of drawing was a passion. Having attained the low standard set by her drawing masters, she went to Mr Madox Brown for finishing lessons. [He] declined to train her as an amateur, but strongly advised her to adopt painting as a life study . . . if it had not been for his encouragement and help she might never have summoned courage to attempt being an artist.[35]

She thus became Brown's pupil in 1864, receiving regular weekly lessons in his studio alongside Cathy and Oliver and becoming a close friend of Lucy, who was the same age. This instruction lasted for the rest of the decade, and well into the 1870s Brown remained her artistic adviser.

Spartali's exhibition debut was at the Dudley Gallery in 1867, with three pictures: *The Pacha's Widow*, *Corinna* and *The Lady Prays – Desire*. The last of these was inspired by *The Faerie Queene* and shows a green-garbed, auburn-haired woman – possibly a self-image – in a Renaissance gown, with book, owl emblem and Greek inscription signifying wisdom [PL. 6]. In the next few years her exhibited titles at the Dudley included *Christina*, *Nerea Foscari*, *Forgetfulness*, *La Romaunt of the Rose* and *Pharmakeutria* or The Love Philtre, showing women concocting a love potion. In 1870, *St Barbara* and *The Mystick Tryst* were sent to the Royal Academy.

During these years of her apprenticeship she sometimes sat to other artists – for portraits by Madox Brown, Burne-Jones and Val Prinsep, and in 1869 to Rossetti for 'three chalk heads' towards his picture of *Dante's Dream on the Anniversary of the Death of Beatrice*. A year or so earlier – probably because the Spartalis had a country estate on the Isle of Wight – she sat to Cameron at her home across the island at Freshwater for a sequence of photographic images. With loose hair and an ivy strand, Spartali was the archaic Greek goddess of memory, Mnemosyne, while in an elaborate beribboned costume she was Hypatia; other subjects included 'The Spirit of the Vine' and 'La Donna Maria'. Portrait photographs by contrast show Spartali with hair neatly braided.

As an artist, she was formally welcomed into the Pre-Raphaelite ranks in 1871, in an article written by William Rossetti which praised her talent and ambition:

> Miss Spartali has a fine power of fusing the emotion of her subject into colour and of giving aspiration to both; beyond what is actually achieved, one sees a reaching towards something ulterior . . . in short Miss Spartali, having a keen perception of the poetry which resides in beauty and the means of art for embodying beauty, succeeds in infusing that perception into the spectator.[36]

The Greek element in Spartali's work was prominent in her most important early picture,

exhibited in London and Liverpool in 1871 and entitled *Antigone Gives Burial Rites to the Body of her Brother Polynices*, taken from Sophocles' drama. The subject perhaps had a contemporary as well as literary–historical meaning, for in the late 1860s Michael Spartali was Greek consul-general in London and as such in contact with Greek exiles at a time when the plight of Cretan nationalists aroused much sympathy, their insurrection against Ottoman occupation being suppressed with some ferocity. Bodies were left unburied in the streets, according to the American consul in Crete, W. J. Stillman, whose own wife committed suicide from grief and depression aggravated by the sufferings of the local people.

The *Academy* critic praised Spartali's 'poetical' picture for its colour and unity, describing the action:

> Polynices is carried out dead . . . the bearers have thrown the body out on the heath and Antigone, who is to suffer death for her piety, laments over it and over the woes of her house, throwing the earth in handfuls upon it.

He commended the 'noble' painting of Antigone's action, but savagely criticised a supposed historical inaccuracy with regard to Theban burial rites.[37]

Subsequent works at the Dudley included *Fear* in 1871 and five pictures in 1872: *Ianthe*, a Greek girl, *A Chaldean Priest*, *In the Cloisters*, *Portrait of a Child* and *On a Balcony*. In 1871 she also produced an extremely accomplished charcoal-and-chalk *Self-Portrait* within the pictorial conventions of Pre-Raphaelitism, showing a pensive half-length figure with a fan who ignores the spectator to gaze into her own thoughts. The artist turned too to the Arthurian subjects favoured in the 'medieval' phase of Pre-Raphaelitism, producing her own version of *Tristram and Iseult*, in which Iseult's dog recognises her lover, and also *Elaine finding Sir Lancelot disguised as a Fool*, both of which were hung at the RA in 1873. The *Art Journal* commented favourably that 'these vistas of garden landscape are conceived in the true spirit of romantic luxuriance, when the beauty of each separate flower is a delight. The figures, too, have a grace that belongs properly to art and which has been well fitted to pictorial expression.' But he objected to the colour, complaining that the tones were 'uncomfortably warm'.[38]

In April 1871 Spartali married William Stillman, hero of the Cretan uprising, who had begun his career as an artist and through his editorship of the *Crayon* promoted Ruskinian ideas in the United States. The marriage was opposed by Marie's family and friends on the grounds that Stillman, a penniless widower with three young children, one suffering from incurable bone disease, had an 'unfailing capacity', as he himself put it, 'to get into hot water'. The couple were steadfast, however, and during the months of their enforced probation Stillman's correspondence shows how keenly both contested the exhortations to prudence; everyone, he complained, seemed to believe that any husband had to provide Marie with a standard of living fit for a 'great lady', when it was insulting to suppose that, with her artistic and intellectual resources, she was incapable of happiness on less than a thousand pounds a year. Marie was of the same mind, and was also angered by the Anglo-Greek community's attitude towards matters of the heart. Some personal emotion may be detectable in the subject of an unexhibited picture completed in 1871, showing Buondelmonte riding to his wedding past the house of the Donatis, as the mother tears off her daughter's veil.[39] This subject refers to the Guelph-Ghibelline quarrel and specifically to family pressure to marry

MARIE SPARTALI

32. Love's Messenger 1885

within the clan. Eventually Mr Spartali was persuaded to accept his daughter's marriage, but it is noticeable that for a long time Greek subjects disappeared entirely from her work.

Marie's daughter Euphrosyne (Effie) was born in 1872. Then Stillman lost his journalistic work in London and suggested moving to America, upon which Michael Spartali offered Marie an income of £400 a year to keep the family in Britain. In 1873 Stillman attempted – perhaps owing to his championship of Ruskin, who was notoriously hostile to Madox Brown – to remove his wife from Brown's tutelage by means of some transparent excuses. 'I need scarcely tell you I was rather taken aback by your informing me the other day that you were considered *too weak to paint now*,' wrote Brown, 'and that moreover you and your husband agreed in thinking my visits were a sacrifice of time on my part such as you could no longer acquiesce in.' He continued:

> I can hardly believe you are in earnest in any intention of leaving off painting. But my object in writing is not to urge you in opposition to the wishes of your husband . . . yet I think it right to make it clear that I have never considered attending to your painting as a trouble . . . therefore I shall continue to consider your work in my care . . . whenever you may think fit to resume it . . .

Stillman's attempt evidently failed. Some years later Brown was still offering advice:

> If at any time you should care to make a tracing of what you are beginning and post it to me, it might save you some trouble as the work progresses. Also if you could find time to send your pictures here before going to the Grosvenor, I might overlook them and possibly find out some defects in drawings that might mar the beauties of your colouring.[40]

Spartali was generally commended for her use of colour, and criticised for her draughtsmanship, especially by those who disliked the 'archaic' Pre-Raphaelite aesthetic. Characteristically, she painted in watercolour, using the density of paint favoured by the Pre-Raphaelites. She was identified as a pupil and disciple of Madox Brown in *Artists of the Nineteenth Century* in 1879, and exhibited her work regularly in Manchester and Liverpool (where 'the principal buyers are', as Rossetti noted) as well as in London. She also sent work to exhibitions in the United States, and it was in an American watercolour exhibition at the National Academy in New York in 1875 that Henry James saw 'four elaborately finished pictures by Mrs Spartali Stillman' – including *Tristram and Iseult* and *Elaine and Lancelot* – which he thought 'the most interesting things' in the show, 'despite a lingering amateurishness', and which he praised not only for their colour but for 'the only thing in a work of art which is deeply valuable . . . imagination, intellectual elevation'.[41] The assiduity with which the artist exhibited is indicative of serious intent and economic need; despite her father's allowance, she painted to sell.

While she was in London finishing her pictures for the 1875 season, Stillman's son died on the Isle of Wight. Here Spartali lived later in the year when Stillman went as war correspondent to the Balkans, covering uprisings against Turkish rule, and a number of landscape paintings depict local scenes. One shows a thatched cottage and a young mother with two infants, attended by a gaggle of geese, receiving a letter from the postman.

From the late 1870s, Spartali regularly selected subjects from early Italian poetry, taking her texts from Rossetti's translations of Dante's *Vita Nuova* and other poets of the period,

republished in 1874 under the title *Dante and his Circle*. The earliest of these was *The Last Sight of Fiammetta*, shown in London and Manchester in 1876 and inspired by Boccaccio's sonnet beginning:

> Round her red garland and her golden hair
> I saw a fire about Fiammetta's head.

Eighteen months later, Rossetti asked Spartali to sit to him for his own vision of Fiammetta. Since her reputation as model has tended to obscure her career as artist and since she is typically said to owe her pictorial inspiration entirely to Rossetti,[42] it is worth noting that in this case her choice of subject evidently stimulated his own, and that by 'casting' Marie as Fiammetta, so to speak, Rossetti implicitly recognised her choice of the theme.

Shortly before this, the Stillmans decided to go abroad. 'I have been very busy painting a picture from Mrs Stillman as she is on the point of leaving England,' Rossetti wrote to Janey Morris in December 1877. 'Her husband is to meet her and the children at Turin and they are to proceed to Corfu for the winter. I have misgivings that they will settle there . . .' Later, he reported that Marie had invited him to visit Corfu, 'where I might compensate her somewhat [for the sittings] by being of use to her work. She showed me two of her latest watercolour pictures – life sized half figures with a good deal of elaborate and excellent imitative painting in the floral accessories.'[43]

From 1878 the family settled in Florence, where in October Marie's son Michael was born (a third child died in infancy), and the following summer she brought him and Effie on a visit to Britain. She was described as well and happy, though Stillman was suffering from 'woeful despondency'. 'Just fancy, while a wife like that is at hand!' exclaimed Rossetti.[44] Their friends had a high opinion of Marie's cheerful, kindly and witty personality, and her obituarist J. W. Mackail spoke revealingly of her 'frankness, simplicity and indomitable spirit' in adverse circumstances, also describing her as 'affectionate and yet subtly malicious'.[45] In the spring of 1880, Janey Morris was also in Italy and wrote for Mrs Stillman's address. 'I should like to call on her and see her happy face in her Florentine home,' she wrote. 'I have never seen her children either.'[46] A month later she was visiting Marie in via Alfieri. The two women were close friends and from 1893 Marie paid regular visits to Kelmscott Manor. After her return to Italy Burne-Jones wrote wistfully:

> You would laugh with the incredulous laugh of yours if I told you how dolefully I passed the streets that led to your house . . . a great deal has gone out of the lives of your friends now you are gone, and we all say it and all feel it and are quite honest about it.[47]

The removals were frequent: after the initial five years in Florence, Marie took the younger children back to Britain for health reasons, where Stillman rejoined them. Then a deterioration in Mr Spartali's business affairs curtailed her allowance, and when Stillman was appointed *Times* correspondent in Italy and Greece in 1886, the family followed him to Rome for a further ten years. Despite these moves and her domestic duties – her husband's absences left Marie responsible for most day-to-day affairs as well as for the care of her children and stepchildren – she continued to paint and send works for exhibition in Britain. Several paintings from this period have Italian landscape backgrounds – *Gathering orange Blossom*, for example, shown in Liverpool in 1879, or *Among the Willows of Tuscany*,

shown in Manchester in 1880. Her main subjects were poetic pieces, and her works showed increasing confidence, although they also reflect a certain isolation from the centres of artistic activity. They exhibit a distinctive Pre-Raphaelite format that represents a personal style, creating a genre of its own with particular emphasis on narrative and dramatic scenes from Dante and Boccaccio, with authentic Italian locations.

Fiammetta Singing, a relatively large work in watercolour with bodycolour, exhibited at the Grosvenor and in Liverpool in 1879 (where it was priced at £125) is representative of these poetic images, taking its text from Boccaccio's sonnet, with a composition showing 'a decorative picture of seven fair women, with background of myrtle trees and distant sea; delightful in quality and colour'.[48]

A subsequent sequence illustrated the phases of Dante's relations with Beatrice, beginning with a *Vita Nuova* scene in which 'Certain ladies of her companionship gathered themselves unto Beatrice where she kept alone in her weeping' (exhibited at the Grosvenor and in Liverpool in 1880, priced at £150) and *Dante and Beatrice on All Saints' Day* (shown in Manchester in 1881, price 120 guineas). These were followed by two pictures exhibited in Liverpool in 1887: *The May Feast at the House of Folco Portinari*, where Dante and Beatrice met as children, and *Upon a Day came Sorrow unto Me*, on the death of Beatrice, with Love as a boy dressed in black and three shrouded figures representing Sorrow, Bile and Pain. These were followed by *Dante at Verona* (Liverpool 1888) illustrating Rossetti's poem on Dante's exile.

Other comparable works depicted *Petrarch and Laura* – the other pair of legendary late-medieval lovers; *By a clear well, in a little field*, a pastoral image from Boccaccio; *Madonna Pietra degli Scrovegni* (shown in Liverpool in 1884 and purchased by subscribers for the collection there); and *Messer Ansaldo Showing Madonna Dianova his Enchanted Garden*, taken from a tale by Boccaccio. This last was among Spartali's most ambitious works, 30 by 40 inches, in gouache, and priced at £375 in Liverpool in 1889. It was reproduced, together with *Upon a Day came Sorrow*, in Percy Bate's book on *English Pre-Raphaelite Painters*, where the artist was described as an 'accomplished lady [who] early fell under the personal influence of Rossetti'[49] although she herself was always careful to credit Brown as her tutor.[50]

As regards her painting practice, she told Samuel Bancroft, the purchaser of *Love's Messenger* (exhibited at the Grosvenor in 1885) [FIG. 33] that the subject – a young woman by a window feeding a bird that has delivered a love-note – was suggested by 'the effect of a fair head in a certain bulls-eye window of a friend's studio where I was working one winter'. She added that it was 'merely a study from a model', identified as her daughter Effie, who 'being then at school was not able to sit for me to complete it from her'. The painting did not sell, however, and the view through the window was added later, in Italy: 'I painted a landscape from the Villa Borghese as background when I made several changes in the picture while in Rome.'[51]

Unpublished letters to the artist from Burne-Jones shed further light on her – and on his – painting practice and friendships. 'I send you a little scribble of suggestions about the dying monk design,' he wrote in response to her request for advice regarding *The Good Monk of Solfiano* (exhibited at the New Gallery in 1892) and *Fra Conrado d'Offida* (exhibited in Liverpool in 1892). He promised to return her coloured sketches by post, and made detailed

MARIE SPARTALI
33. Fra Conrado D'Offida 1892

suggestions for the Monk of Solfiano receiving a phial from the Virgin, displaying all the 'poetical' excesses for which his artistic followers were themselves criticised:

> The new placing of the angels is not to influence you one bit – only I think you will have great difficulty in painting them as your design shows – they may overweight the picture at the right – and may look scattered and confused . . . I have only put them at the foot of the bed for you to see if the switch of them is not perhaps useful for the picture – you could make them gay and lovely perhaps, with eyes all over their wings, of a peacock kind and wreaths of roses and palms in their hands or branches – and little curly gold heads, looking young and celestial and a type of new life.
>
> The whole of the left hand I have copied straight from your design because it is extremely beautiful in composition . . . [but] I have lowered the book in the kneeling monk's hand so that the white of the pages may not come against the white sheet on the bed and so confuse.

He urged her to fill the background with interest, suggesting windows and a view – 'if Assissi

is meant, [it] should show the ridge of the mountain and not look like a city set like Florence in a valley – but perhaps it isn't Assissi' – adding sketches and admitting that 'I didn't work it out in perspective as I meant because I am not accurate, and you will not need it now, for you know enough for this' and concluding: 'When the work is further advanced send a tracing over to me again . . . for *I love helping you* and it is kind of you to pretend I can.'

For the second composition of 'the Vision in the Wood' or *Fra Conrado d'Offida* ('How the Virgin Mary came to Brother Conrad of Offida and laid her Son in his Arms') [FIG. 34] he had 'no such troublesome meddling to suggest':

> the kneeling monk and Virgin & Child only want such change as nature will give you when you begin to make drawings – if the Virgin leaned forward a little to trust the babe safely it might be better – no, she is better upright – and the monk's hands are a little awkward but it is only where nature will at once set you right – this ought to be a lovely little picture and full of care and delight to you and I don't know how it could go wrong anywhere – and you know a wood whose green background is all ready for you – get both done for May – and send me over the tracings later on for final correction and warning . . .[52]

The Stillmans finally returned to Britain in 1898 and settled in Surrey where in 1901 Marie's husband died. Subsequently she exhibited twice in the United States, in Boston in 1904 and at the Oehme Galleries in New York in 1908.

By this time she was in her sixties and turned increasingly to flower and garden paintings. Two watercolour views of Kelmscott Manor, exhibited at the New Gallery in 1906, probably date from her stay there in July 1904. She continued to exhibit regularly at the New Gallery until 1908, chiefly showing landscapes from Italy and the Isle of Wight. Michael Stillman became an architect in the United States, where Marie visited him. Her last major work was *The Pilgrim Folk* (1914), showing a Florentine street scene on the day of Beatrice's death.

She died in March 1927, a few days short of her eighty-fourth birthday – the last survivor, as her obituary put it, of an almost legendary group of women associated with Pre-Raphaelitism. With such remarks her reputation as Pre-Raphaelite artist in her own right was eclipsed.

Spartali's daughter Effie and her stepdaughter Lisa both became artists, the former a sculptor and medallist, the latter an illustrator and portraitist; each regularly showed with Marie at the New Gallery.

Very little is known about either's training. Lisa Stillman [FIG. 32] exhibited at the New Gallery from 1888. Her earliest recorded work seems to have been her illustrations of two pet squirrels owned by her father in Italy during the early 1880s, whose story was published in 1897. She exhibited in Britain until 1909, showing in all sixty-four items at the New Gallery, a portrait of Miss Evelyn Tebbs at the Royal Academy in 1897, three pieces at the Royal Society of Portrait Painters and one at the New English Art Club. In 1927, she inherited her stepmother's 'best easel' and most of her photographs and drawings.

Effie Stillman (1872–1911), sculptor, exhibited from 1892 to 1907, showing thirty-five items at the New Gallery, two in Liverpool and one each at the Royal Academy and Royal

Society of Portrait Painters. Most of her work was in the form of sculpted statuettes and portrait medallions, although she also produced some graphic works. In 1904 two of her pieces, depicting a mature woman in long gown and loose shawl – probably studied from her mother – were on show at an Arts and Crafts exhibition in Brighton; they were illustrated in the *Studio*, which commented: 'The two statuettes by Miss Effie Stillman are finely modelled and do this clever sculptor the greatest credit.'[53] In 1905 she married William Ritchie, a lawyer.

Some years earlier, she had been commissioned by Samuel Bancroft to sculpt the statue of Senator Thomas Bayard to stand outside the Delaware Art Museum in Wilmington; after protracted negotiations this was finally unveiled in 1907. Effie had three sons and died at the relatively young age of thirty-nine.

'My sister began painting as soon as she could hold a brush,' recalled the youngest sibling of Evelyn Pickering (1855–1919), who is better known today under her married name of Evelyn de Morgan. But the family disapproved: in their social circle in the 1860s, art was praiseworthy as an accomplishment, but anathema as a serious profession. 'I want a daughter, not an artist!' complained her mother. From childhood, Evelyn contested such attitudes; on hearing of a cousin lamenting her wasted gifts with the words 'what might I have accomplished had I been forced to work for my living?' she retorted scornfully that 'people who talk like that are born nincompoops!'[54]

Evelyn was the eldest of four children born to a wealthy family who prided themselves on their high birth – her grandmother was daughter of an earl – and ancient lineage. The two girls, after a relatively serious education supervised by their mother, were expected to 'come out' and marry well. Evelyn refused to be presented at court; by the age of sixteen she was devoting her waking hours to art, complaining in her diary of the time wasted on interminable meals, afternoon visitors and evening guests. 'I have to sit in the drawing room and listen to idiots talking about dressmakers and servants!' she noted with rage. 'This enforced idleness is insupportable.'[55] To discourage her excessive interest in art, the drawing master was instructed to tell her she had no talent; she was also forbidden to paint in her free time. In response she would secretly lock herself into her room in order to paint and had a false-bottomed bag in which to conceal her sketching materials when leaving the house.

When discovered, lessons were resumed, but the tutor refused to allow her to study anatomy.

At the age of seventeen she was, with reluctance, permitted to enrol in the recently opened Slade School of Art, where she won prizes for painting from the antique and from life, and also a Slade scholarship. But after two years she left the school to work on her own, and travelled with a companion to Rome, despite parental opposition; here, it is said, 'the classical severity of her earlier manner first blended with the mellow beauty of Italian art'. At this date she produced a massive, sombre bronze head of *Medusa*, with snake locks 'full of nauseating lissomeness'.[56]

At home, she had only pocket money with which to pay for materials and models and many of her studies were thus taken from her younger sister, whom she bribed to sit still, or from 'pretty Jane', the nursemaid Jane Hales. However, 'her work soon attracted public attention from its richness of colouring, its fine brushwork and the power which, in spite of immaturity, it displayed,' noted her sister's memoir. 'No sooner were the pictures seen than they were sold'; sales meant money, and money meant freedom – to paint.[57]

Following her father's sudden death in 1876, Pickering moved to a studio of her own, and in 1877, at the age of twenty-one, she was among the artists invited to show their work at the newly opened Grosvenor Gallery. Here her *Ariadne in Naxos*, showing a grieving classical figure on the seashore, was much admired for its blend of assured handling, depth of colour and intense feeling. At this date, wrote a later commentator:

> Miss Pickering had barely scraped acquaintance with the most noted men of genius who had been influenced by the modern Pre-Raphaelite movement. She had not seen the pictures that Millais painted in his first period, nor had she a chance of becoming familiar with them till they were brought once more to public notice by the Millais exhibition of 1886. With Rossetti's poetry, in 1877, Miss Pickering was well acquainted, but of his genius in painting she knew scarcely anything at all, and it remained almost unknown to her till she visited that fine show of Rossetti's pictures which was held after his death. As regards Burne-Jones, she had certainly been moved by their particular greatness; but the influence of Burne-Jones had not then appeared in her work . . .[58]

Her closest connection with the Pre-Raphaelite school was in fact through her uncle J. R. Spencer Stanhope, who also defied family disapproval to become a professional painter and in 1880 moved to Tuscany, where Pickering was a regular visitor. Her habits of work showed dedication and perfectionism; throughout her career she worked hard and productively – at least a hundred works in oil are known, together with many studies and chalk portraits – and on a relatively large scale. She sent work annually to the Grosvenor – over twenty-five items are listed in the catalogues – as well as to Liverpool, Manchester, Birmingham and Berlin, and later on to the New Gallery. She never submitted to the Royal Academy, apparently in protest against its philistinism. Owing to her social circumstances, it is sometimes thought that she did not paint for exhibition or sale, but the evidence is otherwise, and her pictures certainly sold – to provincial galleries such as Liverpool, through the Fine Art Society, and also to private collectors. One Liverpool patron purchased eight of Pickering's works.

In general, her work at the Grosvenor was well noticed, subject to the prejudices of individual critics. All acknowledged her high aspirations. Thus the *Spectator*'s reviewer commented in 1882 of the *Christian Martyr*, showing a girl tied to the stake, to drown with the rising tide:

> This young lady in her red drapery is less like a living, breathing being, than one of Cimabue's virgins; she is pure with the purity of an ascetic, and we cannot help feeling that her proper place would be in the stained glass window of some chapel . . . Were it not that Miss Pickering is so devoted a student of Art, we should hardly call attention to this picture; but her work is so thorough and unsparing, and her aim so high, that we cannot but recognise the effort, though it is made, we think, in a wrong direction.[59]

The following year, the same journal praised *By the Waters of Babylon* 'both for its faults and its excellences', adding: 'Miss Pickering deserves this praise – that she honestly prefers to fail in the highest school to succeeding in the lowest, and perhaps her chief fault is that she disdains almost too entirely all the cheap attractiveness of modern painting.'[60] The same painting, however, was attacked by the *Athenaeum* for lack of spontaneity, vigour and originality:

> Neither sincere nor robust, neither learned nor brilliant, it shows much labour, yet few genuine studies. The figures are generally ignorant of each other's presence, a not unfortunate characteristic in pictures of ghosts but undesirable in connexion with the subject here depicted. There is no common element of interest in the assembly; the figures are fortuitously disposed . . . and it is not always so clear as it might be to which torso the legs and arms belong. Again, the draperies are in many cases only apparently and not really adapted to, that is to say, moulded on, the wearers. Miss Pickering's inspiration is second-hand; she will do well to exercise herself in searching draughtsmanship.[61]

A more sympathetic defence was proffered in the *Portfolio*:

> Miss Evelyn Pickering shows a capacity for deliberate study and consistent invention in her large picture of the exiled Jews . . . the sad faces, attenuated forms and drooping hands, are mannerisms from which the young artist does not seek to free herself; on the contrary, she looks at nature, whether in the human form or in landscape, more persistently than ever through the medium of the early Florentine School . . . The result is a confirmed and not a healthy mannerism; but apart from this mistaken warp of natural genius, one must allow that the artist's conception is imaginative, and her study of attitude in many cases striking for dramatic intensity, while her colouring is in its arrangement of isolated masses both rich and noble within a grave scale.[62]

This amount of critical attention indicates the seriousness with which the young artist was treated, unlike most women. She was, however, commonly greeted as a follower or disciple of Burne-Jones. The *Portfolio*'s comments appeared alongside a detailed critique of 'the most important feature' of the 1883 exhibition, Burne-Jones's *Wheel of Fortune*; this was at the height of his fame, and some reviewers who traced his influences on her work were offering compliments rather than criticism, although in general such remarks were made to discredit her achievement. In a few of her works the direct influence of Burne-Jones is visible, although this may also be interpreted as a shared response to the work of Renaissance artists such as Botticelli; like Burne-Jones she also produced many sketches in pale chalk on dark

EVELYN PICKERING

35. The Love Potion 1903

papers. Overall, however, her work is distinctively her own, large and symbolic in conception, with an evident disregard of passing fashion. She seems to have believed in the uniqueness of the artist's vision, and there are few if any examples of her seeking or responding to criticism.

In 1885 Evelyn Pickering, at the age of twenty-nine, became engaged – to the surprise of her family, who believed her wedded to art – to the potter William de Morgan, friend and colleague of William Morris and Burne-Jones, and some eighteen years her senior. They were married in 1887 and settled in an old house in Chelsea where she painted and her husband produced the fine lustreware pottery for which he is now famed. The marriage was perceived as a perfect partnership between two unworldly artists whose regard for commerce was notoriously subdued to the demands of art. In practice, the pottery business consumed a good deal of cash, to which Pickering contributed her own money as well as selling pictures to assist family finances.

'Art is more important than you think. But it must be earnest, grim life-earnestness that has no tincture of gain in it, or love of earth-fame' was a view attributed to both Evelyn and William by her sister. Another was: 'Art is of vital importance in the scheme of things [because] it depends for its very existence on certain spiritual laws not known on earth, only guessed at . . .' Both believed in intense faith and great simplicity as the basis of art, but neither was as humourless as these opinions suggest, possessing a full sense of delight in the ridiculousness of life. Their inability to manage servants was legendary, and one friend recalled them taking the cook to the National Gallery, in the hope that this would 'keep her in a good temper'. The de Morgans were firm favourites with the Morris and Burne-Jones families too, and

> few people mentioned them without a smile . . . their delightful irresponsibility, their dauntless pluck [and] their unvarying knack of viewing the great things and the small of life from a standpoint all their own, rendered them refreshingly unique.[63]

In 1893 medical advisers insisted that William de Morgan would not survive if he spent further winters in Britain and so for several years the couple divided their time between London and Florence, where the clear winter light assisted Pickering's painting. She worked productively throughout the 1890s, and at one stage experimented with a new and unique medium devised by William. '*The Soul's Prison House* was painted in London and is framed in an old Italian frame which I picked up in Wardour Street,' wrote the artist.

> It is painted in a method my husband invented that we used to call the 'process'. The colours were ground in glycerine and spirit, and the ground used to paint on was a porous gesso preparation on canvas; the glycerine of course never dried and when the picture was finished it was removed from the paint by means of a sucker plastered on the back of the canvas. The sucker drew out the matrix, that is to say the glycerine with which the picture had been painted; the surface of the picture was then flooded with oil or oil and varnish, to replace the glycerine. It was a ticklish business and I only completed two pictures in this method as, tho' it has a great attraction in the working and a superiority in the tone, the hygrometric quality of the glycerine was very troublesome and obliged one to keep the studio at an even temperature day and night.[64]

In 1904 the artist used the near-legendary Pre-Raphaelite model Janey Morris for her representation of time passing in *The Hour Glass*, an image full of pictorial homage to Pre-Raphaelitism, but also indicative of the artist's friendship with her sitter. According to a note by the artist, this image was conceived as 'an echo of a movement in the Waldstein Sonata of Beethoven' presumably a favourite with both women.[65]

The pottery business was finally closed down in 1905, and in 1909 the couple returned permanently to Britain, the medical advice having proved mistaken. Pickering continued to paint and to exhibit at the New Gallery, and in 1906 she had a solo exhibition in Bruton Street, but in later years she ceased to exhibit, owing in part to the financial success her husband attained in his new and unexpected career as novelist. The age was also out of tune with her kind of painting: according to her sister she viewed the Cubist and Futurist works in Post-Impressionist exhibitions in London in the years around 1910, remarking that they reminded her of the emperor's new clothes.

EVELYN PICKERING

36. Earthbound 1897

Subsequently, 'Evelyn's work never flagged throughout the passing years, but . . . she withdrew more and more from the world, living in that dream world of her own creation and in her selfless devotion to that other life that ran side by side with her own . . .'[66] This comment of her sister's is in keeping with her presentation of Pickering as an unworldly innocent, whereas the works frequently show a full and moral engagement with contemporary issues, albeit in allegorical and historical guise. A large number of her images were concerned with the corruption of riches and the virtue of poverty, under titles such as *Blindness and Cupidity Chasing Joy from the City* (exhibited in Liverpool in 1898), *Earthbound* [FIG. 37] (1897, showing a king counting his gold), *The Marriage of St Francis and Holy Poverty*, *St Christina Giving her Father's Jewels to the Poor* and *The Worship of Mammon* [PL. 12] Perhaps the moral tone of these pictures – showing a rather superior disdain for wealth from one in her class – helped reconcile her mother to the artistic career; certainly Mrs Pickering commissioned a depiction of *Mercy, Truth, Righteousness and Peace* as a gift for her brother, Sir Walter Spencer Stanhope.

Other repeated motifs included images of semi-draped female figures representing Night, Sleep, the Moon and the Sea, as well as pictures inspired by religious subjects, Tennysonian poems and folk tales ranging from the Pre-Raphaelites' favourite *Queen Eleanor and Fair Rosamund* to Hans Andersen's *Little Sea Maid*. The allegorical subjects show more neo-classical traits, while legends tend to be more traditionally Pre-Raphaelite in their detailed drawing and bright colours. A striking example is *The Love Potion* [FIG. 36], a later work from 1903 showing a Circe figure in medieval setting whose subject though not treatment is reminiscent of Spartali's *Pharmakeutria*. Pickering's work was chiefly if not exclusively figurative, and usually on a large scale. Some pictures possess a good deal of narrative meaning, others are more simply aesthetic studies with somewhat fanciful titles. She had a particular passion for angels – once using the wings of humming-birds to colour angelic feathers.

In a critique of Pickering's work, May Morris wrote:

Her pictures have an epic quality and are spacious in conception. The later works show an almost exaggerated insistence on decorative detail. They are remarkable for the beauty of drapery design, for drawing vigorous and delicate, and for sumptuous colour, for great enjoyment of textures. She had astonishing physical endurance and power of work, starting to paint early in the morning and going on swiftly and surely throughout the day. The output in consequence was very great.[67]

In 1914 her remaining pictures were fortuitously shipped back from Italy. The war distressed her intensely; as the fighting progressed, she began a series of pictures on war subjects in symbolic guise, which were shown in her studio in 1916 to raise funds for the British and Italian Red Cross. Her husband died in 1917, and during the following months she completed two of his unfinished novels, as well as designing a memorial stone. Nor did she stop painting, being engaged on a new series of war pictures to be exhibited in 1918. Marie Stillman visited her at this time, and remarked on a new and frightening element in the images – a sense of evil that was in contrast to the serene joys of her earlier work. Evelyn Pickering de Morgan died in 1919, in her sixty-fourth year.

113

THE
THIRD
GENERATION
1880–1910

37. The Little Foot Page (Burd Helen) 1905

s the nineteenth century reached its closing decades, women could look back on a world that seemed very different from that in which they now moved. Considering the situation of women artists in 1880, one woman from an earlier generation commented with feeling: 'I get rather dispirited at my failures, and the want of that knowledge and *finish* I see in all women's work at exhibitions when they have had good training; there was none in my day . . .'[1] This was Louisa, Lady Waterford, born in 1818 and perhaps the best-known amateur artist of the Victorian period, writing to her younger cousin Eleanor Vere Boyle, a respected illustrator and draughtswoman under the initials EVB. Both artists incidentally had been admired by the early PRBs for their drawings and watercolours.

Even more emphatically, one of the pioneers declared that, by 1880, the battle had been won. 'The difficulties which the habits of society of that day placed in the way of a young woman seeking an independent career in Art or, indeed, in any other direction, have now almost wholly passed away,' wrote Anna Mary Howitt in that year, in the preface to the second edition of her book *An Art Student in Munich*.[2]

By the end of the century, there were several prominent women in the field whose fame made them a measure or type for all other female artists. The best known of these were Elizabeth Thompson Butler, whose battle scenes regularly appeared at the Royal Academy; Helen Paterson Allingham, whose watercolours of the picturesque southeastern countryside were seen at the Fine Art Society and in illustrated books; and Kate Greenaway, whose illustrations for children brought her equal popularity with parents. The work of all three was admired and, although none can really be called Pre-Raphaelite, it is an index of the movement's influence over British art as a whole that in his *Academy Notes* of 1875, Ruskin described Butler as Pre-Raphaelite while Greenaway's career, formed in part by her friendship with Ruskin, has sometimes been included in accounts of Pre-Raphaelitism.

But while it was true that much had changed, women artists still did not enjoy equality with men, and in some respects indeed there was a backlash against them during the 1880s and 1890s, as the continuing campaigns for women's rights gathered strength, provoking in some quarters opposition to any further evidence of female emancipation in British society. This was the period when the passing of the second Married Women's Property Act in 1882 gave some substance to women's civil rights, while women's continuing campaign for the vote, following the enfranchisement of virtually all men in 1885, kept up the pressure. In Britain such developments were viewed with great alarm by many men and some women. The female artist of the 1880s, although not necessarily a feminist herself, was often viewed by the die-hard conservative as one of the many irritants to his sex's wellbeing.

This mixture of progress and retrenchment appeared in the art press and in publications directed specifically towards women and girls in the shape of greater acknowledgement of the female artist's existence, but with increased emphasis on her inferiority. She appeared as an amateur, a student, a decorative artist or a teacher far more often than as an artist *tout court*. Typical articles in the *Magazine of Art* through the 1880s included 'Women at work: their functions in Art' (1884) which suggested that while 'a distinguishing mark of modern feminine education is the large part taken in it by art', women and their advisers should not overestimate their talent, and recognise that 'the home, in fact, has endless uses for art'.[3] 'The Love Affairs of Angelika Kauffmann' (1882) similarly trivialised the career of Britain's best-known female artist of the past.

The rise of the Arts and Crafts Movement, as well as the existence of establishments like the Royal School of Art Needlework, founded in 1872, joined with the promotion of home decoration as a fashionable pursuit for middle-class wives to give a persuasive context to this trend. While actual numbers of female artists participating in the professional field continued to increase, the impression given in the media was that the less challenging versions of female creativity were back in favour. Indeed, a four-part, 21-page feature entitled 'Glimpses of Artist-Life' in the *Magazine of Art* in 1887 treated the artist exclusively as male, mentioning women only as models and wives.

We have seen how the establishment of the Slade School offered women new opportunities for art training in London in the 1870s, and this was followed in the next decade by the development of provincial art schools, which proved of considerable benefit to women. In this period, existing schools of design were transformed into schools of art, offering more fine-art training alongside their classes in design and applied art for artisan students. This opened opportunities for women outside London, who could now pursue their studies while remaining within the protection of their families, and incurring no financial outlay on living away from home.

The vast majority of women availing themselves of these opportunities were from the middle classes (although in artisan trades based on female labour, such as pottery manufacture in Staffordshire, art-school training enabled some working women to become designers) and ranged from those who expected to earn their own living — generally as teachers — to those for whom art training was a pleasant and rewarding activity between school and marriage. Towards the end of the century, women students in the provincial schools were strongly influenced by the rise of the Arts and Crafts Movement — the first national exhibition of which was held in 1888 — which extended the definition of art to include work in ceramics, metalwork, stained glass, embroidery and the like. In the social circle of Pre-Raphaelitism, a student such as May Morris, who began her training in the late 1870s, consciously selected a career in design rather than painting, and worked with the aim of eliminating the hierarchy of the fine and applied arts. Although our focus in this book is restricted to two-dimensional art, in this period the boundaries of form were conspicuously flexible.

A notable development in women's art education was the popularity of study in Paris and elsewhere in Europe, which boomed as the continuing emancipation of women in the social sphere made travel from home more acceptable. The feminist press had been promoting this step since the late 1870s, with features like 'New Art Schools on the Continent' in the *English*

Woman's Review in 1877, but mainstream articles such as 'The Girl-Student in Paris' (*Magazine of Art*, 1883) and 'A Paris Atelier' (*Good Words*, 1886) underlined the widespread acceptance of a continental training period in Pre-Raphaelitism's third phase. However, in 1881, a feature in the *Magazine of Art* on 'Lady Art-Students in Munich' (prompted no doubt by the reissue of Howitt's book, although this was not mentioned) revealed almost casually that the situation women students would find there was still quite unequal: the study facilities described were free to men, while the female students had to pay.

The institutions – membership and exhibiting societies such as the RA, the Society of British Artists, the various watercolour associations and the like – which had governed British art since the start of the Victorian era were, by the end of the century, slowly and reluctantly taking down the barriers to women's full participation. In 1893 the RA Schools finally allowed female students a life model, although he was still draped about the loins rather than completely naked as in male students' life classes. In most cases, however, these more liberal moves were motivated by self-interest, as the influence once exerted by the venerable institutions lessened among the men of the younger generation, and women had to be recruited to maintain numbers. In 1889 it was notionally accepted that women could compete for membership of the Academy, but this privilege remained theoretical until well into the twentieth century; the first woman to be elected to associateship of the RA was Annie Swynnerton in 1922, and the first to be admitted to full membership since Kauffmann and Mary Moser had been members of the founding group of Academicians in the eighteenth century was Laura Knight in 1936. Other exhibiting societies gradually allowed women access to membership: Helen Allingham, for example, was elected to the Old Watercolour Society in 1889, but women weren't admitted into the full embrace of the SBA until 1902. It is worth emphasising here, now that the status of such associations has declined, that in the nineteenth century exclusion from artistic bodies severely hindered women artists' advancement, since it was through exhibiting societies that contacts were developed, reputations made and sales secured.

In the last two decades of the century, the newer groups and galleries challenging the established institutions were comparatively more open to the female artist as a fact of cultural life, making neither rules nor exceptions for her. These modern groups included the Grosvenor Gallery, the New Gallery and the Fine Art Society, where women artists featured among exhibitors. Typically, for example, in 1897, the New Gallery showed the work of 76 women and 232 men – a respectable although not startling ratio of 25 per cent female to 75 per cent male. The Fine Art Society was notable for using women art critics and scholars to write its catalogue essays; by the 1890s several were regularly employed to comment on art past and present. The New English Art Club, founded in 1886 to oppose the continuing mediocrity and traditionalism of the Academy and taking its inspiration from modern French art, is a salutary reminder, however, that the story of women and art in the nineteenth century is not a simple one of linear, if gradual, progress towards equality, since it became more misogynistic as it went on, despite having begun as a useful shop window for former Slade students, many of whom were women. And when in 1909 the New Gallery sought to protect its status as a major venue and altered its rules so that subscribing exhibitors had to be elected, rather than simply submitting their works, the number of women elected as painters dropped to four (Evelyn Pickering, Marianne Stokes, Laura Alma-Tadema and Annie

Swynnerton) out of a total of seventy-two, while the numbers in the sections for miniatures and 'handicrafts' rose substantially. Neither process saved the gallery, however; its day was over. In addition to galleries, increasing exposure was available for artists' work in the illustrated press, and women were often employed as artists on the *Graphic* weekly paper, as well as on publications like the *Girls' Own Paper* from which they might more obviously expect employment.

Outside London, a development from which women benefited was the establishment of municipal museums and galleries, often founded on an already existing exhibiting society, as in Manchester and Birmingham. The collections created for these new temples of culture were in many cases based on contemporary art, especially if the city itself was in large part a product of the modern age. For local artists, as well as for those who lived in London but exhibited around the country, these new institutions provided a valuable addition to the patronage available, often opening up a new audience for their work. With work regularly exhibited in, say, Liverpool, and bought for the city gallery, an artist might become quite a local favourite even if she still experienced difficulty in making a name among the ranks of artists competing in London. In addition, municipal galleries were imbued with civic pride, and took an interest in artists of local origin or connections.

National collections – with the exception of the National Portrait Gallery, which bought by subject, not by artist – were less accessible to women, although the Tate Gallery's purchase in 1890 of its first work by a woman was greeted as a benchmark, signifying that women's apprenticeship was over. The painting in question was *Love Locked Out* by Anna Lea Merritt, an American who had adopted Britain as her home in the 1870s, and an exponent of what could be called modern classicism. 'One of the loveliest landmarks in the realms of Art has been discovered within the lifetime of most of us,' declared the speaker on the occasion of the picture's reception. 'I mean the formal, authoritative recognition of the fact that women can paint pictures.'[4]

Myra Louisa Bunce (1854–1919) and Kate Elizabeth Bunce (1856–1927) were sisters and fellow students at the Birmingham School of Art in the 1880s and 1890s, during the period when, under the headship of E. R. Taylor, the school was expanding its work in both the decorative and fine arts and gaining renown as a centre of the Arts and Crafts Movement, particularly in metalwork, stained glass and illustration. 'A change for the better has come over the design of our [art] schools within the last dozen years,' wrote Taylor in 1890, 'and the hard and fast line separating the artist, designer and workman is happily becoming somewhat less marked.'[5] Like other municipal art schools, Birmingham's was in part the result of growing civic pride based on economic prosperity, social progress and cultural advancement, fuelled by a strong sense of local patriotism and belief in the duties of conspicuous citizenship. Kate and Myra Bunce were the daughters of one such prominent Birmingham citizen – John Thackray Bunce, editor of the influential *Birmingham Daily Post* and one of the most important members of the municipal elite as regards art. A reformer and 'fervent adherent of advanced Liberalism', Bunce chaired the School of Art management committee from 1885, was closely associated with the Museum and Art Gallery and received the freedom of the city for his services to art. He took pride in his complete set of Ruskin's works, while his obituary records 'a steadily deepening love and admiration of the work of the Pre-Raphaelite School and especially in its later developments'.[6]

Birmingham was predisposed towards Pre-Raphaelitism because Burne-Jones, the movement's greatest living exponent in the 1880s and 1890s, had been born and bred in the city, and indeed became honorary president of the Royal Birmingham Society of Artists in 1885. The new Art Gallery was opened with an exhibition of work by G. F. Watts and Burne-Jones, followed by two major Pre-Raphaelite exhibitions in 1891 (at which two of Rossetti's medieval subjects were shown, together with the bare-breasted *Venus Verticordia*) and in 1895, while acquisitions created 'one of the finest Pre-Raphaelite collections in the world', containing Millais's *Blind Girl* and Madox Brown's *The Last of England*. In 1894, William Morris delivered a prize-giving address to the art school on 'The Beauty of Life', urging his listeners to get as much pleasure from a Warwickshire meadow as from sublime scenery.[7]

Contemporary photographs of the school show a high proportion of female students, and Kate and Myra Bunce were perhaps among Morris's audience. They are seen in a picture of members of Henry Payne's life class in the late 1880s, at which date they were in their thirties and still living in the family home at Edgbaston. They had been two of five daughters, two of whom died in infancy and a third, Edith, in her twenties. Their mother, born Rebecca Ann Cheesewright, died in 1891. The family was affectionate and close-knit, although very little is known of Kate and Myra's personal or emotional lives. Their father's position meant that neither was financially obliged to earn her own living, nor to seek marriage for economic reasons. Filial love and piety were strong in both women and it may be conjectured that J. Thackray Bunce's achievements and personality dominated their lives; both were over forty by the time of his death in 1899, and neither married.

In 1891 and 1893 Myra Bunce showed two watercolour landscapes at the Royal Academy, one depicting a sunset scene and the other a Cornish cove. Other watercolour views are also known, together with some Christmas illustrations, mostly dating from the 1890s. Records show that altogether Myra exhibited over thirty times, mainly at the annual Birmingham exhibition, but she was chiefly interested in metalwork (introduced at the art school in 1887–88) and most examples of her work now known are in this medium, in partnership with her sister, as decorated frames around Kate's pictures. These include one for *The Keepsake* (1901), a copper surround for the reredos at St Albans Church, Birmingham (c. 1918–19), and for the triptych in Saskatoon Cathedral, Saskatchewan, Canada, where precious stones

belonging to the family are said to be set into the surround. Of these works in the nineteenth-century High Anglican tradition of religious art the finest example is the sisters' jointly executed altarpiece for Longworth parish church in Oxfordshire (their father's ancestral home and centre of the Anglican Lux Mundi group) dedicated to 'the greater glory of God and the memory of Edith, Ann and John Thackray Bunce'. The frame is repoussé silverwork, signed 'Myra L. Bunce 1904', with roundels containing angels and symbolic animals – paschal lamb, phoenix, pelican and signs of the Evangelists – together with vertical panels of wild roses.

Kate Bunce 'inherited literary talent from her father and published a certain amount of verse', according to her obituary, 'but her principal interest was in art. She received her training at the Birmingham School of Art, where she won many prizes, including a bronze medal.'[8] She was among ten contributors to a book of drawings by some of the earliest members of the Birmingham Black and White School of illustrators presented to E. R. Taylor 'as a small token of affection' on his retirement, and several other examples of her illustrative work survive: Christmas cards from the 1890s and pictures for a children's story book by T. Edgar Pemberton, published in Birmingham in 1895. These line drawings are faithful end-of-the-century renderings of Morris's praise to the Birmingham students of 'the peculiar kind of interest and ornamental quality' in medieval design 'caused by the planes of the figures being very near to each other'. They show little influence from *fin-de-siècle* illustration, and indeed the Birmingham school was generally hostile to Decadent and Art Nouveau design (which a later headmaster called 'the Squirm'), preferring a chaster style.

In painting, her earliest known image is a medium-sized watercolour entitled *The Sitting Room* and showing a woman in a white dress seated reading in an interior leading towards a conservatory, with flowers; this is dated 1887 and may well be drawn from Myra, in the Bunce family home. According to the catalogues, Miss K. E. Bunce of 24 Priory Road, Edgbaston, exhibited a deathbed scene at the RA in 1887, under the title *How may I, when he shall ask . . .* This is a quotation from Rossetti's poem 'An Old Song Ended', in which a dying woman leaves instructions for her lover's eventual arrival:

> 'How may I, when he shall ask
>   Tell him who lies there?'
> 'Nay, but leave my face unveiled
>   And unbound my hair.'

These verses had been published for the first time a year earlier, in Rossetti's *Collected Works* (1886); their tone of romantic melancholy is characteristic of Bunce's secular works.

This painting is now lost, as is Bunce's submission to the RA in 1890, *The Minstrel*, and her 1893 work *The Day Dream*, to which another Rossetti quotation was appended: 'She dreams till now on her forgotten book . . .'[9] The line is taken from the poem written to accompany Rossetti's late painting *The Day Dream*, showing a green-gowned woman amid sycamore branches, which had been exhibited at the Rossetti retrospective at the RA in 1883, but it is not known whether Bunce's picture was inspired by Rossetti's painting or by his poem. The *Athenaeum* was caustic:

Under the title The Day Dream Miss Kate Bunce has depicted a dyspeptic-looking damsel in a red dress with a face which soap and water might benefit . . . We fear that Miss Bunce, who has respectable notions of painting, has mistaken her vocation in trying to follow Rossetti.[10]

By the early 1890s decorative mural painting was again in vogue, partly in homage to Pre-Raphaelite endeavours in the field – Ford Madox Brown had executed a series for Manchester Town Hall – and partly as a result of the Arts and Crafts belief in uniting the arts and putting them in public places. In 1893 Kate Bunce's father proposed that Birmingham Town Hall be embellished with a sequence of pictures illustrating the city's historic past. A classical-style building, the Town Hall was the site of a prestigious international music festival – an 'august setting' for such works. The paintings were to be executed by 'capable students' from the art school, under Taylor's direction.

Kate Bunce was allocated two of the eleven historical panels, which together with two allegorical designs for 'Music' and 'Song', contained scenes of Birmingham from the time of the Norman Conquest through to Joseph Priestly's escape from the riots of 1791. As an indication of how art was chosen to 'rise above' or obscure the actualities of nineteenth-century industry and commerce, no images of contemporary manufacturing, on which the artistic patronage depended, were included in the sequence, which centred on the Middle Ages, and Kate's subjects were typically medieval-architectural: *The Guild of the Holy Cross* and *The Alms Houses, Lench's Trust, Founded 1525*. For each panel, a preliminary sketch and colour study were approved by Taylor, followed by a full-size cartoon. The panels were not true murals but oils on canvas, fitting into rectangular spaces beneath the Town Hall windows. Of the ten artists selected, Kate Bunce and Jeanette Bayliss were the only women, while four of the men were already teaching at the art school. Some obscurity surrounds the fate of this project: it seems that one or two of the panels were never installed, and in 1927 all were removed, only to disappear after 1939.[11]

As well as to the RA, where she showed *My Lady* (whereabouts unknown) in 1901, Bunce sent work to the New Gallery, where at the same date *The Keepsake* [PL. 13] was chosen as 'Picture of the Year' and reproduced in the *Pall Mall Gazette*. This is in tempera with brilliant jewel-like colours, and shows a soulful female perched on a strange medieval seat in front of a tapestry loom, attended by a group of women in elaborate headdresses. The figures are elongated and the background spaces filled with images of Arts and Crafts detail: woodcarving, stained glass, embroidery, jewellery. It has been described as 'very much decorative painting on one plane' displaying 'wistful, romantic longing for the past'[12] but it has, at least in intention, a narrative subject, being taken from Rossetti's pseudo-medieval poem 'The Staff and Scrip', and was first shown with this quotation:

> Then stepped a damsel to her side,
> And spoke and needs must weep:
> 'For his sake, lady, if he died,
> He prayed of thee to keep
> This staff and scrip.'

The Keepsake was bequeathed by the artist to Birmingham Art Gallery, where it joined *Melody* (also known as *Musica*). [Front Cover] Presented by Sir John Holder, this is an allegorical treatment depicting a half-length female figure holding an inlaid lute; as in *The Keepsake* this woman avoids the viewer's gaze, as if the artist were unwilling to present her as the object of desire, despite the sensuousness of colour and theme. The silver-gilt vase holding branches of apple blossom suggests a virtuous response to Rossetti's carnal visions of 'women and flowers' such as *Venus Verticordia*, while the circular mirror reflecting not a boudoir but a private chapel with crucifix and stained glass recalls earlier Pre-Raphaelite works. Again the Arts and Crafts references are strong: the gold pendant set with pearls might have been made in the art school, while the mirror, embossed with the word 'Musica' and blue stones, can only be an example of Myra Bunce's jewel-set silverwork.

KATE E. BUNCE
39. The Chance Meeting 1907

The most distinctively Pre-Raphaelite of all Kate Bunce's surviving works is *The Chance Meeting* [FIG. 40], first shown in 1907 at the New Gallery and then at the Coronation Exhibition in Birmingham in 1911. This is a blend of Rossettian themes, for the title is taken from *La Vita Nuova*, one of the encounters between Dante and Beatrice at which no words are spoken, while the quotation attached to the picture, 'Look in my face; my name is Might-have-been,' is the opening line of Rossetti's sonnet 'A Superscription', lamenting 'things unuttered' and ending:

> Then shalt thou see me smile, and turn apart
> Thy visage to mine ambush at thy heart
> Sleepless with cold commemorative eyes.

Such a cold, almost unseeing look passes between the two motionless main figures in Bunce's picture – Dante dressed in black and Beatrice in soft greyish mauve – while subsidiary figures of a woman and child, workman and serving girl, all in rich Renaissance garb, frame the protagonists. This is an ambitious and successful figure painting, including also a dog, a harvest festival of flowers and fruit with birdcage in a courtyard, a private shrine and a landscape view. So packed indeed is the composition that its precise geography is difficult to discern with accuracy, indoors and out being ambiguously distinguished.

Other untraced pictures include *Tabitha Cumi* and *St Warberga*, and between 1887 and 1912 Bunce exhibited a total of forty-one times, in Birmingham, Liverpool, Manchester and in London at the Fine Art Society. But, her obituarist noted, 'her best work was done in church painting, for which, as a deeply religious and spiritual woman, she was temperamentally well equipped'.[13] Both sisters were devout Anglicans and with advancing years – Kate was fifty in 1906 – and changing fashions in the London galleries, the artist concentrated on religious works, painted for specific churches and chapels rather than for exhibition or sale. She was 'much influenced by early Italian painters' and, as a recent writer has noted:

> as a High Churchman [sic] herself, her work also includes precise iconographical details of that Movement. For instance, her angels contemplating the Sacrament have what is known as 'proper custody' of the eyes; that is, they are unaware, through their deep meditation, of any temporal matter beyond the Sacrament. The artist's subjects are entirely conventional: Madonna and Child, Crucifixion, Nativity and such like, together with appropriate patronal saints.[14]

The reredos at Longworth in memory of her parents is a triptych in clear blues and pinks, painted in tempera with a good deal of gold leaf and studded with seed pearls and other semiprecious stones. The central Crucifixion image has a naked Christ drawn from life but hanging somewhat limply, flanked by angels whose golden aureoles and immense pink wings fill the rest of the panel. To the left is the Virgin and Child and to the right the Deposition, each densely surrounded by angels. The decorative effect is magnificently coloured and symmetrically stylised, so that the whole altarpiece glows when seen from the far end of the nave, with the gold nimbi of the ranked angels laid out across the painting in a glistening pattern against blue sky and rose-coloured wings. Seen close to, the carefully painted flowers and birds across the foreground of each panel and the soft patterning of the wing feathers add to the visual richness of the design.

This work was followed in 1906 by four large pictures in oil for the church of SS Mary and Ambrose, Edgbaston, showing the Annunciation, Adoration, Crucifixion and Entombment – classic subjects painted in sober tones from a restricted palette of yellows and browns set in pairs in the angle of the outer wall and chancel. Other church works included a two-panel war memorial picture for Holy Trinity, Stratford-on-Avon (1919), and a triptych (1919), of which the *Birmingham Post* wrote:

> A beautifully painted reredos for the Lady Chapel of St Alban the Martyr Conybere Street has been given by Miss Kate Bunce in memory of her father the late Mr J. Thackray Bunce and her mother and sisters. The painting, which is the work of Miss Bunce, has occupied a number of years of patient work and is a very fine example of Symbolistic [*sic*] art. It represents Our Lord and His Mother, with attendant angels and St Alban and St Patrick.[15]

The altarpiece in Saskatchewan, Canada, is in a cathedral where the dedication was also to St Alban and the bishop was a friend of the artist. This triptych, installed in the 1920s, is based on the Book of Revelations, showing Christ in splendour over a sea of glass, with seven stars and seven angels on either hand; below are two kneeling episcopal saints, Alban and Patrick. Her second cousins visited Kate Bunce towards the end of her life, when she suffered severely from cataracts, and recall that she was continuing to paint, however, and was working on the reredos for Saskatoon Cathedral. A very similar picture, unevenly worked, hangs in St Germain's church, Edgbaston, where the artist worshipped. Both sisters are remembered in the family as religious women for whom the 'giving of their riches to beautify a church reflects their devotion'.[16]

Kate Bunce died at the age of seventy-one in December 1927. In her will, she bequeathed her books to Birmingham University, and the residue of her estate, together with *The Keepsake*, to the Art Gallery. In addition, she allocated £100 to be spent 'on completion of the picture of St Alban which I am painting' for the cathedral in Saskatoon.[17]

Other women were associated with the Birmingham School, most of whom are best known for their work in the decorative and applied arts. This distinction is artificial, especially in the context of the late nineteenth century and the Arts and Crafts Movement, but keeping within the frame of pictorial or two-dimensional work observed elsewhere in this book, we have concentrated on those members of the 'third generation' whose work was chiefly in painting and drawing. Within the pictorial definition, however, other works – in illustration and stained glass, for example – should be included, not least to place the work of painters such as Kate Bunce in perspective. This widening of focus demonstrates how women artists taking their inspiration from Pre-Raphaelite art (a movement containing significant examples of both illustrative and glass art) successfully overcame the supposed division between fine and applied art, and extended the idea of 'late Pre-Raphaelitism'.

The 1890s was thus a golden decade of book illustration, as a result both of technological developments in line and colour reproduction and of the establishment of small presses producing exceptional volumes, such as those from William Morris's Kelmscott Press, whose works were a major influence on the Birmingham School. Several women, on whom the influence of Kate Greenaway's illustrative work, with its elegant pictorial nostalgia and

pleasure in childhood imagery, seems equally important, were well-known illustrators, featuring largely among the National Competition prize lists, for example, as during the 1890s the Birmingham School began to dominate the field. Thus in 1893 Florence Rudland won a silver medal for her designs for La Motte Fouque's *Undine*, published in book form in 1895. Five women – Georgie Gaskin, Evelyn Holden, Violet Holden, Celia Levetus and Mary Newill – were among the eighteen contributors to the illustrated magazine the *Quest* published by the Birmingham Guild of Handicraft in 1894–96, while 16 of the 27 illustrations to the *Life of King Arthur*, the School's wedding gift to the Gaskins, were also women's work. Georgie Gaskin, Mary Newill and Florence Rudland were also contributors to fine illustrated collections of carols and nursery rhymes produced in Birmingham. More work remains to be done on both group and individuals; here we mention briefly only a few of the Birmingham-trained women.

Georgie Evelyn Cave France (1866–1934), who married Arthur Gaskin in 1894, was born in the Birmingham area and studied at the School of Art. Throughout the 1890s she won prizes for her design work in the National Competition, as well as internal awards at the school. Thus in 1891 she was awarded a bronze medal in the National Competition for 'a very pretty ornamental design for a card, remarkably well drawn in pencil', together with a prize for a fan 'which is more than a mere design. It is actually painted on ribbed silk and thus the full design is to be seen.' She also won a national book prize, a free studentship at the art school, a silver medal and prizes for a pictorial design, a wallpaper, a tobacco tin and an embroidery.

In the later 1890s she developed her pictorial career, producing an *ABC: An Alphabet* with rhymes to each illustrated letter, of which the *Bookman* commented: 'Mrs Gaskin is one of the cleverest artists of the Birmingham School . . . there is not one design that is puny or merely imitative.'[18] In 1896 she won a public competition for an illustrated *Calendar of the Seasons*, and was then commissioned to design for a collection of hymns and carols, *Holy Christmas* (1896). Her illustration *The Holy Choir*, showing angels singing, was chosen as a Christmas card by the publishers and reproduced in the *Art Journal*. Iconographically, it incorporates a clear gesture of homage to Rossetti's illustration of Sir Galahad for the Moxon Tennyson – a volume still renowned as a landmark of Pre-Raphaelite illustration.

Her next work was what have been described as 'slightly whimsical' colour illustrations for an edition of *Divine and Moral Songs for Children* by the Protestant hymn-writer Isaac Watts. 'We have rarely, if ever, come across such a dainty and delicate edition of this old and popular children's favourite,' noted the *Bookseller*; 'Mrs Gaskin's designs have a unique charm and a certain quaint originality which make them particularly delightful.'[19] Georgiana Burne-Jones, a friend of the artist, was more forthright. 'I must confess we were appalled at Dr Watts's share in the work,' she wrote. 'I hope you will not be vexed when I tell you that I deliberately took out your pictures and burnt the book!'[20]

Other praised books included *Hornbook Jingles* (1896) and *The Travellers and Other Stories* (1898), which was both written and illustrated by the artist. The reception of such works indicates how female artists were perceived to have a natural affinity for children's tales. 'Mrs Gaskin has a genius for drawing pretty young faces,' remarked the *Bookseller*, 'and a woman's taste for putting her "subjects" into most becoming costumes.'[21] She also

MARY J. NEWILL

40. Sing a Song of Sixpence *c.1900*

designed a number of expressive personal bookplates, one being included in the 1896 *Yellow Book*, and charming Christmas cards [FIG. 42]. From 1900, however, she relinquished illustrative work in favour of jewellery, for which she and her husband are chiefly famed. 'In the jewellery, I did all the designing and he did all the enamel, and we both executed the work with our assistants,' she wrote in 1929.[22] Her daughters were born in 1903 and 1907, and she continued working until her husband's death in 1928 and beyond, continuing jewellery design until within a few months of her own death in 1934.

Mary Jane Newill (1860–1947) also produced illustrations, notably for an edition of Hans Andersen's *The Nightingale* published in Birmingham in 1896, as well as contributing to the *Quest* and to the books of carols and nursery rhymes already mentioned. She also worked extensively in embroidery, and was needlework instructor at the Birmingham School of Art for nearly thirty years from 1892. Through this she became, like Georgie Gaskin, a friend of May Morris and colleague in the Arts and Crafts Movement; when Mary Newill took sabbatical leave to study tempera painting in Florence, her teaching was taken over by May Morris. Newill's designs for embroidery tended to be simple, sometimes with a rough, picturesque quality, like her wall hangings of the *Faerie Queene*, where the figure details are embroidered in crewel work and the trees are patches appliquéd to the coarse silk and linen ground. These formed part of a bedroom display shown at the International Exhibition in Paris in 1900.

An article in the *Studio* in 1895 – by a writer who professed not 'the faintest knowledge of the artist' personally and therefore with 'no preconceived bias for or against' – drew attention to the range of Newill's work in illustration, embroidery and painting. This singled out line drawings that could be easily reproduced, commenting especially on

> some studies of trees quite remarkable for their vigour of line and complete mastery of a convention which by its apparent simplicity tempts many to disaster. The largest of these would provoke admiration wherever exhibited. Not merely is its detail full of interest, it preserves also the broad masses so skilfully balanced that the whole design becomes a notable work of art.[23]

In addition, the magazine reproduced her robust Rossettian illustration of *The Passing of Arthur* with three queens in a Viking boat [FIG 41], a landscape line drawing of Porlock Bay, Somerset, and two chalk or pastel drawings of children. The writer noted: 'Miss Newill has the courage of her conviction and keeps in each case rigidly within the limits of the style she elects to work in . . . with a vivid sense of the importance of selection.' It praised her study of nature and style of simplification, and concluded:

> In the drawings of children the dexterity of touch is apparent, notwithstanding a demure simplicity of purpose has made them appear somewhat formal. The character of the faces is unusually well observed, and the decorative effect gained without straining after archaic mannerisms. Could a selection of her landscape studies be also given, the variety of this clever artist's work would be even more strikingly manifested.[24]

Shortly after this, Newill became one of the handful of Birmingham artists working in stained glass, first producing designs and by 1906 working in her own studio in the city centre. Her earliest designs include windows of William Morris's heroes John Ball and Wat Tyler, made for a house in Sutton Coldfield. Many of her domestic windows have been lost through demolition, but surviving ecclesiastical commissions include a two-light window from 1906 for the lady chapel of SS Mary and Ambrose, Edgbaston (which also contains Kate Bunce's four pictures of the life of Mary), showing Christ approached by a group of women and children before a background of medieval ships and towers above a border of scattered meadow flowers. The links between the arts are made visible in Newill's most striking window designs – part of a commission for a house in Handsworth built in 1898 – showing

MARY J. NEWILL

41. The Passing of Arthur 1894

GEORGIE CAVE GASKIN

42. Christmas Card 1893

Queen Matilda and her ladies working on the Bayeux Tapestry [PL. 15]. Throughout the nineteenth century Matilda was believed to be both artist and executrix of the tapestry, and thus revered as a model for latter-day embroiderers. Mary Newill's Matilda is a young woman such as might be found threading her needle in the classrooms of the art school, whose long sleeves and garment draperies do not impede her work.

Several other women took to designing and making stained glass towards the end of the century. 'Glass painting has of late years received a great impetus in this country and women are taking their part with men in the front ranks of the new movement', wrote Mary Lowndes in 1909, herself a main exponent of the craft and director of a commercial glass studio, noting also that twenty years earlier there had been 'not a single woman glass painter'.[25] The new breed included Florence Camm, who with her brothers took over their father's studio and workshop and enjoyed a long career as designer and glass painter, Caroline Townshend, Veronica Whall, Wilhelmina Geddes and Margaret Agnes Rope, who

130

MARGARET AGNES ROPE

43. Goblin Market 1905

trained at Birmingham and successfully continued her career within the convent walls after joining an enclosed order in 1923. Rope's first recorded work, illustrating Christina Rossetti's *Goblin Market* [FIG. 44] won a silver medal in the National Competition and was described by *The Studio* as possessing 'quite a genuine Pre-Raphaelite flavour'[26]. Later her works were exclusively religious.

In 1908 a survey of *Scottish Painting Past and Present* noted the presence among 'the younger Scottish painters' of 'a number of artists in whose work decorative qualities . . . frequently associated with some intellectual or poetic motive, predominate over the more purely pictorial elements', citing the names of Phoebe Traquair and Jessie King among those whose works 'are in some respects products of the aftermath of Pre-Raphaelitism'.[27] These and other artists, while not forming a 'Scottish school' of late Pre-Raphaelitism, illustrate the various ways in which women artists working in Scotland at the end of the century took the Pre-Raphaelite impulse to create pictorial work of a new and distinctive kind. In the Glasgow school in particular we see Pre-Raphaelitism reach its final destination as an avant-garde art form, which simultaneously chimed with developments in Europe drawing from veins of Pre-Raphaelitism running through Symbolism to Art Nouveau.

Phoebe Anna Traquair, née Moss (1852–1936), was born in Dublin, daughter of an eminent doctor, and attended Dublin School of Art. In 1872 she married a Scottish zoologist and settled in Edinburgh, where her husband became director of the Natural History Museum. Marriage, with 'the duties inherent in her new position', and the birth of a son withdrew her from art for several years, but in the 1880s she resumed art practice, and subsequently enjoyed a long and varied career in painting, embroidery, illumination, bookbinding and metalwork, exhibiting extensively in Europe and America, and winning awards at international exhibitions in London, Paris and St Louis. She was also a prominent member of the Edinburgh Arts and Crafts Club, the Guild of Women Binders and the Royal Society of Painters in Watercolour.

The first work of her mature years were illustrations to her favourite passages of poetry, in the manner of medieval missals. Ruskin lent encouragement and samples to study, and Traquair's evident sense of Pre-Raphaelitism as her guide in this endeavour led her, in March

1885, to employ a mutual friend to introduce her work to the Rossetti family. Mrs Rossetti and Christina recorded a visit from 'Mr Sandeman, who brought us a book of illuminations illustrative of some of Gabriel's poems, and done by a Mrs Traquair; who, calling in the afternoon, fetched away her beautiful performance'.[28]

This work included Rossetti's 'The Blessed Damozel' and was followed by illuminations on vellum for Morris's *Defence of Guenevere* and by illuminated Psalms, Tennyson's *In Memoriam* and Elizabeth Barrett Browning's *Sonnets from the Portuguese*; the last of these was completed in 1897 and exhibited at the Second Exhibition of Artistic Bookbindings by Women held in London at the end of 1898. Two years earlier, a special issue of the *Studio* devoted to modern manuscripts described Phoebe Traquair as one of the two leading artists in the revival of illumination, and quoted her remarks on the medium. 'Purple and gold are delightful things to play with,' she declared, continuing:

> Add to this a love of books and a great desire to project feelings or emotions, and a consciousness that direct transcript from nature did not relieve me of the burden of feeling . . . If I meet with a book that stirs me, I am seized with the desire to help out the emotion with gold, blue, crimson . . .

The law of beauty governed the mode of expression, she added, noting that the smallness of scale made it necessary for the illuminator to excise all nonessentials.[29]

Later, two of Traquair's manuscripts – a version of Dante's *Vita Nuova* and *The House of Life: Sonnets and Songs by Dante Gabriel Rossetti* – were photographically reproduced and published in limited editions in 1902 and 1904 respectively, but the absence of colour makes the work look fussy and dull. An article in the *Art Journal* of 1900, which devoted six pages to her work, concluded that 'the subjective elements' of illumination 'offer this artist admirable opportunity for the exercise of her talent, both as illustrator and colourist'; it continued:

> Keenly sensitive to the prompting of all kinds of imaginative work, she follows the imagery of such poetry with frankness, and pictures the literary symbolism with a directness which illuminates while it charms. And the abstract nature of the ideas, combined with the dignity or the rich sonorous rhythm and harmony of the verbal music, suggest colour schemes full and deep and rich as the rainbow.[30]

The same writer, however, believed that 'Mrs Traquair has found the true métier for her fine talent in mural decoration', which indicated an endeavour with comparable medieval antecedents, but on a wholly different scale. In the *Studio*, the artist described her aim, when painting a wall, 'to make it sing'.

The first of these projects were decorations for the mortuary of the Sick Children's Hospital in Edinburgh, suggested in 1884 by Professor Patrick Geddes. The artist was 'reluctant to embark on an undertaking so much greater in scale and so different from all she had previously done', but rose to the challenge: 'The mortuary was a bare little room, scarcely better than a cellar, but Mrs Traquair, choosing motherhood and the life beyond as subjects, transfigured the walls with beautiful pictures which spoke of love and hope and reunion.'[30] Executed in just over a year, these were not wholly successful, being 'overcharged with meaning', like a missal page writ large. Ten years later when the hospital moved to a new site, the murals were cut out and transferred to a larger mortuary, to which

the artist 'added new pictures and borders, and filled the east and west walls with six great winged figures, with outstretched arms, standing upon spheres, in which are figured the acts of creation', the whole forming a successful ensemble.[31]

In 1885–86, Traquair decorated the choir school of St Mary's Cathedral in Edinburgh with a vast mural work on the side walls 10 feet high and 47 feet long, illustrating the canticle 'O all ye works of the Lord, bless ye the Lord', with further decorations on the east and west gables. The medium was oil mixed with wax on a thick coat of painter's white, which was used in the lights. The scheme was ambitious, depicting on the east gable the clergy and cathedral choir, and on the walls evocations of the Winds, Fire, Light and Darkness, together with Pentecost, the Resurrection and Christ healing the dumb. The execution was assured; according to the *Art Journal*'s contributor, 'the handling is broader, the design simpler, the colour more massed and, if I may use the phrase, more symphonic'.[32]

At this point Traquair visited Italy, to see the work of the early fresco and mural painters, returning to what was considered her magnum opus, begun in 1893, to decorate the Catholic Apostolic Church in Edinburgh with a huge scheme including nave, roof, chancel arch, gables, aisle and side chapel. In the latter two, scenes from the parable of the Wise and Foolish Virgins 'are framed in elaborately-wrought borders, rich in colours and gold, wonderfully inventive and full of massy yet exquisite tracery founded upon natural forms'. Certain passages were enriched with Celtic elements, but the major inspiration was that acknowledged to Pre-Raphaelitism.

The artist's working methods were unusual in that she made no sketches or working designs, but painted directly onto the walls, 'following the promptings of instinct and mood', in the following manner:

> She waits until an idea shapes itself in colour and line in her mind's eye, and then transfers it to the wall at once, thus retaining the vividness and freshness of the conception . . . She has discovered that her ardour cools if checked, and has wisely determined to be content with her first clear impression.

This method, the critic added, had its defects, since the artist's technique and drawing were not always sufficiently 'masterly', yet her work was of the expressive kind 'in which correctness is secondary', and the colour and conception of the depictions 'touch feelings which a more considered procedure would almost certainly fail to reach'. On the west wall

> in the two or three hundred angel figures . . . you can hardly find two alike, while the stillness of the white-robed singers and harpers, contrasted with the tumultuous in-rushing of the brilliantly-robed trumpeters on either side, forms a composition of great power and beauty.[33]

Traquair also worked in oil, watercolour, metal and pictorial enamel. An enamel copper pendant set in gold made in 1904 and entitled *The Song* seems to have been inspired by Rossetti's drawing *Three Sang of Love Together*, which was exhibited the same year in Bradford, and an enamel triptych, *The Red Cross Knight*, was shown at the Arts and Crafts Exhibition of 1906, being commended for its colour and 'pleasant and effective, even noble decoration'.[34] Like many of her contemporaries, she also worked in textile art and, although outside the scope of this study, her pictorial designs for embroidery, which received special

PHOEBE A. TRAQUAIR

45. Pan 1912

attention at the 1903 Arts and Crafts Exhibition, were ambitious, not to say pretentiously artistic, comprising four large panels representing the spiritual and moral phases of life, inspired by Walter Pater's tale of Denys l'Auxerrois in *Imaginary Portraits*. The sequence was begun in 1895 and completed in 1902, and the protagonist is a Botticellian young man dressed in a leopard skin, evidently first cousin to *Pan* [FIG. 46].

Owing to her working methods and lack of specialisation, Traquair was sometimes regarded as less than professional in her approach. But, her champion asserted,

> her art is the spontaneous efflorescence of her imagination, her religion and her love of beauty: and these are of no common order . . . Her work possesses the elusive yet abiding elements of charm and the indefinable yet authentic marks of a noble passion and an exalted inspiration.[35]

The same issue of the *Art Journal* included a short notice on the 'romantic watercolours' of Katherine Cameron (1874–1965), recently exhibited in Glasgow, which placed them firmly within the 'gracious legendary tradition' of Rossetti, Burne-Jones and Morris, singling out her poetic subjects, old ballads and fairy mysteries, together with 'the direct simplicity of her painting, her skilful drawing and composition, and rich feeling for colour'. Trained in Glasgow and Paris, Katherine Cameron was the sister of another Scottish artist, D. Y. Cameron, and produced miniatures, flower pictures and portraits, but was most commended for her imaginative scenes, including a version of 'Proud Maisie', said to be very different in conception from Frederick Sandys's famous head. Her watercolour *Entangled* shows a maiden with flying goblins pulling at her hair, 'painted in deep rose-pink and pale rose-yellow, which are a favourite combination of hers'. Altogether, the article concluded, Cameron was a worthy inheritor of 'the English romantic school' – by which Pre-Raphaelitism was meant – infusing their traditions and poetry 'with as much fresh thought and character as they themselves first did'.[36]

In the last decade of the nineteenth century Glasgow School of Art became a renowned centre of new and innovative art with its roots in Pre-Raphaelitism watered by Symbolism, and among its students were Jessie King and the sisters Margaret and Frances Macdonald. The 'Glasgow Style' stands on its own, but its links with Pre-Raphaelitism are strong and form an appropriate conclusion to this survey, showing how from the end of the Pre-Raphaelite impulse, the women artists of the Glasgow group were able to develop a style and an art practice that looked forward to the art of the twentieth century.

Born at New Kilpatrick to the west of Glasgow, where her father was a Presbyterian minister, Jessie Marion King (1875–1949) is said to have faced and overcome opposition from both parents in pursuit of an artistic career. At the Glasgow School of Art from 1893, she concentrated on drawing and illustrative decoration, and was chosen to illuminate on vellum a history of the school, to be built into the foundation stone of the new building designed by Charles Rennie Mackintosh in 1898. In 1902 she won a gold medal for book design at the International Exhibition of Decorative Art in Turin, where the new Glasgow Style first triumphed. From 1899 she taught design for the bookbinding course at Glasgow School of Art, and later taught ceramic decoration for a single year. Her talents, like Traquair's, were extremely varied, covering theatrical costume, wallpapers, fabrics, posters, gesso panels, bookplates and jewellery; she exhibited successfully in Cork, Berlin and Calcutta as well as in Scotland and England, sending eighty-five works over the years to the Glasgow Institution, for example, and over seventy to the Bruton Street Gallery in London. From 1905 she was a member of the Glasgow Society of Lady Artists.

Her work is notable for its attenuated linear quality and delicate, elusive imagery. Its links with Pre-Raphaelitism are visible in the *fin-de-siècle* compositions with their shallow spaces, flowing lines and stylised motifs, executed with a distinctively chaste hand, and in the choice of Arthurian subjects [FIG. 1]. Like the Birmingham artists, she created graphic and illustrative work to accompany some of the key texts of the Pre-Raphaelite movement. Among King's earliest and most prestigious commissions were illustrated editions of the *High History of the Holy Grail* (1903), William Morris's *The Defence of Guenevere* (1904) – for which she produced twenty-eight full-page illustrations and sixty-seven head- and tailpieces – Milton's *Comus* (1906), and Keats's *Isabella* and *La Belle Dame Sans Merci* [FIG. 48] (1907). In 1909 an exhibition of her drawings entitled *Wilding Things* was held at the Annan Gallery in Glasgow.

JESSIE M. KING

47. La Belle Dame Sans Merci *c.1900–1910*

In his history of Scottish painting J. L. Caw compared her work to that of the 1890s:

> With Miss King a glamorised atmosphere is attained by means in which colour has no part . . . the effects achieved in the limited medium of pen and ink are wonderful. Borrowing technical devices from Beardsley, and influences (as is very evident in the accessories in such drawings as that of a girl reading 'The Magic Grammar' which might have been taken from one of Miss Cranstoun's aesthetic tea-rooms) by the peculiar style of decoration – 'the swirl and blob' – associated with a group of Glasgow designers, it would yet be absurd to describe her work as decadent . . . it is untainted by that distressing morbidity and moral unhealthiness which are the signs of the real decadent.

Caw also linked her style to that of the writer Maeterlinck, describing it as 'mystical, allusive, decorative. The action is slow, rhythmical and symbolic . . . the effect is like that of faded tapestry seen in a dimly lit interior, where what is seen counts for less than what the mind conjures up for itself', and concluded, with a quotation from Morris, that the artist 'is at her best dealing with "old, unhappy, far-off things"'.[37]

In 1908 Jessie King married Ernest A. Taylor and moved first to Manchester, where Taylor worked as a designer of stained glass and their daughter Merle was born, and then to Paris, where from 1911 the couple ran an atelier of painting and applied art. In Paris King responded to the Ballets Russes and the work of Bakst, and her work became bolder in its use of colour, although still retaining its linear stylisation. In 1915 she produced sixteen colour illustrations to an edition of Oscar Wilde's *House of Pomegranates*. She also responded to Modernism, and her mosaic panel of coloured and mirror glass entitled *The Enchanted Faun* displays a stylish blend of green and mauve abstractionism. From this point her art ceased to express the Pre-Raphaelite impulse, although the fairy-tale fancies were never abandoned. The First World War brought the Taylors back to Scotland where they settled in Kirkcudbright and where her work developed through landscape painting and batik fabric designs. She continued to work and exhibit to the end, dying in August 1949.

The origins of the Glasgow Style were recognised as lying within Pre-Raphaelitism. 'Here we have the latest evolution of the imaginative line which has its origin in England,' wrote a Scottish critic in 1905 of the work of Margaret Macdonald. 'As in the mysticism of the poet William Blake, one is carried away to a dream world of shadowy impressions. From Blake, from Rossetti, and the Pre-Raphaelites, there can be drawn a direct line of inheritance right down to the artists of Glasgow.'[38]

Margaret Macdonald (1864–1933) and Frances Macdonald (1873–1921) were born in the West Midlands where their father worked as an engineer before moving to Glasgow in 1890, when both sisters enrolled at the art school. From the mid-1890s they shared a studio in Hope Street, and both became successful as designers, watercolourists and embroiderers, with a personal approach to both medium and manner that developed a stylised, semi-Symbolist, mixed-media art in pictorial and decorative work. At Glasgow School of Art they met the architects Charles R. Mackintosh (whom Margaret married in 1899) and Herbert MacNair (whom Frances married in 1900), forming the artistic partnership known as 'The Four', their work being seen as essentially complementary in style; it is thought that all may have exhibited work together in the art-school show of 1893. The four were among the contributors to the *Magazine*, a hand-illustrated quarterly produced by Glasgow students and associates from 1894, to which Margaret contributed a ghostly image of Guy Fawkes Night.

Frances and Margaret had always worked closely together, and the strange, mystical style of their pictorial work was nicknamed the 'Spook School'. The Glasgow Style, according to a later critic, 'is at its most typical and its most Symbolist in the works of Margaret and Frances Macdonald'. Their images 'defy explanation, but the intended effect is all too clear . . . distorted figures – emaciated and elongated – strong colour (concentrating on blue and green) and symbols of mystery disclose fertile and impressionable imaginations . . .'[39] In 1897–98 the Macdonalds shared the Seasons between them in tall vertical images of Symbolist female figures in swirling mists. Among Frances's work is a pastel *Sleeping Princess* (c. 1895) inscribed with a quotation and set in a beaten metal frame of her own design and making. She also produced a large watercolour design of the Crucifixion and Ascension for a church commission that was never executed, while she and Margaret worked together on a planned

FRANCES MACDONALD

49. 'Tis a long path that wanders to desire *c.*1910

version of the Christmas story, with illustrations in silver and gold bound in a beaten metal cover, which never reached publication. In 1897 they collaborated on their only known etching of the Christ child. Mystical fancies were a main feature of Frances's work, which showed increasingly Expressionist tendencies; among her most strikingly original pictures is an adolescent nude on a pathway with hair circling two males, and the evocatively Rossettian title 'Tis a long path which wanders to desire [FIG. 50]. Another, whose stylised aspects partly conceal the theme, is a variation on the Judgement of Paris, entitled The Choice [PL. 10].

On marriage Frances Macdonald MacNair moved to Liverpool where her son Sylvan was born. She taught embroidery at University College alongside her husband in the architectural department. Together they contributed to the Vienna Secession in 1900, with her image of The Legend of the Snowdrops showing the flowers created from snowflakes by an angel for Eve after the Expulsion, and his painting of The Legend of the Birds. Together they also designed and decorated the much-commended Writing Room for the Scottish Section of the Turin International Exhibition in 1902.

In 1909 the family returned to Glasgow; here Frances taught embroidery and metalwork at the art school for a short while. She exhibited between 1908 and 1911 in Liverpool and London, but few examples of her work survive. Later the couple experienced financial and emotional difficulties, and when Frances died of a cerebral haemorrhage in 1921 her devastated husband withdrew from artistic life. He also destroyed most of his own and his wife's work.

Margaret Macdonald Mackintosh also contributed to the Turin International, as well as to the 1900 Vienna Secession Exhibition, the 1901 Glasgow International Exhibition and the London Arts and Crafts Exhibitions, and her work was illustrated in British and European periodicals. She was elected to the Royal Scottish Society of Painters in Watercolours in 1898 and exhibited with the Glasgow Society of Lady Artists in 1901. A good deal of her work was created as pictorial pieces in different media – gesso, embroidery, metalwork panels – for interiors designed by her husband, such as the Willow and Ingram Street tea rooms in Glasgow, or the house designed for Miss Cranston and her husband at Hous'hill, for which, inter alia, she produced four painted and gilded gesso panels of The Four Queens (1909) for the card room [PL. 14]. She also produced work in pencil and watercolour, with mysterious, fugitive images in sombre, soft colours; among her subjects are two of the drowning Ophelia (1898 and 1908), recalling the very beginnings of Pre-Raphaelitism [PL. 11].

The Mackintoshes left Scotland for London in 1914, and after the war lived in southern France 1923–27, returning to London, where Mackintosh died in 1928. Margaret, who is believed to have virtually given up productive art by this date, died in London in 1933.

The Pre-Raphaelite movement must be viewed as coming to an end with the close of the nineteenth century or, at the latest, with the First World War. Yet the last artist we want to consider had her first major exhibition in 1901, and continued to paint in a Pre-Raphaelite style until well into the 1920s. Eleanor Fortescue Brickdale (1872–1945) was born into a *haute bourgeois* family, the youngest child of the barrister Matthew Inglett Fortescue Brickdale (son of Sir John Fortescue Brickdale of Birchamp House, Newland, in the Forest of Dean) a senior barrister in Chancery and the High Court, and his wife Sarah, daughter of a senior judge at Bristol Crown Court. She grew up at Birchamp Villa, Beulah Hill, in Upper Norwood, Surrey, a suburb to the south of London settled in the mid-nineteenth century by the wealthy professional classes. She had two brothers, one who followed his father into law and one who went into medicine, and two sisters, one of whom died in infancy.

Eleanor Brickdale is said to have revered her brother Charles, who as the eldest son occupied a privileged position in the family. Educated according to his caste at Westminster and Christ Church, Charles had artistic yearnings, taking classes at the Ruskin School of Drawing and maintaining a recreational interest in art through his long legal career as the authority on land titles, for which he received a knighthood. To mark this event, his sister painted his portrait, exhibited at the Royal Academy in 1917.

Less privileged educationally but freer of the economic constraints that propelled her brothers into the professions, she took up the serious study of art at the age of seventeen, first attending the local Crystal Palace School of Art and then, at the third attempt, gaining admittance to the Royal Academy Schools. The fact that RA tuition was free of charge may have influenced her choice, for in 1894 her father was killed in an Alpine accident; their income somewhat diminished, the family moved to Kensington and then, following the marriage of Eleanor's younger brother Jack, to other addresses in the same neighbourhood.

While still a student, Brickdale began to exhibit at the RA, in the black-and-white section – an advertisement design in 1896, *Sir Lancelot du Lake* in 1897 and *Sleeping Beauty* in 1898. Other illustrative work took similar literary and legendary subjects such as *St George and the*

Dragon, The Princess and the Swineherd, Isabella or the Pot of Basil (described by one critic as 'a design which every black and white artist is doomed to attempt sooner or later') and *Knight with the Angel of Death*. Her student career culminated in 1897 in the triumph of a prize for *Spring*, a lunette design for an awkward space in the dining room at Burlington House, and a feature on her work in the *Studio*. Not without criticism of her sense of scale for foregrounded animals (a fawn-sized stag in *Spring* and piglets 'the size of white rats' in *The Princess and the Swineherd*, the article praised Brickdale's vigour and 'admirable power of telling a story'; the 'greedy little princess' was shown 'grudgingly paying her toll of a hundred kisses, to a swineherd drawn with vitality and almost brutal force'.[40]

The £40 prize money for *Spring* enabled Brickdale to begin her first large-scale painting, entitled *The pale complexion of true love . . .* and exhibited at the RA in 1899. Other works in oil included *That overcometh the world* (RA 1899), *Time and the Physician* (RA 1900) and *The Deceitfulness of Riches* (RA 1901). Her earliest published work was a series of seventeen vignettes of views for *A Cotswold Village*, a book written in 1898 by her sister-in-law's brother J. A. Gibbs, followed by line drawings for an edition of Walter Scott's *Ivanhoe* published in 1899. The evidence that Brickdale regarded herself as a professional artist is contained in a pocketbook for 1898–1901 that records her sales: typical prices were thirty shillings for an illustration and five pounds for a watercolour. In 1899 her two oils hung at the RA were sold for a combined total of £35. 5s. 0d. In 1905 a full illustrated edition of Tennyson's *Poems*, with eighteen large and fifty-five small line drawings, earned £145.

This early success and acclaim led, in the summer of 1899, when Brickdale was twenty-seven, to a commission from the London gallery-owners Charles and Walter Dowdeswell for a solo show of watercolours, to be delivered and paid for in quarterly instalments over the next two years. The exhibition, containing forty-five imaginative pictures, opened in June 1901 at the Dowdeswell Galleries in New Bond Street, under the title 'Such Stuff as Dreams are made of!'

The compositions are accomplished and varied and bold, ranging widely over literary, religious or allegorical subjects, chiefly showing figures in period costume engaged in narrative or dramatic scenes, such as the rendering of *The Little Foot Page* [FIG. 38] from the ballad of Burd Helen, a Pre-Raphaelite favourite. Occasionally the subject is a simple single figure, such as the elderly Renaissance matriarch in *The Duenna*; usually the figure compositions are more complex. The exhibition was widely reviewed in the national and specialist press, where the *Morning Leader* described Brickdale as an exponent of 'neo-Pre-Raphaelitism',[41] and *The Times* praised the colours as 'bold and vivid in the extreme', commenting on the 'great force and solidity' of the drawing such as is visible in *Riches*, an intensely drawn grouping of a beggar couple on the roadside embracing their infant.[42] Several of the pictures contain variations on this moral theme, another showing a king passing a quaffing figure in medieval garb under the title *The Cup of Happiness*. *The Deceitfulness of Riches* presumably explores the same idea.

Justice was another favoured theme, beginning with an early headpiece, *Without Prejudice* (c. 1897), and continuing with *Justice Before her Judge* at the RA in 1902, showing Justice blindfolded before the figure of Christ crucified. A variation on this is *Peradventure the darkness shall cover me* (1901), in which 'an Italian murderer, as he passes hurriedly at midnight over a bridge, beholds all at once in a wooden shrine, the figure of Christ upon the

144

Cross, lit up by the moon's light and a taper's glimmer'. This, one critic remarked, complaining of the artist's predilection for long quotations in place of straightforward titles, 'would be none the less impressive if it were labelled *Conscience*'.[43]

Just as Love is allegorically represented by a winged Cupid figure in several of Brickdale's romantic works, angels often feature in her moral subjects. These and directly religious themes such as the *Wise Virgins* represent the artist's choice of traditional subject matter, as well as illuminating what may be interpreted as her own Christian faith, nurtured through late nineteenth-century teaching of the New Testament. One critic noted the 'unaccustomed seriousness and depth of purpose' to be seen in the works, while others responded also to the sense of humour shown in several of the costume pieces, such as *I have married a Wife and therefore cannot come* and *The Travesties of Life*, recalling the 'burlesqued satire . . . in early Elizabethan masques'.[44] The artist also deployed eighteenth-century costume scenes.

Her works were generally received as belonging to the late phase of 'the Pre-Raphaelite revival' alongside work by J. L. Byam Shaw; critics specifically referred also to Rossetti, Madox Brown and Holman Hunt, whose last great Pre-Raphaelite painting of *The Lady of Shalott* was not completed until 1905. Brickdale should in fact be distinguished from other late Pre-Raphaelites like Byam Shaw and Thomas Gotch by her dramatic compositions and vigorous handling; despite the carefully detailed costumes the sense of surface decoration is never dominant, and the works most strongly evoked by her 1900–01 watercolours are perhaps Burne-Jones's *Sidonia the Sorceress* and *Clara von Bork* of 1860. Like the young Burne-Jones, Brickdale often inscribed her initials or monogram on a scroll in the corner of the canvas.

All but two of the pictures in the 1901 exhibition were sold, and the artist was allocated a full-length article, with eight monochrome and two colour illustrations, in the *Studio*. Other critics had noted that, although not concealing it, the Dowdeswell catalogue made no mention of the artist's gender, and this perhaps led the author of the *Studio* article, Walter Shaw Sparrow, to take the opportunity to promote his own views on women and art:

> Miss Fortescue Brickdale is an artist, and her varied and thorough art as a painter in watercolours, now on view . . . proves her to be a lady of real genius. And this being so, what are the qualities of such a genuine woman-artist? . . . Is it her privilege to work under a guidance that is instinctive rather than technical, or should she attempt to vie with men in the use of such a fine artifice of method as cannot be justified as spontaneous or instinctive? In other words, should a woman of genius make herself the imitative slave of men-artists and their ways of work, or should she, controlled by 'her sweet and wayward earthliness', keep us all in mind of the old saying that Intuition is to her sex both Impulse and Law?

Arguing that 'what the world needs now is a general return to womanliness by the ladies who try to be artists', the author criticised Brickdale's earlier pen drawings 'where she aimed at a kind of strength at variance with her own personality', blaming this on the imitation of 'clever studies by young men' during her art-school training. He praised her new work, in which

the medium itself is never paraded, as in most modern watercolours; it is always a quiet,

ELEANOR FORTESCUE BRICKDALE

51. The Guardian Angel 1910

unobtrusive servant to the artist's play of thought, fancy and sentiment; and this result is entirely in accordance with instinctive ways of work most suitable to women of genius.

To add insult to condescension, he claimed that she 'arrives at her ends without becoming conscious of the steps by which she gets there' and praised her versatility: 'like a good actress, she can be her true self plus someone else'.[45]

It is not known to what extent Brickdale agreed with this kind of criticism, but the exhibition certainly established her reputation. Some of the watercolours were shown again six months later in an exhibition at Leighton House, together with oils and other drawings, which coincided with her election as the first female member of the Institute of Painters in Oils and as an associate member of the Royal Watercolour Society. By this date, at the age of thirty, the artist had her own studio in Holland Park Road, not far from the family home, in a residential area favoured by painters and other professional artists. Byam Shaw was among her friends and she taught at his art school, founded in 1911. Later, in an article on careers for women, she noted that teaching 'helped to butter the bread of many a well-known artist'.[46]

Brickdale's works were evidently popular, for a second exhibition was held at Leighton House in May 1904, including twenty-six works from the 1901 Dowdeswell exhibition. This was accompanied by a catalogue whose preface included gratifying remarks by G. F. Watts, the doyen of allegorical painting, who died the same year. The Dowdeswell brothers renewed their commission, and a second exhibition under the same title, 'Such Stuff as Dreams are made of!' was shown in June 1905, containing twenty-five new watercolours. This was accompanied by a leaflet in which the artist explained the subjects, in answer to earlier criticisms of the opacity of meaning.

Brickdale continued to produce at least one oil painting a year for submission to the Royal Academy, but her main work was now in watercolour and in most years from 1902 onwards she exhibited several works at the summer and winter shows of the RWS. In addition, in a manner that increasingly dominated her output, she worked to commission on watercolour pictures for poetic texts, the original works being shown at the Dowdeswell or the Leicester Galleries and reproduced in full colour by the new colour-printing processes in expensive illustrated editions. This had the effect of establishing her reputation as that of illustrator, whereas the earlier works, although frequently inspired by texts and poems, were nevertheless imaginative paintings rather than illustrations. The distinction is a fine one, but it is noticeable that something of the daring and originality – the 'unfeminine' strength and vigour of her early works – tended to diminish with these commissions.

Following the black-and-white illustrations to Tennyson's *Poems* (1905) came eight colour illustrations to Mabel Dearmer's *A Child's Life of Christ* (1906) where the subjects selected illustrate the nature of the artist's Christian piety, with the sentimental and didactic emphases of the age, starting with the Nativity and Christ's childhood, when 'Mary kept all these things in her heart and pondered them', progressing through miracles and parables to the Entry into Jerusalem, the Crucifixion (dramatically but tastefully drawn for young readers with the cross against a dark blue sky and a single red spear rising from the foreground) and the Empty Tomb.

Illustrations to Browning's poems followed in two volumes in 1908 and 1909, several of which tackled the texts very freely and unexpectedly; thus the line 'The world and what it fears' from *Respectability* is rendered by a Cupid and a Scarecrow. Many subjects still focused on the virtues of humility and honest work, showing servants for instance, for whom 'all service ranks the same with God'.

In 1909 the Leicester Galleries in London commissioned a series of twenty-eight Tennyson subjects, delivered and paid for in instalments, at the price of 15 guineas each, which were exhibited in the autumn of 1911. All were based on *Idylls of the King*, the Arthurian legends which formed a mainstay of Pre-Raphaelitism through its various phases, and perhaps this weight of tradition inhibited Brickdale, for her works broke no new ground but seem in a sense to represent summaries of previous endeavours. Enid, the submissive wife of Geraint, and Elaine, who died of unrequited love for Lancelot [PL. 9], are the figures favoured over Vivien, who ensnared Merlin, and the adulterous Guinevere, who is shown, unusually, at the end of her life as a penitent nun. Any artist tackling Tennyson's *Idylls*, however, was more or less obliged to rework the Victorian division of femininity into self-sacrificial, asexual virtue and self-indulgent, sexual vice. A comparable message was contained in the legend of *St Elizabeth of Hungary*, published in 1912, for which Brickdale produced – at a reduced rate of five guineas each, presumably on account of their religious content – eight watercolour illustrations of surpassing sentimentality, beginning with *The Divine Playmate* and including *Saint Elizabeth praying to God to clothe her*.

The characteristic blend of piety, literary archaism and fantasy was not entirely closed to the events of the contemporary world, however, and Brickdale is remarkable as the first and only artist to bring together the imagination of Pre-Raphaelitism with the modern technology of the twentieth century in the field of aviation. Her first works in this genre seem to have been inspired by the death of the Hon. Charles Stewart Rolls (half of the Rolls-Royce partnership) in a flying accident near Bournemouth in July 1910. To commemorate the event Brickdale produced a large watercolour, showing an archangel with mauve wings hovering behind a flying biplane surrounded by a flock of swallows amid a pinkish sunset [FIG. 52]. Below, in a three-section predella characteristic of her work (and, like others, framed to the artist's design) are scenes representing aspects of the history of flight: Leonardo displaying his flying machine, a portrait of Charles Rolls as aviator standing before his aeroplane, and Daedalus fixing Icarus's wings.

A decade later, the subject of Leonardo was enlarged in oils and shown at the Royal Academy in 1920 under the title *The Forerunner*, subtitled *Leonardo da Vinci showing a model of his flying machine to Ludovico Sforza, Duke of Milan, and his Court* [FIG. 53]. By this date, of course, aeroplanes, although still built on the biplane model, had demonstrated their usefulness and potential with the Royal Flying Corps in the First World War. *The Forerunner* was purchased by Lord Leverhulme for 300 guineas.

After the death of her mother in 1909 the artist lived in Kensington with her unmarried sister Kate. She produced further illustrative sequences, being in 1919 commissioned to prepare fifteen watercolours to accompany texts chosen by herself for *Eleanor Fortescue Brickdale's Golden Book of Famous Women*, containing Saint Clare, Saint Catherine of Siena, Kate Barlass (from Rossetti's *The King's Tragedy*), Maud, Guinevere, Rosalind and Celia, Titania, Una, the Queen's Maries, Katherine of Aragon, Joan of Arc, Laura, Beatrice, Fair Rosamund, and Eloise. These were the subjects of her last solo exhibition at the Leicester Galleries in April 1920. Other illustration commissions followed, but although she con-

ELEANOR FORTESCUE BRICKDALE
52. The Forerunner 1920

tinued to send oils to the RA until 1932, in the interwar period her health and sight began to fail.

From 1914 she produced designs for stained glass, many in the Bristol area, where her brother Jack lived. She also created sculpture, designing a war memorial for the King's Own Yorkshire Light Infantry for York Minster which was unveiled in September 1921.

I'm still trying to paint my picture 'All Generations shall call me Blessed' [from the Magnificat] (which of course costs money and probably won't sell), Brickdale told her brother in February 1929: 'but a great many of my dearest friends have been sitting for the heads in it, which saves me a lot. It is a fair size (for me), long and narrow . . . It has a long procession of figures on either side holding banners each one representing one century – from the 1st century up to the present – I am very much enjoying doing it.'[47]

This oil was presented to St George's church, Aubrey Walk, Kensington. Another Lady Chapel altar piece, a triptych showing Mary and Jesus flanked by St Elizabeth, St John and St Anne, mother of Mary, was presented to the parish church in Newland, where Brickdale's brother Charles maintained a summer residence. Other public commissions included a picture of *Knightly Service* (1928) for Winchester College Chapel and *Ariel and Prospero* (1931), for the boardroom at the BBC's Broadcasting House in London. She continued to send to the RWS until 1942, despite suffering a stroke in 1938. She died in London at the age of seventy-three in March 1945.

THE WISH

HOPE TO SING THROUGH ALL THE DAYS

WOMEN'S LIVES
AND
WOMEN'S ART

53. **The Wish** *c.*1910

lthough the facts available on the lives and works of the artists surveyed here render some less visible than others, certain general statements can be made in terms of how women artists responded to Pre-Raphaelitism, the ways in which their careers and reputations were shaped and received, and the kind of pictures they produced. Taken together, the female Pre-Raphaelites form an even more varied group than their male counterparts, and as the material evidence is always more fragmentary than for the men, analytical conclusions must be tentative. But some strands of comparison and contrast can be teased out.

We have seen how, in the early 1850s, the Pre-Raphaelite enterprise appealed to already trained artists such as Howitt and Boyce through its freshness and invention, seriousness and sense of idealism. In loose alliance with the men, these artists were – or seemed – set to develop as successful and innovative painters. For an artist like Siddal, whom family circumstances prevented from obtaining formal training, Pre-Raphaelitism and its social circle offered stimulus through individual encouragement and a positive response to the naive qualities of her work. Other artists, like Brett and Blunden, in relatively constrained and provincial circumstances, responded to a style in sympathy with their aims which valued aspects of art they could encompass – moral and religious subjects, landscapes and sentiment. In its ideas these artists found the stimulus to develop their own art practice, and its appeal to 'nature' and to ideals – openly formulated by Ruskin rather than remaining the property of a closed, metropolitan clique – was welcoming as well as challenging. To this group, the early critical attacks on Pre-Raphaelitism were not proof of worthlessness but evidence of new and attractive qualities.

In this early period, indeed, Pre-Raphaelitism can be defined as generally friendly towards women. It did not, in its presentation or theory, insist on women's unfitness for high art, nor on the kind of painting that was difficult for women to achieve, requiring years of study in the academies or the ateliers of Paris and Rome, nor on the supremacy of subjects based on the heroic male nude and a sound classical education. Furthermore, the young men of the Brotherhood were not chauvinistic in their attitudes to either women or art – whatever they may later have become. A certain liberal egalitarianism pervaded PRB thinking, their own social position making the men keenly aware of the arguments for judging on merit alone. Thus when a group of young male artists gathered at Rossetti's studio with coffee and roast chestnuts one evening at the end of 1852 to examine an illustrative sequence drawn by 'the Hon. Mrs Boyle', they were united in admiration of its beauty 'in feeling, natural simplicity and colour, and in poetical treatment', noting the author's aristocratic origin but not disparaging her sex.[1] In addition, most of the young men of early Pre-Raphaelitism had grown up at home, alongside sisters, rather than being sent away to school, and were thus

accustomed to female company and pursuits. It is therefore not surprising to find women in their families being encouraged to draw and exhibit, even when they did not pursue a career in art, as in the cases of Emily Hunt, Judith Agnes Millais, and Christina Rossetti. Finally, their religious education, whether High Church or Evangelical, stressed the respect and courtesy due to all women as vessels of moral value, although this might be a two-edged sword, easily used to confining or oppressive effect. In summary, although too much should not be made of all this, it is clear that the Pre-Raphaelite impulse did not appear or present itself as hostile or arrogant towards women.

By the time the 'second generation' of artists began their careers in the late 1860s and 1870s, Pre-Raphaelitism had become an established fact of British art, and had evolved in various different ways. For many of our artists, it was already the 'family style', Lucy and Catherine Madox Brown learning from their father and Emma Sandys from her brother. As a pupil of Ford Madox Brown – always generous in his encouragement of women artists – Marie Spartali joined the clan. Pickering also had a family connection through her uncle but seems to have found her own way to Pre-Raphaelitism independently after leaving the Slade School. In this period, too, Pre-Raphaelitism offered artists a style of painting that encouraged imagination and expression rather than erecting criteria of correctness. Its value judgements were based on sentiment and ideas rather than technique; hence the frequent objections, from opponents, to the Pre-Raphaelites' 'bad drawing'.

With the opening of new art schools during the 1870s and 1880s, and concurrent demands for education and professional training, more women were able to embark on artistic careers. By this period Pre-Raphaelitism had ceased to be the vanguard of British art but it nevertheless retained and even regained a place in the spectrum of styles, and our artists of the third generation were among those of both sexes who picked up and re-fired the torch of Pre-Raphaelitism in the 1890s, developing both the symbolic and the aesthetic aspects. Through the Glasgow artists, the Pre-Raphaelite impulse evolved into an artistic style with its own distinctive qualities. Other artists developed one of the original mainsprings of Pre-Raphaelitism in the shape of religious art in church painting and stained glass – an impulse that united, for example, the work of Bunce, Traquair and Brickdale. It thus remained a style many women found congenial to work in.

There was indeed, in some quarters, a sense that Pre-Raphaelitism was altogether too 'womanish' in its nature, both as regards artists and subjects, enabling critics to display the prejudice that femininity was synonymous with weakness and ineptitude. 'It may surprise us that grown men should care for a school of art in which girls play all the parts,' remarked the *Magazine of Art* of the Grosvenor show in 1880, in relation to 'followers in Mr Burne-Jones's footsteps'; 'but the fact undoubtedly remains that such feminine art is interesting to many minds'. Admitting his own preference for 'incidents belonging to the broader masculine life and temper', the writer made a distinction between 'those artists whose emotional poetry charms and touches the imaginative art-lover into forgetfulness of their many technical weaknesses, and those who have nothing to separate them from the most popular and Philistine painters at the Royal Academy, except their affectation':

> the slightest touch of genius explains and excuses much, but we are not infrequently called
> upon in these days to excuse bad drawing and untaught composition for the sake of

mysticism in which there is no poetry, eccentricity in which there is no originality, and effort in which there is no impulse.[2]

This, it may be noted, was addressed to male and female artists alike.

But if women found in Pre-Raphaelitism a relatively sympathetic artistic environment in which to work, it was not absolutely so. The initial friendliness of the early Brotherhood diminished with time, causing Holman Hunt to dismiss his sister's endeavour, and Rossetti to express disappointingly conventional views of female capacity. 'Cathy was saying the other day that she and Lucy would come again when you came to see the picture,' he wrote to Brown about the never finished *Found*; 'but much as I should like to have them, I think on this occasion that the partial view taken by lady-friends might interfere with vigorous criticism, so I'll make another appointment I trust when I see them again.'[3] And while Burne-Jones 'loved helping' Spartali, he was also on record as saying of women artists that 'there aren't any'.[4] As we have noted, the Hogarth Club, whose members included the brothers of both Boyce and Brett, never thought to invite women to join or exhibit in what was perceived as a Pre-Raphaelite showplace. At points like this, the limits of the men's sympathy are revealed.

There were other difficulties, too. Without ascribing to Pre-Raphaelitism itself all the many obstacles to women's art practice which they encountered in the bourgeois culture of nineteenth-century Britain, it is clear that their position in the art world was subordinate. Moreover, within Pre-Raphaelitism's specific terms, the very welcome and tolerance extended to naivety, simplicity and imagination also militated against women's achievement, creating an artistic environment in which they were patted on the head and patronisingly commended for their 'natural' qualities, rather than being required to display ambition and attain technical excellence.

This was truer of some than of others – Boyce, for example, was generally admired as an artist to be praised, not patronised – but seems to have had a limiting effect on their work, so that habits of drawing or composition remained relatively static. It is arguable, for instance, that Siddal might have done better had she not been regarded by Rossetti as a natural genius but encouraged to obtain competent training – as indeed Ruskin indicated when he urged her to draw, sometimes, from 'dull things' and as she recognised when enrolling in a conventional course at Sheffield Art School. It is also possible that Spartali might have painted more interesting pictures without Burne-Jones's soppy advice on angels' wings. On this issue, it may be noted that many male Pre-Raphaelites' work also remained locked into repetitive formulae, but this has neither been ascribed to their sex nor prevented them from being well regarded.

There is also the question of Pre-Raphaelitism's subject matter. In the early phase, landscapes and subject pictures containing both males and females in active or dramatic relation were usual material for Pre-Raphaelite pictures, while in the later phases representations of ideal, allegorical, or decorative female figures and faces – heads with floral accessories, as William Rossetti accurately put it – painted with degrees of sensuous intent became a major feature of Pre-Raphaelitism. These were among the most easily sold works, and their influence on our artists is not to be denied. Indeed, Sandys, Spartali, Cathy Madox Brown and Brickdale produced works in this mode, while Pickering's output included several full-length female figures in a comparably fashionable style. Although the women's works are seldom if ever as vacuous as some of the men's, this focus on female representation in Pre-Raphaelite art was double-edged. On the one hand female figures and groups were within the scope conventionally allotted to women artists in terms of subject (unlike, say, battles or shipwrecks) and also, being generally draped, they were not excluded on grounds of propriety. But the erotic representation of womanhood in alluring or compelling guise directed towards the viewer's gratification is a different exercise for female and male artists, as is the sale of such works to male patrons. Such pictures, whatever other qualities they have, are a product of and a contribution to the articulation of sexuality in the late Victorian period, fittingly described in 1899, in the case of Rossetti's works, as 'images of carnal loveliness'.[5] In this matrix the sex of the artist and the purchaser played a significant role, to the female artist's disadvantage in respect of reputation and sales: it was a sexual arena in which she could not easily compete.

To a certain extent, too, the rise of the Arts and Crafts Movement adversely affected the woman artist. Again, the influence was ambivalent: on the one hand the re-evaluation of the applied arts enabled more women to participate in art practice and share the honours with men; on the other, the division between head and hand, male and female, still tended to be unequal, and to corral women within a 'decorative art' corner, reserving the status of 'fine art' chiefly for male practitioners.

If therefore women artists found the Pre-Raphaelite area a congenial and productive one in which to work, they were also nevertheless disadvantaged within it. Ultimately, Pre-Raphaelitism, as a movement, did not elevate or promote any woman to a position of eminence alongside the early Millais, or Rossetti, Madox Brown or Burne-Jones. And the disadvantages were compounded by external factors.

For adoption of the Pre-Raphaelite style could not insulate women artists from the general conditions of their sex, and it is clear from the brief life histories we have given that the specific material conditions our artists experienced were of prime importance in determining both their personal and professional careers. The chief obstacles to women's art practice lay not within Pre-Raphaelitism but in the wider physical, economic, social and psychological environment.

The first evident condition is that of health, which was differentially experienced in nineteenth-century Britain by gender as well as class. Of our artists, Boyce's career (and life) was ended by puerperal fever, an infection commonly the direct result of unhygienic medical intervention in childbirth and distressingly frequent in Victorian Britain. Ill health can also be seen to have curtailed the careers of Siddal – if, as we believe, her fatal overdose was due in large part to post-natal depression following stillbirth – and those of Brett and Lucy Madox Brown, and probably also that of Emma Sandys, the causes of whose death at the age of thirty-four are not fully known. Early or relatively early death therefore claimed five of our artists and it is no accident that, as is generally the case with male artists, those whose lives were longest, like Spartali, Pickering and Brickdale, also produced the most substantial oeuvres.

Cultural attitudes towards women's health were also significant in that the nineteenth-century cult of female frailty among the middle classes led to the general belief that women's physical constitution was naturally weak; their achievements were thus thought to be determined or limited by their bodies, or gender. From this flowed the idea that women were incapable of hard work, although at the same time they were often accused of being unwilling to work rather than excused for failing.

Wealth, or economic status, is a second important material condition. Economically, our artists lived within a complex web of financial and cultural constraints. In terms of social class, they were drawn from the middle ranks of the bourgeoisie, in a period when commerce and the professions were expanding and consolidating their social position. As an analysis of their fathers' occupations shows, the social range of their families of origin was similar to that of male Pre-Raphaelites. In descending order of wealth and status, Pickering and Brickdale were daughters of successful lawyers, Spartali, Cameron and Boyce daughters of well-to-do businessmen, Traquair the daughter of an eminent physician, Howitt and Bunce daughters of journalist-editors, King the daughter of a clergyman, the Macdonalds of an engineer, the Madox Browns and Sandys of artists (albeit of very different social position), Brett the daughter of an army surgeon, and Blunden and Siddal daughters of small shopkeepers. Significantly, only the last two were economically active before taking up art, the one as a governess and the other as a dressmaker. Below this social level it would have been extremely hard for any woman to become an artist.

Middle-class status meant that women were not expected to pursue or attain independence. None of our artists, not even those from the wealthiest families, seems to have had personally disposable income; all were to some degree dependent on their families when seeking training. At least eight – Howitt, Boyce, the Madox Browns, Sandys, Cameron, Brickdale and Bunce – received some family support in terms of paid training and materials or studio space and tuition, as did other sisters and daughters such as Emily Hunt and Lisa Stillman, although the support was seldom as generous as that allotted to sons. Only three – Siddal, Pickering and King – reported initial obstruction or disapproval. Social class and family support were thus significant factors in these women's careers.

With regard to their own social status as adult artists, although coming from a class in which women were customarily not expected to earn, several had an economic incentive to establish reputations and attract clients equal to that of their male counterparts. From the start Blunden was dependent on her own earning power, while the families of Cameron, Pickering and Brickdale at some time suffered financial anxiety or misfortune (the latter two through the premature deaths of the breadwinner). Both Spartali and Pickering worked at least in part to compensate for their husbands' unsure income, while Boyce, King and the Macdonalds formed 'family firms' or artistic partnerships with their husbands. Brickdale recognised the loss of family support as an incentive to art, and it appears that the existence of just such a cushion actively inhibited Bunce from developing her talent through the art market, although a similar security may well have stimulated Traquair to resume art practice in her thirties. In retrospect, there seems to be much to be said for financial need as a stimulus to production, despite the fact that in the nineteenth century this was the most contentious and potentially shaming justification for her work a 'lady' could make. At the very end of the century, art-school teaching became an additional source of income, of benefit to Brickdale, Newill, King and Frances Macdonald.

These material circumstances had their effect on the art produced. Lack of funds and personal studio space limited the size and scope of the pictures that Brett and Siddal could paint, for example, and also accounts for the medium-sized works produced by Spartali, who had the additional problem of transporting works for exhibition from Italy. The later generation – Brickdale, King and the Macdonalds – were more likely to have their own studios, separate from where they lived; others, like Howitt, Boyce, Lucy Madox Brown and Cameron, had studio space within the family home, with all the occlusion of the distinction between work and domesticity that this entailed. Spartali mentions working in another artist's studio, and using her daughter Effie as model: propriety, expense and lack of professional contacts led female artists to such practices, using willing friends and family members where their male counterparts were more likely to employ professional models.

In terms of geographical location, our sample of women artists benefited in general from proximity to the centres of the Pre-Raphaelite world; those with contacts or who lived in London tended to fare better with regard to exhibition and reputation than those who did not. Thus Brett and Sandys, who spent their lives in provincial locations, did not enjoy the same degree of success as, say, Boyce or Brickdale, who were based in London – and this despite having personal links via their brothers to the centre of Pre-Raphaelitism. However, even given metropolitan residence, the careers of Howitt, Siddal and both Madox Browns cannot be regarded as more successful, in terms of production and recognition, than Blunden in Exeter, or Spartali and Pickering in Italy. Mobility might be a more crucial factor. In contrast with Brickdale, whose early success was due in large part to her position in London, later non-metropolitan artists such as the Bunce sisters and Newill were less favourably placed to attract attention. However, the provincial centres of Birmingham and Glasgow (and also Liverpool and Leeds where doubtless as yet undiscovered female Pre-Raphaelites also worked) formed something of a counterweight to London by the end of the century, enabling artists to develop without servile reference to the capital. Indeed, for the women working in Scotland, distance from the London art world seems to have been a positive asset as far as the development and recognition of their distinctive gifts and styles were concerned.

Nine of the artists discussed here travelled in Europe – again, Brett and Sandys were least fortunate in this respect – of whom six visited Italy and three (Blunden, Spartali and Pickering) worked there. Travel generally benefited artists, enlarging the scope of their art and adding to their experience; curiously, it did not always add to these artists' range of subjects, although the effects of foreign residence are visible in the work of Spartali and King. For Cameron, travel seems to have adversely affected her art practice, no doubt because in Ceylon photographic supplies were as difficult to obtain and handle as were congenial sitters and subjects. In the years that Spartali and Pickering spent abroad, they were able to develop their work, but it is arguable that each might have gained by remaining in London, in closer contact with the centres of the art world with which they identified.

In terms of the marital status of our artists, the majority sooner or later married, while Brett, Sandys, Bunce, Newill and Brickdale remained single. We have little specific evidence of the reasons for marriage or spinsterhood, although the record of Boyce's opinions and the response of Pickering's family suggests that the women's own testimony on this question would be vivid and illuminating.

Of those who remained single, there are no grounds for thinking that any were lesbian – a factor that would probably have been suppressed by contemporaries and descendants – and it is likely that at least Brett and Sandys found themselves in circumstances that discouraged marriage for reasons beyond personal inclination. Social and geographical isolation reduced the numbers of eligible bachelors in their acquaintance, while poor health, allied to lack of money, was regarded as a distinct disadvantage in a prospective wife. At the same time it suited many families to have a daughter remain single to act as unpaid servant, housekeeper and companion, not only in financially constrained households such as those of Brett and Sandys, but also in a wealthy family such as the Pickerings, where Evelyn's sister spent her youth in such attendance on mother, grandmother and aunts, or that of the Bunces, where Kate and Myra appear to have remained at home with their widowed father until it was too late to marry. The positions of Brickdale and Newill were somewhat different, and it may be conjectured that neither married because no man sufficiently in sympathy with their work invited them to do so.

For, although widely perceived to be a woman's profession, marriage was often in conflict with any other serious interest she might pursue, and it was not unusual for wives to abandon, or be obliged to abandon, serious art practice on marriage, just as they would give up other forms of paid employment such as teaching. Generally speaking, married and single women were seen as quite distinct social groups and to carry over the habits of single life, like painting, into the married state was, until well into the twentieth century, a highly controversial ambition. Thus it is clear that Blunden regarded marriage as an alternative to her profession, since as soon as she married she gave up professional art. In addition to prevailing attitudes, any female artist who married, even when her career was well established, knew that the role of wife and, probably, mother would be in conflict with professional work; looking after a family interfered with the regular output of pictures. A married woman artist was expected to continue painting as a pastime rather than a profession. An explicit reference to these assumptions was provided in the *Art Journal*'s critical appreciation of Traquair in 1900 where the author noted that 'the professional painter . . . whose ideal of professional standing is an annual income from his work and a full quota of pictures in the annual exhibitions, is apt to speak of all Mrs Traquair's work as amateur'.[6] In estimation, a great gulf divided the amateur and professional artist.

In radical and liberal circles, a less conventional understanding of the differences between the married and single state prevailed, and it is significant that of the women discussed here who married, the majority did so within a social circle known for its bohemianism and freedom from rigid prescriptions. Of the dozen or so marriages among these female Pre-Raphaelites, seven married fellow artists and three others – both Madox Browns and Spartali – married men who worked in comparable cultural fields. Of the few who did not, Blunden, who evidently wished to become Ruskin's wife, married an engineer in rather unusual circumstances, while both Cameron and Traquair began their art careers in middle life; these marriages therefore occurred either before or at the end of the woman's professional career.

That a sympathic spouse was something to remark on is shown by the fact that the husbands of Howitt, Boyce, Siddal, Lucy Madox Brown, Pickering and King, to our knowledge, were noted by contemporaries for encouraging artistic rather than domestic activities in their womenfolk, in ways that were evidently unexpected. The men, too, drew attention to the fact on their own account. 'Indeed and of course my wife *does* draw still,' insisted Siddal's husband, while his brother, Lucy Madox Brown's husband, recorded with some pride his offer of the painting room within the marital home. In his correspondence and autobiography, Spartali's spouse paid lip service to his wife's artistic ambitions, although we may suspect that it was his absence rather than assistance that enabled her to paint so consistently. Cameron's husband was viewed as extremely tolerant of his wife's demanding and messy new career in photography, yet in the end his desire to live abroad curtailed her possibilities. Pickering's marriage clearly would not have taken place unless her husband had shared her priorities with regard to postnuptial working arrangements, while King and the Macdonalds belonged to a generation where newer egalitarian ideas prevailed, although husbands' careers still took precedence, notably in the case of Margaret Macdonald. In general, therefore, the female Pre-Raphaelites received at least some domestic support in their artistic endeavours, even though it was not always whole-hearted.

They needed such psychological support, since the disincentives to women artists were great and we can see the effects of discouragement on two at least of our artists – Howitt and Cathy Madox Brown – as well as perhaps also on Brett, Blunden, and Sandys, whose confidence was limited or sapped by lack of personal encouragement. Others might be mentioned here: the brief appearance in our story of Emily Hunt – who after exhibiting a number of times at the Royal Academy gave up art on marriage – suggests or stands in for a host of other women who were attracted to Pre-Raphaelitism but never achieved so much as a mention in the histories and whose lives cannot now be recovered. Of course, there were men who aspired and failed, too, but the ramifications of gender were not the cause of their failure, while women's circumstances were such that many who showed talent and enterprise were defeated by dismissive teachers and demanding families, as well as by an internalised view that women could achieve nothing worthwhile. Here we may also note the fate of Georgiana Macdonald, who studied drawing and wood-engraving at South Kensington prior to her marriage to Edward Burne-Jones, and then laid aside her pencils and tools. 'It is pathetic to think how we women longed to keep pace with the men, and how gladly they kept us by them until their pace quickened and we had to fall behind,' she remembered long afterwards. 'I stopped, as so many women do, well this side of tolerable skill, daunted by the path which has to be followed alone if the end is to be reached.' And also, we may add, by distinct lack of encouragement at home.[7]

If marriage did not of itself destroy the careers of those artists discussed in this book, from their life stories it is clear that the domestic consequences of marriage, especially pregnancy, child care and care of other relatives, had a substantial impact on their opportunity to work as well as, in some cases, on their desire to do so. The dictates of propriety, the constraints on freedom of movement and travel, above all the time-consuming daily and social duties required of women affected their time and opportunities to paint, in a way that was seldom if ever true of men.

Most conspicuously, child-bearing was inimical to creative work. If, as Burne-Jones claimed, 'children and pictures are too important to be produced by one man',[8] how much more incompatible might they be for women? As we have seen, childbirth killed Boyce and perhaps indirectly also Siddal. Both Madox Browns seem to have been effectively defeated by

ELEANOR FORTESCUE BRICKDALE

9. Farewell, Fair Lily 1911

FRANCES MACDONALD

10. The Choice *c.*1910

MARGARET MACDONALD

11. Ophelia 1908

EVELYN PICKERING

12. **The Worship of Mammon** 1909

KATE E. BUNCE

13. **The Keepsake** 1901

MARGARET MACDONALD

14. The Queen of Diamonds 1909

MARY J. NEWILL

15. Queen Matilda 1898

EVELYN PICKERING

16. The Red Cross 1918

the demands of motherhood – allied to ill health – and quasi-maternal duties. Cameron, a woman of remarkable energies, took up her career when child-bearing was over. She and Spartali, who bore three children and cared for three stepchildren, are the only ones from our sample who succeeded in both raising a large family and pursuing a successful career. Pickering had no children, whether by choice or default – given her absorption in art, one suspects the former – while Blunden, who married late, had one daughter. It would seem that the last generation profited from contraception, since Traquair, Frances Macdonald and King each had only one child. Margaret Macdonald was childless. While child-rearing and art were therefore not wholly antipathetic, a career was clearly easier to achieve with a small family or none at all.

Evidence on such questions is signally lacking from the women themselves. Our artists lived in a century when the issues of women's lives were under active discussion and change, and many benefited personally from the changes we have outlined in respect of women and art practice, but there are few records of their own views on this. Howitt took, perhaps, the most publicly feminist position, although her withdrawal from the professional world drastically limited this contribution. Of the others, Boyce and Pickering privately expressed similar views on the importance of independence, while Siddal and Spartali effectively experienced it while continuing to paint. The Madox Brown sisters grew up and passed on to their children generally progressive views, but neither they nor the other artists are on record as supporting campaigns for women's emancipation or the vote. We cannot conclude that they were therefore not feminists, or anti-suffragists: the evidence is too inadequate for such deductions. All of them, even the solidly respectable Traquair, Bunce and Brickdale, must have been aware of inhabiting an unusual, anomalous position as professional artists in a male world.

For female artists, producing work was the first struggle, exhibiting it the second, and selling it the third. The last two stages of success involved both luck and judgement.

The worth of artists is customarily determined according to their reputations: that is to say, it is generally assumed that reputation is a reliable guide to an artist's worth. Yet female artists' reputations generally speaking derive from and are determined by a complexity of prejudice and habit by which such artists are judged firstly as women, and secondly as painters, sculptors or whatever. In the nineteenth century, artists' reputations lay in the hands of critics, collectors, latterly dealers, and audiences; additionally, in the case of those involved with Pre-Raphaelitism, a critic, viewer or potential patron brought their view of the school to bear on a particular artist's specific work. The women artists of Pre-Raphaelitism were thus placed within a web of critical constraints. To succeed, they needed critical attention and then the income which sales and patronage brought.

Pre-Raphaelite artists were fortunate in having several critical voices on their side, and a number of committed patrons. Not only was John Ruskin a tireless promoter of the style, but one of the original PRB, F. G. Stephens, was art critic for the *Athenaeum* from 1861, and another, William Rossetti, wrote the art reviews for the *Spectator* from 1850 to 1858. Ruskin also had many wealthy associates who looked to him for advice on collecting, and the Oxford connections of several Pre-Raphaelite figures were also productive of patronage.

Critical praise was obviously most desired, but because the prestigious exhibitions were so large and diverse in content, any form of critical attention, positive or negative, could help an exhibitor, since a painting could pass virtually unnoticed by the gallery-going public unless mentioned in the press or at least given word-of-mouth publicity. So important was this that if a work was purchased before being shown publicly, either through commission or personal connection, valuable public exposure would be lost, and often an artist would specifically request of the buyer that the work be shown at a forthcoming exhibition rather than going straight into the buyer's hands. A vivid instance of this was Howitt's first exhibition appearance, with *Margaret* at the Portland Gallery in 1854, which was sold before its showing. The artist persisted nevertheless in exhibiting it, even though it was rejected by her first choice, the British Institution, and was further assisted by the *Athenaeum* with a piece of gossip to this effect, a week or so after its initial favourable review, with the following note:

> It is positively said that the gem of the Portland Gallery, Miss Howitt's 'Margaret returning from the fountain', the finest picture so far of the year and one of the best pictures – both as to the conceiving imagination and the executing hand – ever painted by a woman, was rejected as unworthy of a place on the walls of the British Institution!

With the judicious addition of a well-known name, the first-time exhibitor was handsomely launched with the paper's readership thus:

> Among the many who would have bought it was Miss Burdett-Coutts: – being too late as a purchaser for the present effort of the young artist, this lady took care to secure the next work from the same easel by means of a commission.[9]

Social convention, however, prevented women from currying the favour of critics in the ways open to men in the course of their everyday lives. It is inconceivable that, as a single woman, Boyce could have been invited to dine by Ruskin, as was her brother, in order to meet the art critic of *Blackwood's Magazine*. Nevertheless, Ruskin's role was such that many looked to him as their potential promoter. Blunden went so far as to ingratiate herself by letter, Brett hoped that her brother could introduce the great man to her work, and Rossetti secured his attention for Siddal. Later, Cameron wrote to solicit an opinion as if from the oracle itself. Mention in Ruskin's *Academy Notes* or in one of his increasingly frequent public lectures on the new art was just the exposure to benefit an aspiring Pre-Raphaelite. Once Ruskin praised Blunden's *Past and Present* at the RA in 1858, not only was that particular picture promoted, but the artist's existence was registered by his audience and his critical colleagues; from that year, Blunden's exhibits were regularly noticed in the papers. In this light, the abrupt destruction of Howitt's career by Ruskin seems more understandable; if critics could make an artist's reputation, they could also break it, especially if the critic were Ruskin and the artist an aspiring Pre-Raphaelite.

Critics had the power, too, of defining exhibited work. Women artists found throughout the nineteenth century that, on the whole, critics would relate their work to that of some male exemplar, thus not only limiting its merits by the suggestion that it lacked originality, but also categorising it in terms of its pedigree. In the 1850s, 1860s and to a lesser degree in the 1870s, this critical habit usually took the form of linking the artist to the father, brother or husband with whose work the reviewer was familiar, and the invariable effect of which was to present her as but a pale shadow. How condescending this could be is demonstrated by the *Illustrated London News* review of Sandys's last public appearance, at the Society of Lady Artists in 1874:

> The ladies appear to be dependent on teachers – the works often recall the styles of male painters of the same surnames as those of the exhibitors. It is not hard to divine what may be expected in a drawing of 'Fair Rosamund' by Miss Emma Sandys (which is very firmly pencilled though hardly a feminine type of female beauty) or in the pretty little pictures by Mrs E. M. Ward and Miss Flora Ward, or in the contributions of Misses Gastineau, Linnell, Rebecca Solomon and others.[10]

Such an appraisal says more about the critic's prejudiced lack of good will than about the work's merit, as is shown by comparing the *Art Journal* review of the same exhibit, which noted that '"Fair Rosamund" by Miss Emma Sandys is yet another example distinguished by a power and thoroughness not to be found in most of the drawings here', with never a mention of the artist's fashionable brother.[11]

Even where the comparison was intended to commend the artist, her presentation as a relative creature confirmed her status, as with the *Critic*'s well-meant notice of Emily Hunt's exhibit at the RA in 1861, that 'Miss Emily Hunt's very preRaffaelite head of a "Shy Damsel" claims a glance on its own account, and for her kinsman's sake'.[12] A family connection was thus a mixed blessing for a woman artist, especially as she started out.

Given the familial character of Pre-Raphaelitism, this critical habit could, indeed, have proved chronic: in the cases of Brett, Boyce, the two Madox Browns and Sandys, as well as occasional exhibitors such as Siddal and Agnes Millais, this form of dismissal would have been easy. It is perhaps a testament to the strength of their work that such invidious comparisons were only rarely made, although Brett, for one, initially evaded them by the use of a pseudonym. Boyce made her own reputation before her brother, and was immune to such relative judgements. In the second generation, critics were somewhat less obsessed with female artists' referees, although Lucy Madox Brown and Marie Spartali were discussed in the shadow of Madox Brown, as is implied in *The Times*'s comment that they were 'trained in the same school'.[13] This could, of course, be simple recognition of affinity with the Pre-Raphaelite school, yet it was more markedly confined to the work of women, and commonly used to demote or peg down the exhibit rather than elevate it. When Howitt's first exhibit was defined by the *Critic* reviewer as 'an attempt in the Millais school',[14] it was clearly the writer's opinion that the value or success of the essay was in doubt, while Spartali found herself treated as old hat by some opponents of Pre-Raphaelitism on her very first exhibition ('Miss Marie Spartali, in her "Corinna", gives us once more the tiresome old ugly face and the red disorderly hair,' said the *Saturday Review* of the Dudley in 1867[15]) on this basis. In the same vein, as we have noted, Bunce's *The Daydream* was dismissed by the *Athenaeum*'s critics at the RA of 1892 with the remark: 'We fear Miss Bunce, who has respectable notions of painting, has mistaken her vocation in trying to follow Rossetti.'[16] Pickering was struck by the same journal when showing *The Spear of Ithuriel* at the New Gallery in 1900; calling the painting 'a pseudo Burne-Jones', the critic continued: 'It is weaker in its design than anything of his, and devoid of the splendours of his colour, his love for beauty, and the sumptuousness of his tones.'[17] The third generation, in fact, found it hard to escape being reviewed as copyists, whether of Madox Brown, Rossetti or Burne-Jones. The *Athenaeum's* critic – consistent if cruel – wrote of *Messer Ansaldo's Garden* at the New in 1889 that 'Miss Spartali's example has about it something which suggests to us, at a distance, a Rossetti, translated, if that were possible, by Mr Ford Madox Brown'.[18] Where a male artist might benefit from comparison with an established figure, the female artist was brought down: Spartali's artistic genealogy is here identified correctly but the observation was made in a manner and within an ideological context that placed male artists in a father-and-son chain but defined female artists as imitators and dependants, lacking originality.

In a more positive vein, critical attention could provide the artist with guidance, which was especially necessary if she had only had a scraped-together art training and worked in relative isolation, like Blunden or Brett. Even when working within an artistic circle, on a personal level women might meet with gallantry rather than constructive criticism. Generally speaking Victorian critics did not shrink from advising artists where they had gone wrong or what they might do for the better, although those with the most opinionated tones might be those with least aesthetic sense. If, like those of Brett or the two Madox Browns, the artist's efforts to exhibit were repeatedly frustrated by rejection or bad hanging, she lost the response of the informed critic to assist her development as much as the potential sale. This constructive aspect of press criticism may well have been the main factor in persuading artists who weren't dependent on sales from exhibitions to continue showing their work publicly. Without public exposure, an artist like Siddal could not benefit from such feedback; however positive the opinions of friends, they were always partial. In addition, the general view was that an artist who didn't exhibit remained essentially an amateur.

A businesslike artist such as Blunden found the admonishments of critics very useful. They not only provided an idea of the level of accomplishment but also indicated what potential collectors, often guided by critics, might look for. During the 1860s, Blunden attracted a lot of free advice from reviewers of the London exhibition round. 'For her own sake,' wrote the *Art Journal* critic of her British Institution exhibit in 1866, 'it were wise to exchange the dotted method of miniature painting landscape for a manner more broadly generalised.'[19] Similarly, *Morning Mist* at the Dudley in 1867 was, wrote the *Saturday Review*, 'exceedingly delicate in tone and colour, but slightly injured by too much of system in the touching of the trees'.[20] Here was an idea of strengths and weaknesses from which the artist could move forward.

The teacherly vein of criticism could also, of course, threaten the attempt to engage an audience, with its awarding of points won and lost, and its assumption that the artist was not only seeking advice but answerable as in an examination. The *Times* critic illustrates the destructive potential of the judgemental as opposed to advisory role. Lucy Madox Brown's first appearance, in 1869, was greeted with encouragement: 'In spite of a niggling execution and many signs of a timid and unpractised hand, there is in the figure of the girl a naturalness in her action and a harmony in the colour which lift this drawing out of the ruck,' wrote the reviewer (without apparently recognising the subject as Cathy Madox Brown, also appearing in the same exhibition with her own work). The next year, the tone was markedly cooler: 'Miss Lucy Madox Brown . . . repeats all the defects, but does not attain the merits, of her last year's drawing.' With *Romeo and Juliet* the year after, the artist persuaded the critic back to her side, earning a long paragraph which concluded that 'with all its very obvious faults, this is a drawing of rare sentiment, and the execution, also, shows uncommon power and warrants high expectations of the young artist's future'. But the following year, 1872, she fell from grace in no uncertain terms, although her Dudley exhibit, *The Magic Mirror*, continued in the same vein as her previous work. 'We are sorry to pronounce Miss Lucy Madox Brown's "Magic Mirror" a mistake and a failure in every point' was the damning verdict.[21] *The Times* of course had never been a friend to Pre-Raphaelitism, but the critic's response shows how works were judged as if on trial. In one respect, the artist was lucky to attract the consistent attention of such an influential critic while exhibiting mainly in watercolour, for this medium would never command the same respect of traditional organs as oil painting did. Tantalisingly, no evidence survives of her response to this continuous assessment, and it is impossible to know how potential admirers were affected by this widely read reviewer's opinions.

The same critic had a similar relationship with Spartali. Of *Pharmakeutria* and *Nerea Foscari* at the Dudley Gallery in 1869 he noted that 'among the affectors of the Archaic School', Miss Spartali 'probably is entitled to the prize for bad drawing', although 'at the same time, it would be hard to deny [her] the uncommon quality of rich and solemn colour'. The following year, he remarked that while the characteristics of this Archaic School were still visible in her large half-length *Romance of the Rose*, 'there is a splendour of low sunlight in the face and bosom and a pervading power of grave colour, which go far to redeem such blots as the branches which adhere to the head, and the gracelessness and bad drawing of the head'. By 1871, with *Antigone*, she was still improving, although far from perfect. 'Miss Spartali has never exhibited so powerful a drawing,' opined *The Times*, 'though it betrays the old weakness, the one unvarying Camelot face, with the long hatchet jaw and the protruding chin, which the school borrowed from their master Rossetti.'[22] The grudging tone must have been wearying for the artist thus addressed, and was not necessarily an improvement on the more facile type of review that substituted coy gallantry for judgement. Overall, Boyce was the best treated by critics, her evident strength, imagination and visual exploration gaining her considerable respect in the art press.

A further type of critical attention, of which the female artist generally in this period received very little, was the monograph or feature devoted to the 'profiling' of a single artist. The *Art Journal* ran a series of such profiles in the 1850s and 1860s, paying scant attention to Pre-Raphaelitism as a whole and none to its female exemplars. The *Magazine of Art* made much of artists as personalities, but gave female artists very little individual promotion. The *Studio* by contrast publicised all manifestations of the Pre-Raphaelite and Arts and Crafts field, but was not established until 1893, so that only the third generation benefited from its patronage in their early careers. Traquair, Brickdale and Pickering were promoted in the magazine, which also employed several female graphic artists to produce headings, vignettes and full-page illustrations.

With regard to patronage and sales, Ruskin proved of most help to the female artists of Pre-Raphaelitism. He saw the promotion of young artists and the promulgation of Pre-Raphaelitism as a proper part of his self-ordained service to art and, although seething with contradictory perceptions of both art and women, gave of his time and attention to petitioners such as Blunden in considerable measure. His usefulness as an agent is clear from his correspondence to her in late 1858. 'I can't be of immediate use to you, for I have my hands quite full at present,' he wrote, 'but if you will send me any drawings you want disposed of, I will try to do so, provided you write me no more nonsense.' Three weeks later, he wrote again, saying, 'Primarily, send me the things you want to sell, and I'll give you something to do for me when I have it.' The commissions he promised her were copies of works of art which he might use in lecturing and teaching, giving another dimension of exposure to the fortunate protégée. Blunden was thus more or less getting the services of a dealer free of charge, with a notable distinction in the matter of commission. 'Have you fixed a price on that drawing of the blue sea and cliffs?' he wrote in December 1859. 'I should like to know in case I could find a purchaser.' Three days later (from which it is evident with what alacrity Blunden replied) he sent a cheque for the full price of ten guineas, saying, 'If I cannot sell it for you, I shall keep it, for I like it.'[23]

His services to Siddal had the same well-intentioned but unpredictable results. After Rossetti had carefully prepared the ground, Ruskin

> saw and bought on the spot every scrap of designs hitherto produced by Miss Siddal. He asked me to name a price for them, after asking and learning that they were for sale; and I, of course, considering the immense advantage of their getting into his hands, named a very low price, £25, which he declared to be too low *even* for a low price, and increased to £30. He is going to have them splendidly mounted and bound together in gold, and no doubt this will be a real opening to her, as it is already a great assistance and encouragement.[24]

Later the same year, Ruskin settled an annual payment of £150 for any work she might produce, with the intention of acting as agent, promising her the difference in price of any pictures he succeeded in selling. He publicised her art among his friends such as Henry Acland in Oxford (to whom Siddal presented *We Are Seven* in recognition of medical attention, thus placing the picture in a place where it would be publicly seen by Acland's wide acquaintance) and Ellen Heaton, a serious patron in Leeds, to whom he commended Siddal as a deserving artist for whom 'some day or other a commission may be encouragement and sympathy be charity'.[25] Her first independent sale, of *Clerk Saunders* from the Russell Place exhibition, was to Ruskin's friend Professor Norton.

Not all Pre-Raphaelite artists had such useful contacts. Just as Blunden used Ruskin's name to impress the Exeter public, Brett might have boasted of her brother after his name was made in order to secure commissions, but does not seem to have done so. Sandys may have been recommended by her father at a local level and then by her brother, once he had become fashionable in the early 1860s, and, judging by common aspects in their art, she did obtain some work through this connection.

On a local level, equally useful was the support of prominent figures in the region, which could be advertised in exhibition catalogue entries, local press comment, and in the titles of pictures. Brett, as a landscapist, evidently disdained to exploit this possibility in the sites she portrayed, which might have been exhibited as 'Such-and-such Manor, the property of Lord and Lady So-and-so', but Sandys, on the other hand, used her portrait sitters' potential to impress. Being represented at the Royal Academy with *Lady Winifred Herbert, daughter of the Earl of Caernarvon* (1870) or *The Duchess of St Albans* (1874) was of more benefit than simply showing 'Portrait of a Lady'. Similarly, in her very first exhibition in Norwich, the fact that *Girl with a Butterfly* was listed in the catalogue as 'lent by William Dixon Esq.' increased Sandys's credibility with the aim of attracting another patron.

None of the artists discussed here found royal patronage – indeed there is no evidence to suggest that Pre-Raphaelitism was popular in Victoria and Albert's circle with anyone but Princess Louise, herself an artist who was invited to exhibit at the Grosvenor Gallery – but some of the new patronage from the recently enriched middle classes did come their way. The patrons most visible in conventional accounts of Pre-Raphaelitism – the Combes of Oxford, the stockbroker Thomas Plint, the industrialists James Leathart and Thomas Fairbairn – paid brief attention to some of the women practising in this modern style. Howitt sold *The Castaway* to Fairbairn, who exhibited it in the important Manchester Art Treasures exhibition in 1857, while Boyce sold her version of a similar subject *The Outcast* (subsequently known as *No Joy the blowing Season gives*) to Thomas Plint. Later, Harold Rathbone, Madox Brown's pupil and patron, bought Catherine Madox Brown's *Cromer* and also collected funds from subscribers to buy Spartali's *Madonna Pietra* for Liverpool Art Gallery in 1884. Pickering attracted the support of Thomas Imrie, who bought at least eight of her works. But in general the women Pre-Raphaelites did not obtain consistent and prolonged support from patrons and, given the competition for sales, it is evident that the Pre-Raphaelite promoters and intermediaries felt that the need of male artists to secure professional standing and income came first. In any case, women were socially disadvantaged when it came to meeting prospective patrons, as George Boyce's diaries indicate, recording several instances when he was introduced to potential purchasers. In April 1863, for example, he dined with Rossetti to meet Leathart whom he afterwards escorted to his hotel; two days later Leathart called and bought three drawings. Women simply did not have such opportunities.

In the three generations of women artists here, Boyce, Cameron and Brickdale are examples of those who benefited from their observed connection with the movement, but owed their professional success largely to their own husbanding and deployment of resources. Boyce combined Pre-Raphaelitism with her own independently formed ideas; Cameron carved out a place for herself in the relatively new and controversial field of photography; and Brickdale achieved a long and commercially successful career. The last two were helped by the rise of the art dealer, a development which had in general little impact on other Pre-Raphaelite women who, like their male colleagues, preferred to continue using the exhibiting societies and shows as shop windows. Dealers, however, could make a successful artist very successful indeed, through promotion and publicity for individuals or specific works, introducing one-artist shows, exploiting reproductive possibilities with copyright and so on. Holman Hunt in particular benefited from his association with the dealer Gambart, although few other Pre-Raphaelites had such success with this new force in the British art world. Cameron was able to use Colnaghi's successfully because she could initially pay for their services and exploit the professional marketing strategies that this entailed, exposing her work to a wider clientele. She possessed, too, the social confidence and prominence that helped guarantee public response to a solo show, while of equal value was the illustriousness of some of her sitters, in an age that valued portraits of famous individuals for their own sake,

rather than for that of the artist. Brickdale had a profitable relationship with dealers partly because she was working at the very end of the period discussed here, when the old patterns and forms were being replaced by dealer-led marketing, and partly because her work straddled the dividing line between fine art and commercial illustration. As the catalogue to her commemorative exhibition in 1972 remarked, 'there was no doubt that Walter and Charles Dowdeswell had sufficient faith in the marketability of her talent to risk the outlay for the exhibition at their fashionable gallery'.[26] This faith was repeated in 1905, with her second exhibition, but thereafter the market for Brickdale's easel paintings contracted: no longer encouraging her to produce whatever she liked, confident that it would sell, the Dowdeswells and the Leicester Galleries took to exhibitions linked to publication of her watercolours in book form, thus downgrading the work. The less illustrious direction Brickdale's output took, therefore, was largely influenced by the dealers.

For later artists, dealers played the part of patron (although Colnaghi's took no risk) just as their first-generation sisters looked to Plint, Fairbairn and perhaps Burdett-Coutts. They also benefited from the innovation of the solo exhibition, developed by dealers from the 1860s onwards but not accorded many female Pre-Raphaelites. Spartali was never honoured with a solo show, while Pickering was given one only in 1906, at the end of her career, when she was no longer in such need of sales. She is, however, the only artist here to have been paid the compliment of a virtual museum of her own work, created when her sister endeavoured to buy back the paintings as a memorial to the artist's talent. Funds were never found for suitable premises, however, and it is largely by luck that the De Morgan Foundation's collection is now displayed, at Old Battersea House and elsewhere. Generally speaking, women Pre-Raphaelites fared badly with museums and public galleries, only a very few enjoying the patronage of such institutions – chiefly in Liverpool – in their own lifetimes. Of the work by women Pre-Raphaelite artists now in public collections, most was bequeathed by the artists or their families as, for example, Brickdale's work in Bristol and Bunce's in Birmingham.

The third generation of Pre-Raphaelites enjoyed one further type of patronage, that of the church. Certain High Church patrons and congregations were attracted to the modern and yet medieval work produced at the overlap of Pre-Raphaelitism and the Arts and Crafts Movement from the 1870s on in the fields of mural painting, stained glass, embroidery and metalwork. The Bunce sisters, Traquair, the stained glass artists and Brickdale are notable here insofar as their own religious convictions gave such commissions an especial appeal, and no doubt appealed equally to the clergy employing or accepting their work. For the Bunces and Traquair, church patronage extended their first medium of painting into different realms, while for Brickdale it meant the additional medium of stained glass in later life as her sight began to fail. For all three, large-scale compositions for church walls extended the scope of their work in the public arena but also paradoxically removed it from critical exposure. Perhaps surprisingly, given her ability to produce figurative compositions on a large scale and her interest in moral subjects, Pickering did not enjoy church patronage along with her contemporaries; perhaps, although she possessed the technical qualifications for such commissions, she could not claim the spiritual ones, being no churchgoer.

Yet overall, the account of how and to whom the women artists sold their work is thin and indicative of a general lack of loyal patronage. Added to their difficulties with regard to

regular exhibition and the cultivation of sustained critical support, the female artists of Pre-Raphaelitism had mostly to scrape together their reputations within their own lifetimes. Since their deaths, their involvement with the movement has been erratically remembered and much of the evidence of that involvement – their paintings, drawings, photographs and other pictures – has been dispersed and lost. Pre-Raphaelitism has therefore been recounted, defined and preserved without their pictures being included in the account. Yet their work is part of Pre-Raphaelitism and, when amassed and consulted, enriches our overall knowledge and understanding of the style.

The work of the women artists associated with Pre-Raphaelitism is indeed as varied as that of their male colleagues. Taken as a whole, it shows the same early enthusiasm for truth to nature, the subsequent move towards imaginative realism and the absorption of historical themes and figures, and the end-of-century divergence into the decorative, symbolic and poetic which continued the vividness of early and mid-term Pre-Raphaelitism. As with male Pre-Raphaelites, some of the women's work is Pre-Raphaelite by conviction, some by connection, giving a range of pictorial appearance which is sometimes easier to identify as Pre-Raphaelite by background knowledge rather than simply by surface recognition, although it can seldom be identified with any other style.

Again like their better-known male colleagues, female Pre-Raphaelites' work shows a range of commitment to the movement dependent on the artist's circumstances at the time of discovering the style and the role of art in their life. Some enthusiasts of both sexes surrendered themselves completely to Pre-Raphaelitism, while others – Boyce and Ford Madox Brown and the Glasgow Four, for instance – injected into it aims and ideas formulated from other sources. Being a Pre-Raphaelite clearly attracted female artists in differing ways, and no more generalisations can be made about their work than are possible, as it is now realised, with male Pre-Raphaelites.

However, like the Pre-Raphaelite work already known and accepted as such, the work of the artists in this book ploughed certain familiar furrows of nineteenth-century British art. In the first generation, the English countryside – fields, coasts, rural scenes with their inhabitants and workers – preoccupied Brett, Boyce and Howitt, as is seen in Brett's numerous local views where a figure works or wanders, and in her *Old House at Farleigh* [PL. 8] where a specific site is brought into particular focus. Also in this generation, Blunden, Boyce and Howitt demonstrate the concern of the early Pre-Raphaelites to discuss topical social questions and types from modern life: working women, 'fallen women' and other contemporary political issues appear in their paintings and drawings. The recurrence of Gretchen or Margaret from *Faust* – Howitt, Boyce and Cameron all treated this figure – shows the extent to which the questions of seduction and prostitution concerned our artists, also handled by Siddal in *Pippa Passes*. Blunden's *Song of the Shirt* [FIG. 15] and Boyce's *Heather Gatherer* represent the wide range of women workers to be found in their work as a whole, while Blunden's *Uncle Tom's Cabin* [FIG. 4] broached the extremely topical issue of slavery. The treatment of contemporary issues exercised later artists too, from Spartali's representation of Greek subjects to Newill's images of democratic heroes. Brickdale and Pickering discussed the questions of their day – materialism, social relations, war and

womanhood – rather in allegorical or historical guise, replacing the actual scenes of mid-Victorian Britain presented by the first generation with an imaginative parallel world that drew on the enduring Pre-Raphaelite fascination with mythology and medievalism. Thus Pickering portrayed *The Worship of Mammon* [PL. 12] while, in an interesting representation of the Judgement of Paris in *The Choice* [PL. 10], Frances Macdonald commented on the contemporary awareness of male selection of women in the marriage market. Spartali with her picture of St Francis and Brickdale with her various images of the evils of wealth and virtues of poverty also addressed contemporary social problems.

The historical and literary dimension which formed such a conspicuous part of Pre-Raphaelitism throughout its lifetime, weaving its way through the work of three generations, is clear in the work of many artists, notably Boyce and Siddal in the first generation. Boyce's *Elgiva* [PL. 2] and *Veneziana* [FIG. 55] exemplify how history could be plundered for female role models, while *Clerk Saunders* [PL. 1 & FIG. 18] shows Siddal exploring the visual possibilities of ancient balladry. This imaginative strand dominates in the second and third generation, guiding if not characterising the pictures of Cameron, Spartali, Lucy Madox Brown, Sandys, Pickering and Brickdale in a host of works drawn from historical and literary sources. Lucy Madox Brown is particularly notable for the range of historical periods represented, including the eighteenth century of *After the Ball*. Later, Brickdale drew on a full range of periods for her illustrative work, frequently using both the Renaissance and Augustan eras. The religious or pious element that was strong in early Pre-Raphaelitism is seen in early works such as Boyce's *Children's Crusade* or Siddal's *Nativity* and *Madonna*, but emerged most forcefully in the third generation as Anglo-Catholic devotional practices brought religion and art together in the latter years of the century in the works of Traquair, Bunce, Brickdale and others.

Another already recognised aspect of Pre-Raphaelitism which the women's work confirms is the predominance of woman as the style's chief visual character, although the women's woman, so to speak, is markedly more varied than in male Pre-Raphaelitism. The female artist's interest in woman as a subject, although in some cases obviously learned from male exemplars, has of course a different significance, for the artist is in some measure portraying herself, not the interminable Other of the male artist. As a result, the numerous and varied female figures were presented with a great deal less lubriciousness and more understanding and sympathy than in comparable images from male artists.

In the context of the heightened gender-consciousness which characterised the second half of the nineteenth century, the female artist would have been aware of discussing her own kind when picturing women. Of our artists, only Howitt and Boyce could be called feminists, but several others, including Siddal, Lucy Madox Brown, Spartali and Pickering, explicitly or implicitly rejected the prevailing view of weak, dependent womanhood, and the careers of all demonstrate an attempt to challenge contemporary definitions of femininity. It is therefore interesting to note that women artists within Pre-Raphaelitism presented a wide range of female subjects drawn from poetry, drama, fiction, history and modern life, and with a wide spectrum of reference and meaning. In certain cases they selected figures now traditionally associated with Pre-Raphaelitism – Siddal's *Lady of Shalott* was among the earliest depictions of this subject, for example, while both Cameron and Margaret Macdonald tackled Ophelia – but treated them in very different ways. Other examples of common subject and

JOANNA M. BOYCE
54. La Veneziana 1861

MARGARET MACDONALD

55. Fantasy 1906

differing treatments include Elgiva painted by both Boyce and Millais; Viola by both Deverell and Sandys; Onora, although from different poetic sources, by both Sandys and her brother, and Fiammetta by both Spartali and Rossetti. In its later generations, Pre-Raphaelitism became somewhat incestuous: artists fed off earlier images and texts and were commissioned to illustrate the same subjects – such as Brickdale's versions of Browning and Tennyson or King's illustrations for *The Defence of Guenevere* – that had inspired the first generation, although seldom if ever in a spirit of pastiche: the subjects still had resonance for the artists. In addition, artists of both sexes were proud to look, as did Spartali, Bunce and Traquair, to Rossetti's own poetry for inspiration. Our recovery of the careers of Bunce and Traquair, indeed, considerably enlarges this aspect of later Pre-Raphaelitism.

Within all this, however, it is noticeable that our artists' heroines include many original and varied subjects: Boadicea (Howitt), Undine (Boyce), Lady Macbeth (Siddal), Hypatia (Cameron), Margaret Roper (Lucy Madox Brown), Antigone (Spartali), Medea (Pickering), Queen Matilda (Newill). Many of these subjects display a thorough understanding of the literary and historical sources that is different in emphasis from that discernible in their male counterparts' work. Moreover, some apparently historical or legendary subjects had contemporary meaning, for instance Spartali's lament for the Greek victims of oppression, and Pickering's protest against plutocracy with her image of *St Christina giving her father's jewels to the poor*. Among the female figures portrayed, a number can be seen as emblems of women's oppression, like the betrayed Gretchen, Spartali's Procne, and Pickering's captive in *The Gilded Cage*. It is in some ways sad to note that when commissioned to produce a series on Famous Women, late in her career, Brickdale relied almost entirely on literary and legendary heroines, rather than seeking out historical or living role models, apparently finding few real-life figures to set beside her unexpected aviator Charles Rolls and his forerunner Leonardo.

While the early Pre-Raphaelite female artists seem to have presented single or double-figure treatments putting women in the forefront, Brickdale and Pickering tended to present social questions as the province and concern of both sexes, even while they also used the female with allegorical, iconic or rhetorical intent in other pictures. Pickering often presented the two sexes as a quasi-androgynous race (as did Burne-Jones), exhibiting drastically few gender characteristics. How this should be interpreted is a complex question but contrasts markedly with Brickdale's formula of equal vigour for her men and women, rather than equal delicacy. Pickering was also capable, as was Spartali, of presenting women as powerful witches and sorceresses – *The Love Potion* and *Queen Eleanor* by the former and *Pharmakeutria* and *Medea* by the latter.

An expansion of this already rich catalogue of womankind occurred in the work of the third generation, where female figures drawn from private sources, neither supported nor legitimised by literature or history, are particularly noticeable in the work of the Macdonald sisters [FIG. 50], King [FIG. 54], Pickering and Brickdale. The general retreat from realism which characterised European avant-garde art towards the end of the century encouraged purely imaginative and symbolic presentations of woman in the work of both male and female artists.

The female Pre-Raphaelites determined their images of women and men from crucially different sources than their male colleagues, and thus escaped the monotony of work derived

from desires or ideals transfixed by one or two actual images, as in the work of Rossetti, Burne-Jones and Frederick Sandys. The nearest any female artist came to such repetition is where Cameron fastened on Mary Hillier as the embodiment of the Madonna or holy mother. Cameron's oeuvre shows that men could be generalised into a preferred type in the same way as her male contemporaries liked to merge women into a model of womanhood; the search in her pictures for a heroic yet spiritual male yields the largest masculine presence to be found in the Pre-Raphaelite work of women. In the other artists, the few dominant male figures that appear are holy knights such as Sir Galahad and St George in the work of Siddal, Spartali, Brickdale and Bunce, or persons from Dante and Boccaccio, like Spartali's *Fra Conrado* [FIG. 34] and Bunce's *The Chance Meeting* [FIG. 40]. These presentations suggest that the women had difficulty in finding masculine subjects from their own society to suit their artistic purposes.

Women's Pre-Raphaelite work thus accords woman a central place, but also deploys her across a much more varied spectrum of female possibilities than is usually perceived in Pre-Raphaelitism – and, it may be noted, not exclusively drawn from white people. The formal means by which Pre-Raphaelite woman was represented in the work of the female practitioners also shows great variety.

For a confident and well-trained artist like Boyce, variety of means and methods was one of the delights of painting. Her oeuvre is regrettably small but nevertheless contains a number of different formats, from the closely framed head of *Sidney* [PL. 3] to the full-length figure of *Gretchen* and from composed groups at middle distance, like *Nativity*, to the naturalistic rendering of a few figures in a domestic interior, like *Peep-Bo*. Some artists found effective or favourite formulae which they used over and again, but the arrangement of pictorial elements within the picture space was generally one aspect of practice in which Pre-Raphaelites altogether differed widely. Thus, for instance, Sandys used an almost invariable format of head-and-shoulders against an associative background wall shutting off the space inhabited by the figure, as in *A Fashionable Lady* or *Viola* [FIGS. 20 & 2]. Siddal – despite her inexperience in figure drawing – presented her women whole either in boxlike areas which confine them, as in *Clerk Saunders* [PL. 1] and *St Agnes' Eve*, or in open spaces, as in *Lovers Listening to Music* [FIG. 19] and *The Ladies' Lament*, according to the mood of the narrative; indeed it is precisely because the full figure is related to an imagined physical environment that the emotional content is conveyed. Similar formal qualities are apparent in the work of Lucy Madox Brown in *Romeo and Juliet* [FIG. 23] where the power of the image is conveyed by the disposition of the figures in the tomb, and in *Margaret Roper* [PL. 4] where the horror of the subject is emphasised by the compositional daring of the scene in the boat under London Bridge.

A comparison of *The Lady Prays – Desire* with *Love's Messenger* [PL. 6 & FIG. 33] indicates Spartali's versatility in creating distinct moods and atmosphere by the disposition of two similar but contrasting half-length figures within the picture space. Sandys's women, on the other hand, are presented obviously and directly, for the artist spent less energy on exposition of her subjects' history or experience, except by including elements of costume or accessories to carry the narrative burden, especially if the character came from a well-known literary source; *Viola* [FIG. 2] shows how, with a character familiar to the public, judiciously chosen and placed references to Shakespeare's text (including a quotation) could identify and amplify the subject at the same time. Focusing on Viola's undisclosed love, the artist uses the mirror and the figure's gaze beyond the picture space to articulate that which is unspoken.

Bunce showed impressive variety of compositional forms, too, ranging from the iconic figure of *Musica* [cover], all eyes and hair and dense decorative framing, to the full-length females of *The Keepsake* [PL. 13] and the multifigured scene of *The Chance Meeting* [FIG. 40], while her domestic interiors and religious scenes display even more varied formats.

Spartali and Pickering frequently placed their figures in complex groups inhabiting relatively large and often open spaces. Spartali's are usually within a context that holds the characters in a narrative or dramatic scene, such as *The Vision of Fra Conrado* [FIG. 34] or her many images from Dante, while Pickering used multiple figures for allegorical purposes, as in *Blindness and Cupidity* and *Mercy and Truth, Righteousness and Peace*. Pairs and smaller groups are also deployed for symbolic purposes, for example her many images of Night and Darkness. Storytelling characterised Brickdale's work, which was varied and unpredictable and always adroit (as Spartali's and Pickering's work did not invariably succeed in being), using the figures' relationship to the pictorial space to psychological and formal effect. The single figure of *The Little Foot Page* [FIG. 38], in its dense natural background with the bright colour and detail characteristic of early Pre-Raphaelitism, is as accomplished as the large complex image of *The Forerunner* [FIG. 53] showing the court of Ludovico Sforza.

Form and treatment were determined by the destination of the image, whether for a canvas to hang in a room or gallery, a picture for the page of a book, a photograph, or a painting or window for a church. Like many other fine artists of the period, Siddal, Traquair, King and Brickdale worked extensively with book illustration in mind. With Siddal's *Clerk Saunders* the various treatments can be seen, the subject beginning as a woodblock illustration and developing into a watercolour. Most of Brickdale's watercolours, as opposed to her oils, were conceived for book reproduction with the new colour-printing techniques of the time. For Cameron, whose pictures were produced both out of enthusiasm and as marketable commodities, format was to a degree learned from works of art which the photographer was aiming to emulate, and thus consciously borrowed from other Pre-Raphaelite works whose public she wished to share. With stained glass, both the technical limitations and glories of stained glass were to be welcomed, according to Veronica Whall. 'Light is our medium and light is our colour', she wrote. 'We have to mix it with our colours; we have to harness it; to tie it down; to make it stop where we want it, or let it pour through – a stupendous, living, ever-changing force'.[27]

Size and scale varied within each artist's oeuvre, although the specific conditions under which each woman worked led to certain habitual practices. Thus, as already noted, Brett's smallness of scale, Sandys's repeated medium-sized vertical images, Pickering's epic scale, Cameron's choice of a square plate and King's characteristic use of square and oval shapes and delicate drawing suitable for book-page reproduction. Women working at home, without the use of a studio, had generally less choice over these matters, and in Spartali's and the two Madox Browns' work the extent to which their output was hedged about by their domestic situations can be told from the pictures' size and content as well as their subjects and sitters.

Landscape work by the women of Pre-Raphaelitism reflects these conditions. Nature in its rural and garden manifestations was available over the back fence, as it were, or on family holidays and excursions: the works of Brett and Spartali or Blunden and King in later life

ANNA M. HOWITT
56. Elizabeth Siddal 1854

illustrate such scenes. Exotic or dramatic landscape was seldom available. Several female Pre-Raphaelites seem hardly to have tackled landscape at all, apparently preferring – or perhaps constrained – to work on interior scenes. Only as the social changes affecting women continued through the second half of the century did the world at large become accessible. Despite their occasional travels, unconditional mobility was rarely theirs at home or abroad, and then only if family and friends were not enslaved to notions of respectability. Brett's quiet persistence [FIG. 13], Blunden's determination [FIG. 16] and Howitt's private pursuit of landscape views demonstrate the difficulties of producing Pre-Raphaelite depictions of nature in the first generation, when this seemed to represent the essence of the movement. Blunden, Spartali and Pickering all worked as well as travelled in Italy (considered by some the spiritual home of Pre-Raphaelitism) and while what is known of Blunden's Italian landscape work is unremarkable and Pickering's backgrounds were more imaginary than actual, Spartali's work reflected her places of residence both in landscape subjects and as locations for her poetic pictures such as *Fra Conrado*. In Italy, she was able to use Florentine backgrounds for subjects from Dante and Boccaccio, as well as regularly painting straight landscape scenes such as *Among the Willows of Tuscany* and the scenes of Perugia exhibited in 1893. British scenes from the Isle of Wight feature in both her early and very late work.

There are equally distinct conclusions to be learned from the work of women artists in other genres. In portraiture, the range and social status of a male artist's sitters tell us something about his own professional standing. Typically, a female artist's sitters tell us of her limited mobility and restricted social sphere. Portraits by the artists under discussion here, for instance, include Brett's mother, Boyce's baby and nursemaid, Pickering's husband and her sister's lady's maid, Cathy Madox Brown's mother and father, Lucy Madox Brown's sister, and the artists themselves. Unrelated and unknown sitters appear in Brett's and Sandys's work, and probably did so also in Blunden's, although no material evidence remains. Sandys's portraits form half her oeuvre, as it is known at the moment, most of which were clearly standard commercial commissions relied upon by the professional artist. Even so, the sitters were invariably women and children similar to those dominating the other Pre-Raphaelite women's portrait output and generally prevailing in women artists' work in this period. Self-portraits (Siddal and Spartali) and pictures of each other (Howitt [FIG. 57], Boyce, Lucy Madox Brown) parallel their male colleagues' mutual biography, although the women's works are less substantial than the men's; they remained sketches, or were never exhibited, thus staying essentially private images. Perhaps the finest of those included here is Cathy Madox Brown's portrait of her father [FIG. 25], which is of course also the portrait of a fellow artist, a figure frequently depicted within Pre-Raphaelitism.

Travel widened an artist's dramatis personae as well as landscapes, and although neither of the Madox Browns nor the landscapist Brett appears to have brought back portraits from their trips abroad, Boyce made several portrait paintings on her holidays in Britain as well as on her major continental tour, when she drew and painted fellow travellers, passers-by and local types. Spartali, not otherwise known for portraiture, did at least one portrait while abroad – that of Mrs William Hutton, painted in Venice in 1880 [FIG. 58]. The ability to draw on a broad human spectrum makes Cameron, a woman with a wide acquaintance and the social position denied to less privileged women, an obvious exception in this group of artists. She could portray friends, relatives, famous contemporary figures, working people (including the captive volunteers in her own employ) and eventually members of another ethnic group in their native setting. Men and women, boys and girls, real-life persons and symbolic figures, celebrities and unknown individuals people her oeuvre, making it at once the most highly populated and most varied of all.

This initial survey of women's Pre-Raphaelite work by no means represents a complete and definitive account, but rather a basic study on which further investigations can be built. It is worth noting, therefore, that as far as can be judged from the uneven evidence currently available, the women exhibit as wide a diversity of ability as the male artists of Pre-Raphaelitism. While much was made at the outset of the movement of its failure to meet conventional standards of excellence, much has also been subsequently made of the discrepancies in traditional painterly skills between the work of the various artists subsumed under the Pre-Raphaelite banner. Assessments based on allegedly agreed-upon notions of excellence are fraught with ideological bias, but it is nevertheless useful to recognise in the diversity of accomplishment within Pre-Raphaelitism the fact that the style attracted a wide range of artistic talent and achievement. This attests to the democratic appeal of the movement, and also its appeal to women artists, whose circumstances made conventional

notions of artistic achievement perhaps the most intimidating aspect of the arguments about women artists that raged through the nineteenth century. Between ideas of polished professional competence and the idiosyncratic rejection of such standards, Pre-Raphaelitism offered female artists hope, encouragement, an arena in which their work was not automatically discounted, and possible although never assured status and fame. The belief that the artist's attitude was as important as ability gave women opportunities within Pre-Raphaelitism generally reserved for their more privileged male counterparts, whatever the actual level of ability reached and displayed. Indeed, unevenness of achievement is as much a characteristic of Pre-Raphaelitism as vivid colour, detailed observation, intensity of mood or rejection of academic convention, and limited expertise in one aspect or another of image-making neither prohibited an artist, male or female, from entering Pre-Raphaelitism nor precludes an artist from serious consideration as a Pre-Raphaelite now. Both the strengths and the weaknesses of the artists discussed in this book played a part in making Pre-Raphaelitism recognisably different from other movements in British art, and kept the developing style distinct from other contemporary trends from generation to generation. Considered in ignorance of the women artists' curious, exciting, beautiful, idiosyncratic and revealing works, Pre-Raphaelitism is seen less than fully and in categorical terms that falsify its complexity.

MARIE SPARTALI

57. Mrs Hutton in Venice 1880

BIBLIOGRAPHY

This bibliography contains all works quoted in the text and cited in the Notes and References that follow, together with other relevant works; it is not a comprehensive bibliography of the Pre-Raphaelite movement as a whole.

Place of publication London unless otherwise stated.

Armstrong, Thomas (1912) *A Memoir 1832–1911*.
Arts Council of Great Britain (1975) *Burne-Jones*, exhibition catalogue, ed. John Christian.
Ashmolean Museum (1972) *Eleanor Fortescue Brickdale*, exhibition catalogue, ed. G. L. Taylor, Oxford.
Atkinson, J. Bevington, ed. (1871) *English Art of the Present Day*.
Bartram, Michael (1985) *The Pre-Raphaelite Camera*.
Bate, Percy (1899) *The English Pre-Raphaelite Painters, their Associates and Successors*.
Bell, Quentin (1982) *A New and Noble School: the Pre-Raphaelites*.
Billcliffe, Roger (1978) *Mackintosh Watercolours*.
Birmingham Museums and Art Gallery (1981) *Arthur and Georgie Gaskin*, exhibition catalogue, Birmingham.
Bornard, Odette, ed. (1977) *The Diary of William Michael Rossetti*.
Boyd, Elizabeth French (1976) *Bloomsbury Heritage*.
Brighton Museum and Art Gallery (1974) *Frederick Sandys*, exhibition catalogue, ed. Betty O'Looney, Brighton.
Bryson, John with Troxell, Janet (1976) *Dante Gabriel Rossetti and Jane Morris: Their Correspondence*, Oxford.
Burne-Jones, Georgiana (1904) *Memorials of Sir Edward Burne-Jones*, 2 vols.
Callen, Anthea (1979) *Angel in the Studio: Women in the Arts and Crafts Movement 1870–1914*.
Casteras, Susan P. (1987) *Images of Victorian Womanhood in English Art*, London, New Jersey and Ontario.
Caw, James L. (1908) *Scottish Painting Past and Present 1620–1908*, Edinburgh.
Cherry, Deborah (1980) 'The Hogarth Club', *Burlington Magazine*, vol. 117.
Cherry, Deborah, and Pollock, Griselda (1984) 'Woman as sign in Pre-Raphaelite literature: a case study of the representation of Elizabeth Siddal', *Art History*, vol. 7.
Clayton, Ellen (1876) *English Female Artists*, 2 vols.
Clement, Clara Erskine, and Hutton, Laurence (1879) *Artists of the Nineteenth Century and their Works*, 2 vols.
Cook, E. T. and Wedderburn, A. D. O. eds. (1902–12) *The Works of John Ruskin*, 39 vols.
Cormack, Peter (1985) *Women Stained Glass Artists of the Arts and Crafts Movement*, exhibition catalogue, Walthamstow.
Crawford, Alan, ed. (1984) *By Hammer and Hand: the Arts and Crafts Movement in Birmingham*, Birmingham.
Delaware Art Museum (1976) *The Pre-Raphaelite Era 1848–1914*, exhibition catalogue, eds. Rowland and Betty Elzea, Wilmington, Delaware.

Doughty, O., and Wahl, J. R. eds. (1965) *The Letters of Dante Gabriel Rossetti*, 4 vols., Oxford.
Elzea, Rowland (1984) *The Samuel and Mary R. Bancroft Jr and Related Pre-Raphaelite Collections*, Wilmington, Delaware.
Fitzgerald, Penelope (1975) *Edward Burne-Jones*.
Fredeman, W. E. (1965) *Pre-Raphaelitism: a Bibliocritical Study*. ed. (1975) *The PRB Journal*.
Hare, Augustus (1893) *Two Noble Lives*, 3 vols.
Harker, Margaret (1983) *Julia Margaret Cameron*.
Hilton, Timothy (1970) *The Pre-Raphaelites*.
Holme, Geoffrey, and Salaman, Malcolm (1923) *British Book Illustration Yesterday and Today*.
Hopkinson, Amanda (1986) *Julia Margaret Cameron*.
Howitt, Anna Mary (1853) *An Art Student in Munich*. Reissued 1880.
Howitt, Mary (1889) *Autobiography*, ed. Margaret Howitt.
Hueffer, Ford Madox (1896) *Ford Madox Brown*.
(1897) 'The younger Madox Browns', *The Artist*, no. 19.
Hunt, William Holman (1905) *Pre-Raphaelitism and the Pre-Raphaelite Brotherhood*, 2 vols.
Irwin, David and Francina (1975) *Scottish Painters at Home and Abroad 1700–1900*.
James, Henry (1956) *The Painter's Eye*, ed. J. L. Sweeney.
Lago, Mary, ed. (1982) *Burne-Jones Talking: Conversations 1895–1898 preserved by his studio assistant Thomas Rooke*.
Lewis, Roger C. and Lasner, Mark Samuels eds. (1978) *Poems and Drawings of Elizabeth Siddal*, Wolfville, Canada.
Marillier, H. C. (1899) *Dante Gabriel Rossetti: An Illustrated Memorial of his Art and Life*.
Marsh, Jan (1985) *Pre-Raphaelite Sisterhood*.
(1987) *Pre-Raphaelite Women: Images of Femininity*.
(1988) 'Imagining Elizabeth Siddal', *History Workshop Journal*, no. 25.
du Maurier, Daphne, ed. (1951) *The Young George du Maurier: A Selection of his Letters 1860–1867*.
Meizener, Arthur (1971) *The Saddest Story: A Biography of Ford Madox Ford*.
Miller, Frances, ed. (1974) *Catalogue of the William James Stillman Collection*, Schenectady.
Nunn, Pamela Gerrish (1986) *Canvassing*.
(1987) *Victorian Women Artists*.
(1988) 'Rosa Brett', *Burlington Magazine*, vol. 126.
Packer, Lona Mosk (1963) *Christina Rossetti*, California and Cambridge.
Parris, Leslie, ed. (1984) *The Pre-Raphaelite Papers*.

Praz, Mario (1958) *La Casa della Vita*, Milan.
Rochdale Art Gallery (1987) *Painting Women: Victorian Women Artists*, exhibition catalogue, ed. Deborah Cherry, Rochdale.
Rose, Andrea (1977) *The Pre-Raphaelites*, Oxford.
    (1981) *Pre-Raphaelite Portraits*, Oxford.
    ed. (1979) *The Germ*, Oxford and Birmingham.
Rossetti, W. M. ed. (1895) *Dante Gabriel Rossetti: His Family Letters with a Memoir*, 2 vols.
    ed. (1899) *Ruskin: Rossetti: Pre-Raphaelitism, Papers 1854–1862*.
    ed. (1900) *Pre-Raphaelite Diaries and Letters*.
    (1903) 'Dante Rossetti and Elizabeth Siddal', *Burlington Magazine*, vol. 1.
    (1906) *Some Reminiscences*, 2 vols.
    ed. (1908) *The Family Letters of Christina Georgina Rossetti*.
Sellars, Jane (1988) *Women's Works*, exhibition catalogue, Liverpool.
Shonfield, Zuzanna, ed. (1987) *The Precariously Privileged: A Professional Family in Victorian London*, Oxford.
Soskice, Juliet (1921) *Chapters from Childhood*. Reissued 1972.
Sparrow, Walter Shaw (1905) *Women Painters of the World, from the time of Caterina Vigri to Rosa Bonheur and the Present Day*.
Staley, Alan (1973) *The Pre-Raphaelite Landscape*.

Stillman, W. J. (1901) *Autobiography of a Journalist*, 2 vols.
Stirling, A. M. W. (1922) *William de Morgan and his Wife*.
    (1924) *Life's Little Day: Some Tales and other Reminiscences*.
Surtees, Virginia (1971) *The Paintings and Drawings of Dante Gabriel Rossetti (1828–1882) A catalogue raisonné*, 2 vols., Oxford.
    ed. (1972) *Sublime and Instructive: Letters from John Ruskin to Louisa Marchioness of Waterford, Anna Blunden and Ellen Heaton*.
    ed. (1980) *The Diaries of George Price Boyce*, Norwich.
    ed. (1981) *The Diary of Ford Madox Brown*, New Haven and London.
Tate Gallery (1984) *The Pre-Raphaelites*, exhibition catalogue.
Taylor, E. R. (1890) *Elementary Art Teaching*.
Taylor, Ina (1987) *Victorian Sisters*.
Troxell, Janet (1937) *Three Rossettis: Unpublished Letters to and from Dante Gabriel, Christina, William*, Cambridge, USA.
Watkinson, Ray (1970) *Pre-Raphaelite Art and Design*.
Weaver, Mike (1984) *Julia Margaret Cameron*.
Williamson, Audrey (1976) *Artists in Revolt: the Pre-Raphaelites*.
Wood, Christopher (1981) *The Pre-Raphaelites*.

REFERENCES

Chapter 1: 'Direct and Serious and Heartfelt'

1. Bate, 1899, 117.
2. Tate Gallery, 1984, 11.
3. W. M. Rossetti, 1895, i, 135.
4. W. H. Hunt, 1905, i, 130–1.
5. *Household Words*, 15 June 1850.
6. *Athenaeum*, 1 June 1850, 590.
7. Cook and Wedderburn, 1904, xii, 157.
8. Cook and Wedderburn, 1902, iii, 624.
9. *Illustrated London News*, 4 May 1850, 306.
10. *Fine Arts Quarterly*, January 1864, 260.
11. Tate Gallery, 1984, 23.
12. *Saturday Review*, 31 May 1873, 717.
13. quoted Arts Council, 1975, 11.
14. John Hoole, Foreword, *The Last Romantics: The Romantic Tradition in British Art: Burne-Jones to Stanley Spencer*, ed. John Christian, Barbican Art Gallery, London, 1989, 7.
15. *The Studio*, 1898, xiii, 70.
16. Tate Gallery, 1984, 18.

Chapter 2: The First Generation

1. see Callen, 1979, 30, n. 54.
2. A. M. Howitt, 1853, i, 232.
3. *Lady's Pictorial*, 1847, i, 390.
4. BRP[arkes] Papers IV, Girton College, Cambridge. For permission to quote we are indebted to the writer's descendants and the Mistress and Fellows of Girton College.
5. BRP Papers V, Girton College, Cambridge.
6. M. Howitt, 1889, ii, 181.
7. ibid., i, x.
8. ibid., ii, 56.
9. A. M. Howitt, 1853, i, 38–9.
10. *Athenaeum*, May 1854, 346.
11. *Illustrated London News*, May 1854, 278.
12. *Critic*, May 1854, 163.
13. Doughty and Wahl, 1965, i, 214.

14. *Athenaeum*, July 1855, 648.
15. *Athenaeum*, June 1856, 510.
16. M. Howitt, 1889, ii, 117.
17. ibid., ii, 165.
18. ibid., ii, 149.
19. Bornard, 1977, 35.
20. M. Howitt, 1889, i, xi.
21. *The Friend*, 1884, i, 214.
22. From the unpublished biography compiled by the artist's daughter in family papers. We are indebted to the artist's descendants for permission to quote from this.
23. *Athenaeum*, 27 January 1861, 121.
24. Family papers.
25. Surtees, 1981, 138.
26. Cook and Wedderburn, 1903, xiv, 31.
27. *Saturday Review*, 10 May 1856, 31–2.
28. Family papers.
29. ibid.
30. Troxell, 1937, 8.
31. *Critic*, 27 July 1861, 109.
32. *Spectator*, 20 July 1861, 783.
33. *Critic*, 27 July 1861, 109.
34. Family papers.
35. ibid.
36. ibid.
37. ibid.
38. ibid.
39. ibid.
40. *Spectator*, 5 June 1858, 624.
41. Family papers.
42. Family papers.
43. Clayton, 1876, ii, 196.
44. *Western Times*, 22 July 1854, 5.
45. Surtees, 1972, 87.
46. *Western Times*, 21 August 1858, 5.
47. Surtees, 1972, 115–6.
48. *Spectator*, 13 April 1861, 389.
49. *Spectator*, 27 July 1861, 812.
50. *Spectator*, 18 June 1864, 711.

51. *Art Journal*, 1 May 1867, 145.
52. Clayton, 1876, ii, 202.
53. *Art Journal*, 1 May 1870, quoted in Clayton, 1876, ii, 202.
54. Clayton, 1876, ii, 221.
55. *Edgbastonia*, xviii, no. 209, October 1898, 205–9.
56. *Birmingham Post*, 14 December 1915, 164.
57. 'Mrs D. G. Rossetta' [sic], press clipping in Sheffield Local Studies Library.
58. Doughty and Wahl, 1965, i, 167.
59. BRP Papers V, Girton College, Cambridge.
60. Doughty and Wahl, 1965, i, 245.
61. Marillier, 1899, 74–5.
62. Cook and Wedderburn, 1912, Letters i, 206.
63. ibid., 229.
64. *Spectator*, 6 June 1857.
65. letter signed 'A.S.', press clipping in Sheffield Local Studies Library.
66. Doughty and Wahl, 1965, ii, 384.
67. W. M. Rossetti, 1903, 295.
68. label on back of picture, Fitzwilliam Museum, Cambridge.

Chapter 3: The Second Generation

1. *Examiner*, 3 March 1871, 229.
2. *Art Journal*, 1 January 1873, 6.
3. Shonfield, 1987, 64.
4. *Magazine of Art*, 1883, 325.
5. Family papers, for which we are indebted to Mrs Ann Moore for permission to quote.
6. *English Woman's Review*, 1867, 219.
7. *Art Journal*, 1 June 1870, 168.
8. Bate, 1899, 21.
9. Hueffer, 1897, 49.
10. Surtees, 1981, 126, 141–2.
11. Clayton, 1876, ii, 118.
12. Hueffer, 1897, 50.
13. Hueffer, 1896, 252.
14. *Athenaeum*, February 1869, 247–8.
15. Atkinson, 1871, 48.
16. Doughty and Wahl, 1965, iii, 1152.
17. Rossetti, 1906, ii, 432.
18. Soskice, 1921, 204.
19. Hueffer, 1897, 51.
20. quoted Phillips sale catalogue, 4 November 1985, lot 191.
21. Soskice, 1921, 202.
22. *Art Journal*, 1 March 1884, 73.
23. Boyd, 1976, 11.
24. Hopkinson, 1987, 3.
25. Weaver, 1984, 155.
26. Harker, 1983, 5.
27. quoted Weaver, 1984, 154.
28. Boyd, 1976, 23.
29. *Galaxy*, July 1875, reprinted in James, 1956, 92–3.
30. Delaware Art Museum, 1974, 172.
31. *The Times*, 8 March 1927.
32. du Maurier, 1951, 31.
33. Armstrong, 1912, 195.
34. Praz, 1958, 255.
35. Clayton, 1876, ii, 136.
36. see Atkinson, 1871, 48.
37. *Academy*, 15 February 1877, 133.
38. *Art Journal*, July 1873, 240.
39. Clayton, 1876, ii, 136.
40. Miller, 1974, WJS 36 and 35.
41. James, 1956, 92.
42. *Country Life*, 30 December 1965, 1780.
43. Bryson, 1976, 45.
44. ibid.
45. *The Times*, 8 March 1927.
46. Bryson, 1976, 175.
47. Burne-Jones papers xxvi, Fitzwilliam Museum.
48. *Grosvenor Notes*, 1979, 44.
49. Bate, 1899, 112.
50. letter dated 19 September 1903, now in Delaware Art Museum.
51. quoted Delaware Art Museum, 1976, 174–6.
52. Miller, 1974, WJS 53 and 54.
53. *Studio*, 1904, 255. A full account of Effie Stillman's career is now available in Philip Atwood 'Effie Stillman Sculptor and Medallist', *The Medal*, no. 14, Spring 1989, 48 ff.
54. quotations from Stirling, 1922, 172; and Stirling, 1924, 23, 27.
55. Sterling, 1922, 177.
56. ibid., 185.
57. ibid.
58. quoted ibid., 190.
59. *Spectator*, 24 June 1882, 830.
60. *Spectator*, 9 June 1883, 738.
61. *Athenaeum*, 12 June 1883, 609.
62. *Portfolio*, 1883, 125.
63. Stirling, 1924, 233.
64. ibid., 232.
65. National Trust guide to Cragside, 1985, 48.
66. Stirling, 1922, 350.
67. ibid., 192.

Chapter 4: The Third Generation

1. Louisa Waterford, 23 February 1880, quoted Hare, 1893, iii, 400.
2. A. M. Howitt, 1880 edition, preface.
3. *Magazine of Art*, March 1884, 98.
4. Wyke Baillis, quoted Arts Council of Great Britain, *Great Victorian Pictures*, 1978, 59.
5. E. R. Taylor, 1890, 153.
6. *Birmingham Daily Post*, 26 September 1899.
7. 21 February 1894, in *The Collected Works of William Morris* (1910–14) vol. xxii, 425 ff.
8. *Birmingham Post*, 22 December 1927.
9. The verse in fact reads: 'towards deep skies . . . She dreams; till now on her forgotten book Drops the forgotten blossom from her hand'.
10. *Athenaeum*, 21 May 1892, 67?.
11. see Crawford, 1984, 62.
12. ibid., 77.
13. *Birmingham Post*, 22 December 1927.
14. Crawford, 1984, 78.
15. *Birmingham Post*, 27 June 1919.
16. Information from the Misses Joyce and Myra Kendrick, granddaughters of J. Thackray Bunce's sister.
17. *Birmingham Post*, 18 February 1928.
18. *Bookman Supplement*, ix, December 1895, 12.
19. *Christmas Bookseller*, 1896, 96.
20. letter dated 21 November 1896, quoted Birmingham Museums and Art Gallery catalogue, 1982, 31.
21. *Christmas Bookseller*, 1896, 21.
22. Birmingham Museums and Art Gallery catalogue, 1982, 77.
23. *Studio*, special supplement, 1895, 56.
24. ibid., 63.
25. Programme for the Quinquennial Congress of the International Woman Suffrage Alliance, 27 April 1909, quoted Cormack, 1985, 1.
26. *Studio*, vol. xxxv, 320, quoted Cormack, 1985, 12.
27. Caw, 1908, 354.
28. Rossetti, 1908, 232.
29. quoted *Studio* special no. 1896–7, 51–2.
30. *Art Journal*, 1900, 144; *Studio*, 1896 – see Callen, 1979, 122–3 and

226 for further details.
31. *Art Journal*, 1900, 144–6.
32. ibid.
33. ibid., 147–8.
34. *Studio*, 1906, 213–4.
35. *Art Journal*, 1900, 148.
36. ibid., 149.
37. Caw, 1908, 416–7.
38. B. E. Kalas, essay written 1905, republished Mackintosh Memorial Exhibition catalogue, Glasgow, 1933, 5.
39. Billcliffe, 1978, 12.
40. *Studio*, 1898, 104.
41. *Morning Leader*, 28 June 1901.
42. *The Times*, 13 June 1901.
43. *Studio*, 1901, 42.
44. ibid.
45. ibid., 31–42.
46. *Women's Employment*, 15 January 1932, quoted in Ashmolean Museum, 1972, 5.
47. Ashmolean Museum, 1972, no. 35.

Chapter 5: 'Sisters in Art'

1. Surtees, 1980, 8.
2. 'Pictures of the Year VI', *Magazine of Art*, 1880, 474–5.
3. Doughty and Wahl, 1965, iii, 1032.
4. Lago, 1982, 136.
5. Marillier, 1899.
6. *Art Journal*, 1900, 148.
7. Burne-Jones, 1904, i, 218.
8. Lago, 1982, 11.
9. *Athenaeum*, 25 March 1884, 380.
10. *Illustrated London News*, 21 March 1874, 282.
11. *Art Journal*, 1 May 1874, 146.
12. *Critic*, 11 May 1861, 606.
13. *The Times*, 11 February 1871, 4.
14. *Critic*, 15 March 1854, 163.
15. *Saturday Review*, 23 February 1867, 236.
16. *Athenaeum*, 21 May 1892, 672.
17. *Athenaeum*, 28 April 1900, 534.
18. *Athenaeum*, 25 May 1889, 669.
19. *Art Journal*, 1 February 1866, 71.
20. *Saturday Review*, 9 March 1867, 691.
21. *The Times*, 15 February 1869, 4; 14 February 1870, 4; 11 February 1871, 4; 13 February 1872, 4.
22. *The Times*, 15 February 1869, 4; 4 February 1870, 4; 11 February 1871, 4.
23. Surtees, 1972, 120–1.
24. Doughty and Wahl, 1965.
25. Surtees, 1972, 157.
26. Ashmolean, 1972, 4.
27. 'Glass, Lead and Light', *Stained Glass*, vol. xx, no. 1, quoted Cormack, 1985, 2.

INDEX